# Matthew:
## Structure,
## Christology,
## Kingdom

# MATTHEW: STRUCTURE, CHRISTOLOGY, KINGDOM

by
JACK DEAN KINGSBURY

FORTRESS PRESS          Minneapolis

First Fortress Press paperback edition 1989

*Library of Congress Catalog Card Number 75–13043*
ISBN  0–8006–0434–2
4926D75      Printed in U.S.A.      1–434

To  Barbara

# Contents

# Preface

To be quite candid, I am gratified indeed to see this book made available again for use by colleagues and students. Within the context of my own research, it occupies an important place. With few exceptions, the positions I take here still constitute the cornerstone of my understanding of Matthew's Gospel. Over the years, these positions have been adapted, refined, and elaborated, but scarcely abandoned. The subtitle of the book describes its contents: It deals with the structure of Matthew's Gospel (chap. 1); with the identity and significance of Jesus (chaps. 2 and 3); and with the central theological concept of Matthew, his notion of the Kingdom of Heaven (chap. 4). Whereas the chapter on the Kingdom seems to have found widespread approval among scholars, the chapters on the structure and christology of the Gospel have stirred no little discussion.

Concerning the structure of Matthew's Gospel, I speak of a topical outline in three parts (1:1—4:16; 4:17—16:20; 16:21—28:20), with the respective verses 1:1; 4:17; and 16:21 marking the beginning of each part. Attendant to this outline is a scheme of salvation-history in two epochs: "the time of Israel (OT)" and the time of Jesus (earthly—exalted)." As regards the outline, I do not pretend to be the first to argue that the three parts just cited are the main ones into which the Gospel falls.[1] As far as I know, however, I am the first to use this threefold division so as to determine the nature and

---

1. Without attempting to be exhaustive, F. Neirynck ("APO TOTE ĒRXATO and the Structure of Matthew," *Ephemerides Theologicae Lovanienses* 64 [1988]: 21) traces this way of dividing Matthew's Gospel back to the nineteenth-century scholar Theodor Keim (*The History of Jesus of Nazara*, trans. A. Ransom [2d ed.; London: Williams and Norgate, 1876], 1: 71–72, esp. 71 n. 2). Keim's book, first published in German in 1867, was translated into English as early as 1873.

purpose of the Gospel. In line with 1:1; 4:17; and 16:21, Matthew initially describes Jesus' person (1:1—4:16) and then tells of his public ministry (4:17—16:20) and of his journey to Jerusalem and his passion (16:21—28:20). When combined with Matthew's scheme of salvation-history, one sees that the First Gospel is essentially a story of Jesus' life (topical outline), the purpose of which is to depict Jesus as being decisively significant for the salvation of both Jews and Gentiles (scheme of salvation-history).

I just designated Matthew's Gospel as a story of Jesus' life. Presently, some scholars prefer to speak of it instead as an example of ancient biography. In principle, I agree with this. The problem, however, is that "ancient biography" has become an umbrella term encompassing quite different notions of the character, and therefore also of the aim, of Matthew's Gospel.[2] As a result, it is less than apparent, at least thus far in the scholarly discussion, exactly how the insistence that Matthew's Gospel belongs to the genre of ancient biography contributes to a better understanding of its "peculiar" nature and purpose.

As narrated by Matthew, the story of Jesus' life is one of conflict between Jesus and Israel. Israel is made up of the religious authorities and the crowds. The three parts of the story constitute its beginning, middle, and end. In the beginning (1:1—4:16), Matthew presents Jesus to the reader. In the middle (4:17—16:20), he tells of Jesus' ministry to Israel of teaching, preaching, and healing (4:17—11:1) and of Israel's response to Jesus, which is that of repudiation (11:2—16:20). And in the lengthy end section (16:21—28:20), Matthew tells of Jesus' journey to Jerusalem and of his suffering, death, and resurrection.

The clues for understanding Matthew's story along these lines are to be found within the story itself. In the beginning, the story culminates in the baptismal pericope (3:13–17), where God "presents" Jesus as the Son who is empowered for messianic ministry. Events prior to the baptismal pericope lead up to it, just as those that follow flow from it. Also, whereas Jesus tends to be passive throughout 1:1—4:16, beginning with 4:17 he seizes the initiative and vigorously acts.

The middle of the story, in turn, divides itself into two phases. In the first phase (4:17—11:1), the key summary-passages 4:23; 9:35; and 11:1 indicate that the focus is on Jesus' ministry of teaching, preaching, and healing,

2. For a discussion of this trend, cf. J. D. Kingsbury, *Matthew* (Proclamation Commentaries; 2d ed. rev. and enl.; Philadelphia: Fortress, 1986), 9–13. For a more recent statement on the necessity of understanding the canonical Gospels as ancient biography, cf. C. H. Talbert, "Once Again: Gospel Genre," *Semeia* 43 (1988): 53–73.

whereby he proffers salvation to Israel.[3] In the second phase (11:2—16:20), the key passages 11:2–6 and 13:53–58 indicate that the focus is on the way people respond to Jesus' ministry. Throughout this phrase, the twin themes of repudiating Jesus ("taking offense" at him; cf. 11:6; 13:57) and of wondering about his identity (cf. 11:2; 13:55) govern the story.[4] To be sure, even though repudiated by people in Israel, Jesus does not simply cease teaching and healing. The thing to note, however, is that beginning with 11:2 these activities as such no longer direct the story's plot, or flow of events.

In the long end section of the story, Jesus' three passion-predictions (16:21; 17:22–23; 20:17–19),[5] which are called to mind at 26:2, lend unity to the narrative and guide the flow of events. These predictions indicate the controlling themes of Jesus' journey to Jerusalem and his suffering, death, and resurrection. As these themes are elaborated, the story moves through three phases. In the first phase, Matthew tells of Jesus' journey itself, in the course of which he principally instructs the disciples (16:21—20:34). In the second phase, Jesus enters Jerusalem and remains in and around the city, clashing with the religious authorities in the temple, pronouncing woes against them, and delivering his eschatological discourse (21:1—25:46). And in the third, climactic phase, Jesus suffers, dies, and is raised (26:1—28:20). The stress in this phase is on both the deceit the authorities practice in bringing Jesus to the cross and on God's vindication of Jesus.

The conflict Matthew describes in his story finds its resolution in Jesus' death on the cross. As Matthew shows, Jesus' death is willed not only by

3. In 4:17, the stress is on the gospel of God's inbreaking kingdom that Jesus proclaims; in 5:1—7:29, it is on the Sermon on the Mount as the example par excellence of Jesus' teaching (cf. 5:2; 7:28–29); in 8:1—9:34, it is on miracles Jesus performs, whereby he heals (cf. 8:16–17); and in 9:35—10:42, it is on Jesus' disciples as preaching and healing after the manner of Jesus himself (cf. 10:1, 7–8).

4. To see exactly how Matthew develops these two themes, cf. J. D. Kingsbury, *Matthew as Story* (2d ed. rev. and enl.; Philadelphia: Fortress, 1988), 72–75.

5. Concerning the number of passion-predictions Jesus makes in Matthew's Gospel, I disagree with those scholars who (a) construe 16:21 not as a passion-prediction but as a "redactional statement" and (b) combine 26:2 with 17:22–23 and 20:17–19 and understand these to be the three passion-predictions in Matthew's Gospel (cf. T. B. Slater, "Notes on Matthew's Structure," *JBL* 99 [1980]: 436; Neirynck, "Structure of Matthew," 47; also M. M. Thompson, "The Structure of Matthew: A Survey of Recent Trends," *Studia Biblica et Theologica* 12 [1982]: 231). As regards 16:21, although these words are uttered by Matthew and not Jesus himself, Matthew nonetheless attributes them to Jesus: "From that time on Jesus began to show his disciples that he must go to Jerusalem and suffer many things. . . ." Also, these words plainly tell of events still to come. Accordingly, attributed by Matthew to Jesus, these words constitute Jesus' first passion-prediction. As regards 26:2, Jesus' words here can clearly be seen not to be a passion-prediction. On the contrary, Jesus uses them, not to foretell the future, but to summon the disciples to recall the passion-predictions he earlier gave them (16:21; 17:22–23; 20:17–19). Notice the way Jesus begins his utterance: "You know that. . . ." In short, then, the passion-predictions do indeed number three, and these three are 16:21; 17:22–23; and 20:17–19. By the same token, 26:2 is a retrospective reminder of these three predictions.

the religious authorities but also by God and Jesus. The religious authorities will the death of Jesus because they believe he is a false messiah (27:63) and consequently a threat to both themselves as Israel's leaders and the very existence of Israel. Jesus wills his death because he, as the obedient Son of God, wills what God his Father wills (26:39, 42). And God wills the death of Jesus (16:21) because through it God establishes a new covenant whereby Jesus atones for sins (26:28) and mediates salvation to all (1:21; 24:14; 28:19). In bringing Jesus to the cross, the authorities believe that they are acting in a manner well-pleasing to God. God, however, raises Jesus from the dead, thus vindicating him (28:5–6) and exalting him to all authority in heaven and on earth (28:18). The upshot is that in Matthew's story God decides the conflict between Jesus and Israel in favor of Jesus. By the close of the story, therefore, Jesus' death has become emblematic not of his destruction but of the salvation God accomplishes in him for all humankind.

To read Matthew's Gospel as a story of Jesus' life being told in terms of a three-part, topical outline raises the question of how the expression "topical outline" is understood. The use of this expression is manifestly not intended to suggest that Matthew's Gospel is to be thought of statically as three, self-contained blocks of material.[6] On the contrary, Matthew's Gospel is, as I have said, a story, and the three parts constitute the beginning, middle, and end of this story. Necessarily, one encounters numerous turning points within a story, some of which are of primary significance and some of which are of secondary, tertiary, or even lesser significance. In Matthew's story, the function of the passages 4:17 and 16:21 is to alert the reader to the two most important turning points of the story: Jesus, after being presented to the reader, undertakes (4:17) a public ministry in response to which Israel (though not the disciples) repudiates him; turning toward Jerusalem (16:21), Jesus journeys there and submits to suffering and death. Accordingly, as I understand them, the passages 4:17 and 16:21 mark the major transitions of Matthew's story: The beginning gives way to the middle and the middle to the end. When these passages are so construed, one sees that the expression "topical outline" is being understood in dynamic, not static, terms.

My own threefold approach to Matthew's Gospel is, of course, only one of several approaches. Because, in fact, no single approach commands the approval of all scholars, a few question whether Matthew's Gospel can even

6. This misunderstanding seems to lie at the basis of the remarks by D. Senior (*What are they saying about Matthew?* [New York: Paulist Press, 1983], 26–27).

be said to evince a topical outline.[7] The vast majority, however, believes that it does. There are also a few who play down or even ignore the presence of any topical outline on the grounds that Matthew's Gospel has been written to promulgate some scheme of salvation-history.[8] It is alleged, for example, that Matthew's Gospel was written to present the church as the true Israel,[9] or the life of Jesus as the way of righteousness,[10] or the time of Matthew as the time of the Gentile mission,[11] or to proclaim God's faithfulness to his OT promises as seen in the new covenant he has made with the church.[12]

A survey of all those who do espouse some form of topical outline for Matthew's Gospel reveals that, apart from the threefold approach I take, they favor one of three approaches. Most advocate Bacon's outline[13] or some variation thereof. Taking their cue from the fivefold formula "And it happened when Jesus finished [these sayings],"[14] these scholars tend to argue that the emphasis in Matthew's Gospel is on the great discourses of Jesus.[15] Other scholars advocate a chiastic outline, which leads them to identify either chapter 11[16] or chapter 13[17] as the focal point of the Gospel. And still others advocate an outline based to a greater or lesser extent on matters of geography.[18]

---

7. Cf. already F. V. Filson, *The Gospel according to St. Matthew* (Black's New Testament Commentaries; London: Adam and Charles Black, 1960), 21–24. Also Thompson, "Structure of Matthew," 238; Senior, *What are they saying about Matthew?*, 25; G. Stanton, "The Origin and Purpose of Matthew's Gospel: Matthean Scholarship from 1945–1980," in *Aufstieg und Niedergang der römischen Welt* (Berlin: Walter de Gruyter, 1985), 2. 25/3. 1905; U. Luz, *Das Evangelium nach Matthäus* (Evangelisch-Katholischer Kommentar zum Neuen Testament 1/1; Neukirchen-Vlyn and Zurich: Neukirchener Verlag and Benziger Verlag), 16.

8. For a more thorough treatment of this issue, see this book, 25–39; also D. R. Bauer, *The Structure of Matthew's Gospel: A Study in Literary Design* (Journal for the Study of the New Testament Supplement Series 31; Bible and Literature Series 15; Sheffield: Almond, 1988), 45–54.

9. Cf. W. Trilling, *Das wahre Israel* (STANT 10; München: Kösel-Verlag, 1964).

10. G. Strecker, *Der Weg der Gerechtigkeit* (FRLANT 82; Göttingen: Vandenhoeck & Ruprecht, 1962).

11. R. Walker, *Die Heilsgeschichte im ersten Evangelium* (FRLANT 91; Göttingen: Vandenhoeck & Ruprecht, 1967).

12. H. Frankemölle, *Jahwebund und Kirche Christi* (NTAbh 10; Münster: Aschendorff, 1974).

13. See this book, 2–3.

14. Cf. Matt 7:28; 11:1; 13:53; 19:1; 26:1.

15. For a long list of scholars who follow Bacon's approach to Matthew's Gospel, see Bauer, "Structure of Matthew's Gospel," 151 n. 15.

16. Cf., e.g., H. B. Green, "The Structure of St. Matthew's Gospel," *Studia Evangelica* IV (TU 102; Berlin: Akademie, 1968), 47–59.

17. For a list of scholars taking this position, cf. Bauer, "Structure of Matthew's Gospel," 36, 153 n. 35.

18. Cf., e.g., W. Farmer, *Jesus and the Gospels* (Philadelphia: Fortress, 1982), 146, 155. For the names of other scholars who likewise advocate a geographical approach to the structure of Matthew's Gospel, cf. D. Verseput, *The Rejection of the Humble Messianic King: A Study of the Composition of Matthew 11—12* (European University Studies 291; Frankfurt: Peter Lang, 1986), 315 n. 29.

To assess these various approaches to Matthew's Gospel, the advent of literary, or narrative, criticism provides scholars with an important new tool.[19] Without doubt, Matthew's Gospel shows itself, as I noted, to be a story having a coherent Plot revolving around conflict between Jesus and Israel[20] and finding its resolution in the death of Jesus. Elementary as this observation is, it is not without implication for determining the structure of Matthew's Gospel. Specifically, it implies that the way one determines this structure is by determining the boundaries of the beginning, middle, and end of Matthew's story. If this is correct, two things follow. The first is that one will not adopt too quickly the skeptical notion that Matthew's Gospel evinces no topical outline. And the second is that any approach to Matthew's Gospel which is incompatible with its character as story can be ruled out. Thus, any salvation-historical or geographical approach leading one to find the culmination of Matthew's Gospel at a point other than the death (and resurrection) of Jesus can quickly be dismissed. Similarly, the untenability of both the Baconian and the chiastic approaches also becomes apparent: The chiastic approach misguidedly finds the center of Matthew's Gospel in either chapter 11 or chapter 13; and Bacon's approach suffers from the twin defects that, as a matter of principle, it subordinates narrative to discourse and, correspondingly, erroneously identifies not the death of Jesus but his great discourses, especially the Sermon on the Mount, as the climactic feature of the Gospel.

To elaborate on this critique of Bacon's approach, there is certainly no denying that Jesus' great discourses are a highly significant feature of Matthew's Gospel. The thing to observe, however, is that their place is "within," not "above" or "apart from," the narrative. To illustrate, the second part of Matthew's story (4:17—16:20) falls, as was stated, into two phases. In the first phase (4:17—11:1), Jesus embarks on his public ministry of teaching, preaching, and healing (4:23; 9:35; 11:1). Within this phase, the Sermon on the Mount is the example par excellence of Jesus' teaching (5:2; 7:28–29). Similarly, Jesus' missionary discourse contains his instructions to the disciples on doing as he has been doing, preaching and healing (10:7–8). In the second phase (11:1—16:20), Israel responds to Jesus' ministry by repudiating him. In his discourse in parables (13:1–52), Jesus himself reacts to Israel's repudiation by speaking in parables, that is, in speech which the Jewish crowds cannot understand (13:10–13) but which the disciples can understand (13:51–

19. For a narrative-critical approach to the First Gospel, cf. Kingsbury, *Matthew as Story*, esp. chap. 1.
20. Concerning the "plot" of Matthew and the "conflict" it portrays, cf. Kingsbury, *Matthew as Story*, 3–9.

52). In the third part of Matthew's story (16:21—28:20), Jesus journeys to Jerusalem and suffers and dies. This part falls into three phases, and discourses of Jesus occur in two of them. In the first phase (16:21—20:34), which is the journey itself, Jesus mainly instructs the disciples on their life together, and part of such instruction is his discourse on the church (18:1–35). And in the second phase (21:1—25:46), Jesus, immediately prior to his suffering and death offers the disciples his eschatological discourse of the events they will experience in the time after his resurrection and leading up to his Parousia (24:1—25:46). To repeat, significant as the great discourses of Jesus are, they are not the central element of Matthew's Gospel; instead, they are firmly embedded within the story Matthew tells of Jesus' life.

In contrast to the various approaches just discussed, the threefold approach to Matthew's Gospel I advocate does harmonize with the latter's character as story. This does not prove, of course, that my outline of Matthew is the only one that is viable. Some literary critics, for example, take a threefold approach to Matthew's story but divide it in terms of setting, complication, and resolution[21] or of initial state, process, and goal.[22] While the strength of these approaches is that they take the narrative or story character of Matthew's Gospel seriously, the problem with them is that they mark off the "beginning," "middle," and "end" of Matthew's story without paying due attention to formal indicators found in the text itself.[23] One of the great advantages of the threefold approach as I construe it is precisely that it does rely on formal indicators in determining where Matthew's story invites one to draw the boundaries between beginning, middle, and end.

Although my particular threefold approach is only one of several approaches to Matthew's Gospel, a survey of the scholarly literature indicates that it has not been unsuccessful in gaining the assent of others.[24] Still,

---

21. Cf., e.g., H. J. Combrink ("The Structure of the Gospel of Matthew as Narrative," *Tyndale Bulletin* 34 [1982]: 75, 80, 84), who divides Matthew's Gospel as follows: 1:1—4:17 (the setting); 4:18—25:46 (the complication); and 26:1—28:20 (the resolution).

22. Cf. D. O. Via, Jr. ("Structure, Christology, and Ethics in Matthew," in *Orientation by Disorientation: Studies in Literary Criticism and Biblical Literary Criticism*, ed. R. A. Spencer [Presented in Honor of William A. Beardslee; Pittsburgh: Pickwick, 1980], 202, 205, 208), who argues for these three divisions in Matthew's Gospel: 1:1—4:16 (initial state); 4:17—27:34 (process); and 27:35—28:20 (goal).

23. F. Matera ("The Plot of Matthew's Gospel," *CBQ* [1987]: 233–53) takes yet a different literary approach to Matthew's Gospel. Matera believes that by distinguishing "kernels" (major events) from "satellites" (events dependent upon kernels), one can mark off the "narrative blocks" of Matthew's gospel-story (1:1—4:11; 4:12—11:1; 11:2—16:12; 16:13—20:34; 21:1—28:15; 28:16-20). My objection to this approach is that it operates without the use of formal criteria. Unless one can specify the "marks" of a kernel, one is unable to demonstrate that the events one has identified as kernels are in fact such.

24. On this score, Neirynck ("Structure of Matthew," 23, 24 nn. 13–14) has compiled something

whereas D. R. Bauer is one of its staunchest proponents,[25] F. Neirynck holds that it is in need of correction.[26] In calling for correction, however, Neirynck

---

of a list of those who have adopted the threefold approach as I advocate it. Some named by him are the following: W. G. Kümmel (*Introduction to the New Testament*, trans. H. C. Kee [Nashville: Abingdon, 1975], 103–05), but with modification; Slater ("Notes on Matthew's Structure," 436); L. Sabourin (*The Gospel according to Matthew* [Bombay: St. Paul Publications, 1982], 1:52–61), but with 28:16–20 regarded as the conclusion of the whole of Matthew's Gospel; R. Schnackenburg ("Petrus im Matthäusevangelium,") in *À cause de le'Évangile. Etudes sur les Synoptiques et les Acts* [In honor of J. Dupont; Lectio Divina, 123; Paris: Cerf, 1985], 120–21; idem (*Matthäusevangelium* [Die Neue Echter Bibel; Würzburg: Echter, 1985], 1:5–6); J. Gnilka (*Das Matthäusevangelium* [Herders Theologischer Kommentar zum Neuen Testament 1/1; Freiburg: Herder, 1986], 1:vii); A. Sand (*Das Evangelium nach Matthäus* [RNT; Regensburg: Friedrich Pustet, 1986], 5–11), but with modification; Verseput (*Rejection of the Humble King*, 18–21); W. Schenk (*Die Sprache des Matthäus: Die Text Konstituenten in ihren makro- und mikrostrukturellen Relationen* [Göttingen: Vandenhoeck & Ruprecht, 1987], 36); idem ("Das 'Matthäusevangelium' als Petrusevangelium," *BZ* 27 [1983]: 71). S. Freyne (*Galilee, Jesus and the Gospels: Literary Approaches and Historical Investigations* [Philadelphia: Fortress, 1988], 76. 11. For further discussion of the place of the threefold approach as I understand it within the context of modern scholarship, see Bauer, "Structure of Matthew's Gospel," 40–45.

25. Ibid.

26. Neirynck, "Structure of Matthew," 24 (cf. also J.-C. Ingelaere, "Structure de Matthieu et histoire de salut," *Foi et Vie* 78 [1979]: 20–24). One who is more critical than Neirynck of the threefold approach to Matthew which I take is M. M. Thompson ("Structure of Matthew," 226–33). In Thompson's view, scholars in general have made too much of the structure of Matthew's Gospel, for Matthew is to be likened to a storyteller who moves his narrative along without dividing it into any specific parts ibid., 236–38). Indeed, even to find a clear-cut outline in Matthew's Gospel is going to extremes (ibid.). In terms of my approach in particular, Thompson adjudges it to be misguided on five major counts (ibid., 228–32).

Before we turn to Thompson's five objections, there is a prior issue I should like to address. As I just indicated, underlying Thompson's entire survey of scholarly views on the structure of Matthew is her conviction that it is illegitimate to construct any outline of Matthew's Gospel. With this conviction as her guide, she of course proposes no outline of her own of Matthew's Gospel. Relieved of this burden, her task becomes obvious: to cast doubt on the proposals of others. The reason I point this out is that there is a direct correlation between the way Thompson conceives of her task and her mode of argumentation. In great measure, Thompson operates at the level of assertion: she tends to advance criticisms or alternative interpretations without sufficiently grounding them, and she makes little attempt to show the reader how her construal of any given point makes for a better understanding of Matthew's text or story. The upshot is that, in the last analysis, Thompson's survey falls short of its goal: it remains unconvincing, because her treatment of the evidence is so skimpy and superficial that the reader is finally put in the position of simply having to accept her assertion that Matthew's Gospel admits of no outline (rather than some outline).

Thompson's first objection (ibid., 228–29) to my approach focuses on the twofold formula, "From that time on [*apo tote*] Jesus began to preach [to show his disciples] . . ." (4:17; 16:21). On my view, this formula is literarily and thematically distinctive (cf. this book, 7–9). In contrast, Thompson opines that it is not clear on what basis this formula can be so regarded. The answer is that it can be so regarded because of the "readerly" attention it draws to itself. On another note, Thompson also contends that the phrase *apo tote* looks back as well as forward. But this is not so; in contradistinction to 26:16, *apo tote* at 4:17 and 16:21 is asyndetic: it "looks ahead" and not behind.

Thompson's second objection ("Structure of Matthew," 229–30) is that 1:1—4:16 does not constitute a unit with 1:1 serving as the superscription. Since in asserting this, Thompson raises no point I do not myself deal with in this book (cf. esp. 9–11), I simply refer the reader to that discussion.

Thompson's third objection ("Structure of Matthew," 230–31) concerns the two sets of three

disclaims any intention to contest "the significance of 4,17 and 16,21 in the general outline of the Gospel."[27] Instead, it is his intent to emend the approach, to wit: (a) in place of 4:17 and 16:21, the pericopes 4:12–17 and 16:13–23 are to be regarded as the respective beginnings of Jesus' public ministry and of his journey to Jerusalem;[28] and (b) the strict definition of 4:17—16:20 as the middle and 16:21—28:20 as the end should be abandoned, on two[29] counts. First, Jesus' preaching, which commences in the first half

summary-passages: (a) 4:23; 9:35; and 11:1; and (b) 16:21; 17:22–23; and 20:17–19. Concerning (a), two of Thompson's contentions are so frivolous as to require no answer. The third one is that the section 4:17—16:20 in reality contains five summary-passages (cf. 14:34–36; 15:29–31) not three, so that my count is off. The underlying issue here is the unity of 4:17—16:20. As I see it, 4:17—16:20 treats of the public ministry of Jesus in Israel, and this ministry divides itself into two phases. In the first phase (4:17—11:1), Jesus preaches (4:17), teaches (chaps. 5—7), heals (cf. chaps. 8:1—9:34), and dispatches his disciples to preach and heal (9:35—10:42). Because the summary-passages 4:23; 9:35; and 11:1 stress these selfsame activities, the correspondence between these summary-passages and the flow of Matthew's story reveals that these summary-passages reflect the leitmotif of the section 4:17—11:1. In the second phase (11:2—16:20), the flow of events stresses Israel's response to Jesus' ministry, which is that of repudiation. Since 14:34–36 and 15:29–31 do not correspond with this overall flow of events, one can see that they have a different purpose to serve in Matthew's story than 4:23; 9:35; and 11:1 and that this purpose is other than to convey the leitmotif of the section 11:2—16:20. Concerning (b), Thompson charges, respectively, that I am inconsistent in my use of 4:17 and 16:21, that the passion-predictions cannot be regarded as "summaries," and that since 26:1–2 is also a passion-prediction, the passion-predictions in reality number not three but four. On all three counts, however, Thompson errs. First, the consistency in my use of 4:17 and 16:21 lies in the fact that I regard these two passages as marking the two main turning points in Jesus' life: at 4:17, Jesus begins his public ministry to Israel; at 16:21, he turns toward Jerusalem, where he suffers, dies, and is raised. Second, the reason the passion-predictions can be accounted as "summaries" is that they correspond in what they foretell with the flow of events throughout 16:21—28:20: Jesus journeys to Jerusalem and enters upon his passion. And third, Thompson notwithstanding, 26:2 is not a fourth passion-prediction but a retrospective reminder (note the words: "You know that . . ." [cf. above, n. 5]) by means of which Jesus recalls the three passion-predictions he earlier gave the disciples at 16:21; 17:22–23; and 20:17–19.

Thompson's fourth objection (ibid., 231) is that my understanding of the structure of Matthew's Gospel does not correspond with my understanding of Matthew's view of salvation-history. On the contrary, the correspondence between "structure" and "view of salvation-history" in Matthew's Gospel is to be found, as I see it, in the emphasis that both place on the figure of Jesus Messiah, the Son of God. On the one hand, the structure of Matthew's Gospel focuses on the person, the public ministry, and the suffering, death, and resurrection of Jesus Messiah. On the other hand, the focus of Matthew's concept of salvation-history is on Jesus Messiah as being of decisive significance for all people, Jew and Gentile alike.

Thompson's final objection (ibid., 231–32) is that, in determining the structure of Matthew's Gospel, I do not take sufficient account of Matthew's use of Mark. In making this observation, Thompson is, of course, correct. The thing to notice, however, is that far from regarding this as a weakness, I regard it as one of the great strengths of my approach. To base one's understanding of the structure of Matthew's Gospel on discerning Matthew's use of Mark is to introduce all the uncertainties of the synoptic problem into the already complex task of ascertaining the structure of Matthew. My position is that to determine the structure of Matthew, Matthew must be read not in terms of Mark, but of Matthew.

27. Neirynck, "Structure of Matthew," 58.

28. Ibid., 25–26, 31, 55 n. 190.

29. In addition to these two reasons, Neirynck ("Structure of Matthew," 33–35) also has a third reason for disputing the notion that Matthew's story can be divided into the two main parts

of the middle (4:17—11:1), continues beyond the close of the middle. Second, Israel's repudiation of Jesus, which is highlighted in the second half of the middle (11:2—16:20), also continues beyond the close of the middle.[30]

Upon scrutiny, neither aspect of Neirynck's dual emendation commends itself. To take Neirynck's second point first, the contention that Matthew's story cannot properly be divided into the two main parts 4:17—16:20 and 16:21—28:20 because Matthew's treatment of the motifs they highlight is not coterminous with the sections themselves reveals that Neirynck and I have different perceptions of the purpose an outline serves. As I see it, the chief purpose of an outline is to indicate the motif that governs a story in any given section. Thus, although Neirynck's claim that Jesus is depicted as preaching *(kēryssein)* throughout most of Matthew's story is lexically incorrect,[31] Jesus does indeed teach and heal thoughout most of the story. This notwithstanding, the only phase of the story in which Jesus' public ministry of teaching, preaching, and healing can be said to constitute the motif governing the story is 4:17—11:1. Following 11:1, Jesus may still be depicted as teaching and healing, but teaching and healing are no longer the motif around which the story revolves. In similar fashion, the motif governing

---

4:17—16:20 and 16:21—28:20, to wit: Neirynck holds that the section 26:1—28:20 constitutes yet another main part of Matthew's story (ibid., 57–58). On this score, Neirynck contends that 26:16 ("And from that time on [*kai apo tote*] he [Judas] was seeking an opportunity that he might betray him") is to be regarded as parallel to the formula occurring at 4:17 and 16:21 ("From that time on [*apo tote*] Jesus began to preach [to show his disciples] . . ."). Just as 4:17 (embedded in the pericope 4:12–16) marks the beginning of Jesus' ministry and 16:21 (embedded in the pericope 16:13–23) marks the beginning of Jesus' journey to Jerusalem, so this "new turn in the life of Judas [at 26:16, which is embedded in the pericope 26:1–16] is in fact the beginning of the passion narrative in Mt" (ibid., 33).

Neirynck's view that 26:16 parallels 4:17 and 16:21 and that the passion account constitutes one main part of Matthew's story alongside other main parts strikes me as unconvincing on several counts. Literarily, it is difficult to see how 26:16 can be regarded as a parallel to 4:17 and 16:21 when the only element it has in common with them is the expression *apo tote*. Materially, 26:16 also differs noticeably from 4:17 and 16:21 in that the subject of the sentence is not "Jesus" but "Judas." True, Judas's history is indeed, as Neirynck observes, "linked with" that of Jesus (ibid., 33). Regardless, Jesus, not Judas, is the protagonist of Matthew's story, and it is Jesus who inaugurates "primary" turning points in the story. Third, against the view that the passion account itself (chaps. 26—28) constitutes one main part of Matthew's story stand the passion-predictions (16:21; 17:22–23; 20:17–19), which are recalled at 26:2. Together, these four passages attest to the unity of the entire section 16:21—28:20, for they capture in a nutshell the tenor of Matthew's narration: Jesus' journey to Jerusalem and his suffering, death, and resurrection. One does best, therefore, to construe the passion account, not as a main part in its own right, but as the climactic subsection of the end of Matthew's story (16:21—28:20). And on a minor note, it is also not apparent to me that 26:1–16 presents itself as the "introductory pericope" to the passion account. Strictly speaking, the principal players in the passion account are God, Jesus, and the religious and Gentile authorities (16:21; 17:22–23; 20:17–19). Narratively, therefore, the "introductory pericope" to the passion account proves to be not 26:1–16 but 26:1–5.

30. Neirynck, "Structure of Matthew," 58.

31. Lexically, the last passage in Matthew's story in which Jesus himself is said to "preach" *(kēryssein)* is 11:1 (but cf. 11:5).

Matthew's story in 11:2—16:20 is that of Israel's response to Jesus' public ministry, which is that of repudiation. Correctly, Neirynck sees that Israel's repudiation of Jesus does not cease at 16:20. What he fails to recognize, however, is that as Matthew's story continues, this motif of repudiation becomes transmuted into controversy in Jerusalem leading to suffering, death, and resurrection. The result is that the leitmotif guiding Matthew's story throughout 16:21—28:20 is not simply repudiation but, as the passion-predictions attest, journey to Jerusalem and suffering, death, and resurrection. The point is, Neirynck calls for the emendation of my outline of Matthew's story, but I cannot see that he has either given it its due or that what he proposes in its stead[32] does greater justice to the evidence.

To turn to Neirynck's first point regarding the places in Matthew's story at which Jesus begins, respectively, his public ministry and his journey to Jerusalem, the critical issue dividing us is sharp disagreement over how Matthew's Gospel is to be read. Neirynck insists that if one is to understand how Matthew has structured his Gospel, one must read Matthew's Gospel in terms of Mark.[33] When Matthew's Gospel is so read, it becomes apparent, Neirynck asserts, that Matt 4:12–17 is the redacted counterpart of Mark 1:14–15[34] and that Matt 16:13–23 is the redacted counterpart of Mark 8:27–33.[35] Accordingly, just as Mark 1:15 and 8:31 (cf. *kai* ["And"]) are linked, respectively, to Mark 1:14 and 8:27–30, so Matt 4:17 and 16:21 are linked by means of *apo tote* ("From that time on") to 4:12–16 and 16:13–20. In Matthew's story, therefore, not 4:17 but 4:12–17 marks the beginning of Jesus' public ministry, and not 16:21 but 16:13–23[36] marks the beginning of Jesus' journey to Jerusalem.

32. Cf. Neirynck, "Structure of Matthew," 57–58.

33. Ibid., 27–59.

34. Cf. ibid., 30–31, 34–35.

35. Cf. ibid., 50–55.

36. On a side note, Neirynck ("Structure of Matthew," 32–33, 57 [note the headings on 25, 46]) hypothesizes that Matthew begins main parts of his Gospel with "introductory pericopes," most notably 4:12–17; 16:13–23; and 26:1–16. In the case of 16:13–23, Neirynck (ibid., 49–50) establishes the unity of this pericope not only by reading Matthew in terms of Mark (cf. ibid., 50–55 and the body of the discussion above) but also by attributing a "structural function" both to Peter (cf. esp. 16:16–17 with 22–23) and to a play on the word *anthrōpos* ("man") in the expressions "the Son of man" and "the things of men" (cf. 16:13 with 16:23). On this matter of "structural function," the question is whether it is legitimate to ascribe structural significance to a figure such as Peter or a term like "man." If it is legitimate, what specifically are the criteria on the basis of which one can know in reading through Matthew precisely when a character such as Peter or a play on a word like "man" does or does not bear structural significance? In making decisions like this, interpreters most often seem to operate on little more than scholarly assertion. Moreover, they are not always consistent in the way they proceed. For example, Neirynck himself (ibid., 47 n. 149; 55 n. 190; 59 n. 209) opines that 20:34 marks the end of one section of Matthew's Gospel (16:13—20:34) and that 21:1 begins a new section. If one

Whatever the merit of this argument, where I part company with Neirynck is already at the point where he insists that the way one determines the major divisions in Matthew's Gospel is by reading Matthew in terms of Mark. [37] The expression *apo tote* at Matt 4:17 and 16:20 is asyndetic. When, therefore, it is read in light of Matthew's use of the syndetic expression *kai apo tote* ("*And* from that time on") in 26:16, it is clear that it does not link 4:17 and 16:21 to the respective pericopes 4:12–16 and 16:13–20, but does just the opposite: Asyndetic *apo tote* signals that 4:17 and 16:21 stand apart from the preceding pericopes 4:12–16 and 16:13–20. The only basis for Neirynck's assertion of linkage instead of separation as regards 4:17 and 16:21 is his contention that one must revert to Mark if one is to ascertain the structure of Matthew. Since I disagree with this contention, I see no reason to change my position that, again, 4:17 and 16:21 mark the beginning, respectively, of Jesus' public ministry and of his journey to Jerusalem and his suffering, death, and resurrection.

From the discussion thus far, one can see that since this book was first published, the scholarly debate over the structure of Matthew's Gospel has been lively indeed. I said at the outset, however, that this book has stirred discussion not only regarding the structure of Matthew but also regarding its christology. Christology, in fact, is the concern of half the book (chaps. 2—3).

---

glances at the preceding pericope 20:29–34 on the one hand and at the following pericopes 21:1–11 and 21:12–17 on the other, one observes that in all three the title "Son of David" stands out prominently. These observations prompt two related questions: If in connection with 16:13–23 it is legitimate to claim that the figure of Peter or a play on a term like "man" bears structural significance, why is one not also compelled to assert that the same holds true in the case of Matthew's use of the christological title "Son of David" in the section 20:29—21:17? On what grounds can one properly claim that the section 16:13–23 cannot be "broken" at 16:21 because of the figure of Peter but that the section 20:29—21:17 can be "broken" at 20:34 despite the prominent use, in both what precedes and follows, of the title "Son of David"? As is apparent, in a gospel-story in which the narrator's spotlight, with very few exceptions, continually rests on the protagonist Jesus, I reject the notion that a character like Peter or a term like "man" will be made to bear major "structural" significance.

37. Neirynck's insistence that Matthew's Gospel is to be read in terms of Mark's Gospel comes to expression throughout his article, but it is particularly apparent in his closing remarks ("Structure of Matthew," 59). How pivotal this Markan approach to Matthew is to the whole of Neirynck's argument is perhaps best illustrated by his attempt to show that I, too, have obligated myself to read Matthew in this way (cf., e.g., this remark: "For Kingsbury, who admits Matthew's dependence upon Mark . . . , a 'Markan' division of Matthew should include the following parallel structure" [ibid., 28]). What Neirynck is after is this: If he can claim that I, too, have obligated myself to read Matthew in terms of Mark, he can then also claim that I am inconsistent in my approach to Matthew's Gospel if I do not revert to Mark in establishing the structure of Matthew. The truth of the matter, however, is that following the publication of my doctoral dissertation (*The Parables of Jesus in Matthew 13* [London and Richmond, Va.: SPCK and John Knox, 1969]), I abandoned the redaction-critical view that the best way to approach Matthew was through Mark. In this book, for example, I made a point of not basing my understanding of Matthew's structure on the notion that the way to approach Matthew is by first consulting Mark.

It is important to recall how things stood in the area of scholarly research on Matthew's christology when this book first appeared. For the most part, the research was characterized by two related factors. First, there were prominent scholars who stoutly maintained that, when it came to christology, Matthew reflected very little on the identity and significance of Jesus. Essentially, Matthew was content to take over title of majesty from the tradition and to pass them on.[38] Indeed, Matthew exercised so little creativity in working with titles of majesty that one can even detect inconsistency in the materials he incorporated into his Gospel.[39] Second, no unanimity whatsoever existed among scholars on which titles of majesty, if any, could legitimately be emphasized (see pp. 41–42). One scholar, for example, stressed multiple titles; another, "Son of David"; another, "Messiah"; another, "the Son of man"; another, "Kyrios"; another, "Son of David" and "Kyrios"; and another, "Kyrios" and "the Son of man." Virtually the only title most scholars seemed reluctant to stress was "Son of God." Apparently, the reason for this was partly historical and partly redaction-critical. On the one hand, historical research could point to little or no evidence that "Son of God" had been used messianically in Jewish tradition.[40] On the other hand, Matthew, in comparison with Mark and Luke, employs the title "Son of David" with great frequency (eleven times as opposed to four times each for Mark and Luke). From these observations, scholars were inclined to conclude that whereas Matthew inherited and largely transmitted the title "Son of God," his real interest lay in portraying (the earthly) Jesus as the "Son of David."

The notion that Matthew exhibits no great interest in christology and the striking diversity with which scholars approached what christology he proffered were major factors prompting the writing of this book. In analyzing

38. Cf., e.g., the following statement by G. Bornkamm ("End-Expectation and Church in Matthew," *Tradition and Interpretation in Matthew*, trans. P. Scott [New Testament Library; Philadelphia: Westminster, 1963], 32–33), who in 1975 was still at the height of his career: "In only a few passages does Matthew's Gospel reveal any theological reflections on the relation of . . . titles of honour to each other; in the first place he [Matthew] is satisfied with the evidence that they are all based on Scripture."

39. On this score, E. Schweizer (*Matthäus und seine Gemeinde* [SBS 71; Stuttgart: KBW Verlag, 1974], 65) declares: "To be sure, with Matthew neither the ecclesiology nor the christology has been systematically thought through. One should not wonder, therefore, if statements stand side by side that are not in complete accord with one another."

40. On this point, cf. J. A. Fitzmyer, "The Contribution of Qumran Aramaic to the Study of the New Testament," *A Wandering Aramean: Collected Aramaic Essays* (SBLMS 25; Missoula, Mont: Scholars Press, 1979), 90–94, 102–07. The apparent lack of a messianic use of "Son of God" in Jewish tradition posed a problem for Matthean scholars because most held that, if Matthew had any intention, it was to paint a portrait of Jesus that would have direct relevance for persons of Jewish background. As I note above in the body of the discussion, one title used frequently in Matthew that, scholars believed, possessed such direct relevance is "Son of David." Still, if one sets aside for a moment the historical problem and focuses on Matthew's Gospel itself, there can be no question but that "Son of God" has the character of a messianic title (cf. 16:16; 26:63).

the evidence, I found myself led to a view of Matthew's christology having little in common with the positions taken by the scholars alluded to above. I concluded, for example, that Matthew did not unreflectively adopt a portrait of Jesus from the tradition and that the portrait he did sketch is not flawed because of inconsistency. Quite the contrary, Matthew's portrait of Jesus is both well-defined and coherent. Indeed, fundamental to Matthew's characterization of Jesus is that he is the "Son of God": Jesus, the Messiah-King from the line of David and of Abraham, is the royal Son of God. The reason "Son of God" lies at the heart of Matthew's christology is that Matthew construed this title as best expressing the deepest mystery of Jesus' person: "Son of God" points directly to Jesus' unique relationship with God, for, conceived and empowered by the Spirit, he speaks and acts on divine authority.

It would be too much to say that there exists today, as a result of this book, a consensus among scholars that "Son of God" is Matthew's preeminent characterization of Jesus. It is, however, fair to say that because of this book scholars today readily acknowledge the critical importance of Son-of-God christology in Matthew's Gospel.[41] Still, to raise the question of the importance of Son-of-God christology in Matthew is necessarily to raise a further question, to wit: If "Son of God" is Matthew's preeminent title for Jesus, how does it relate to "the Son of man"?[42]

My answer to this question is that whereas "Son of God" is a title by means of which Jesus' identity is declared or confessed, "the Son of man" is the title by means of which Jesus refers to himself in public. "Son of God," therefore, is of the nature of a confessional title, whereas "the Son of man" is of the nature of a public title. This notwithstanding, as Matthew depicts

41. Simply as one indication of this, note, for example, the words with which D. J. Verseput ("The Role and Meaning of the 'Son of God' Title in Matthew's Gospel," *NTS* 33 [1987]: 532), who refers to this book in a footnote, begins his article: "In recent years the importance of the title 'Son of God' for Matthew's Gospel has received well-deserved recognition. There needs to be no hesitation in acknowledging the programmatic role which it plays in the christological development of the First Gospel."

42. In his book *The Vision of Matthew: Christ, Church and Morality in the First Gospel* Theological Inquiries [New York: Paulist Press, 1979], 217-19), J. P. Meier poses this selfsame question, and the answer he gives contrasts pointedly with my position. He writes: "we should think of an ellipse with two foci, *Son of God* and *Son of Man*, with the Son floating somewhere in between" (italics his). The reason I am unable to adopt Meier's view is that, for me, "Son of God" and "the Son of man" are, by nature, two different kinds of terms. "Son of God" (along with, e.g., "Messiah," "King of the Jews [Israel]," "Son of David," and "Son of Abraham") are "messianic terms." They explain "who Jesus is" and thus communicate some particular understanding of both his identity and his significance. By contrast, "the Son of man" simply means "the (this) man" (e.g., 8:20: "Foxes have holes, and birds of the air have nests; but this man [the Son of man] has nowhere to lay his head"; 24:37: "As were the days of Noah, so will be the coming of this man [the Son of man]"). The term "the Son of man," therefore, does not explain "who Jesus is" and hence stands apart from these other terms.

the exalted Jesus returning for judgment at the Latter Day, the titles "Son of God" and "the Son of man" "coalesce": The Jesus who, this side of the Parousia, cannot be confessed to be the "Son of God" except by divine revelation is at the same time "the Son of man" who, at the end of time, will appear in the sight of all humanity as its Judge. At the consummation of the age, therefore, humans everywhere will see with their eyes what heretofore has been perceived only by faith: that Jesus is in truth the Son of God.

Since having written this book, I have reflected further on "the Son of man" in Matthew's christology and have modified my position with respect to its status.[43] To be sure, "the Son of man" is indeed the designation by means of which Jesus openly, in public or to his disciples, refers to himself. The Greek equivalent of "the Son of man" may be translated as "the man," or "the human being."[44] In English, one can perhaps best capture the force of the term by rendering it as "this man," or "this human being."[45] If one substitutes the expression "this man" each time the term "the Son of man" occurs in Matthew's Gospel, one can see how it functions: "The Son of man" is the designation Jesus openly uses to refer to himself, yet in using it he does not at the same time divulge his messianic identity. Or to put it differently, because in designating himself as "the Son of man" Jesus in effect refers to himself as "this man," it is apparent that no matter how openly or frequently he utters this term, it never discloses to others "who he is."

Because "the Son of man" is not used by Jesus to divulge his identity, it proves not to be a title of majesty. By definition, titles of majesty, when applied to Jesus, communicate some understanding of his identity and significance. Still, although "the Son of man" is not a title, this is not to say that it is therefore simply used generically to mean "a man" or as the equivalent of a pronoun to mean "I" or "me." The reason these latter options are ruled out is that "the Son of man" in Matthew's Gospel never refers to any human other than Jesus and is always definite in form (" 'the' Son of man"). Accordingly, one does best to regard "the Son of man" as a technical term. Like other technical terms (e.g., "righteousness," "the kingdom of Heaven"), "the Son of man" bears a precise meaning within the Gospel of Matthew

---

43. For a more detailed treatment of Matthew's use of "the Son of man," cf. Kingsbury, *Matthew as Story*, chap. 5.

44. For a succinct treatment of the philological background of "the Son of man," cf. J. A. Fitzmyer, "The New Testament Title 'Son of Man' Philologically Considered," in *A Wandering Aramean*, 143–60.

45. On this point, cf. the remarks by G. Vermes, *Jesus and the World of Judaism* (Philadelphia: Fortress, 1984), 99.

("the [this] man," referring exclusively to Jesus). At the same time, it does not, like christological titles such as "Son of God" or "Son of David," inform the reader or the characters in the story of the identity of Jesus.

Except for this change of view concerning "the Son of man," my endorsement of the other positions I take in chapters 2—3 on the christology of Matthew remains firm. The same is true of the views I express on the Kingdom of Heaven in chapter 4.

To conclude this preface, I should like to express my hearty thanks to John A. Hollar, Senior Editor of Fortress Press, for taking the initiative in having this book reissued. As a result, he has provided me with this opportunity to take stock of it once again, and for this, too, I am grateful.

J. D. K.

*Union Theological Seminary in Virginia*
*Advent, 1988*

# Preface to First Edition

In an initial study of the first Gospel (*The Parables of Jesus in Matthew 13* [London and Richmond, Va.: S.P.C.K. and John Knox, 1969]), I was impressed with the great diversity of scholarly approaches to the christology of Matthew. Since then such diversity has, if anything, been on the increase. One man, for example, places "Prophet" at the heart of Matthew's christology, another the "earthly Messiah," another "Son of Man," another "Kyrios," and still others different combinations of titles, such as "Son of David" and "Son of Man," "Son of David" and "Kyrios," "Kyrios" and "Son of Man," or all of the latter and "Son of God" as well. Most recently, one commentator has seen fit to carry this trend toward diversity to its ultimate conclusion, asserting that the key to Matthew's christology is the note of "fulfillment"; Jesus simply fulfills across the board every christological title Matthew is disposed to attribute to him. In this scheme, all titles are seen of course as lying on the same plane.

There are two major reasons why students of the first Gospel have thus far achieved no agreement as to how to approach the christology of Matthew. One reason is that the relationship Matthew establishes between the structure of his Gospel and its christology has been assessed variously. So it is that those who adhere to some form of Bacon's outline of the Gospel almost inevitably cast the Matthaean Jesus in the mold of prophet, new-Moses, teacher, preacher, or lawgiver and regard the Gospel as a whole as a catechism, lectionary, manual of instructions, or book of sermons embedded in narrative. Alternatively, those who hold that Matthew has organized his Gospel in the main according to a concept of salvation-history, whereby the "time of Jesus" is boldly marked off from the "time of the church," distinguish sharply between the earthly Jesus, identified most often as the Messiah and Son of David, and the exalted Jesus, identified as the Kyrios or Son of Man. In some instances, commentators prefer to designate Matthew's Gospel in broad terms as a "life of Jesus" or a new edition of Mark or a kerygmatic portrait of history. These designations give little hint as to how the respective commentator envisages the structure of the Gospel in relationship to its christology.

In an attempt to come to terms with the structure of Matthew's Gospel, I have had to break both with Bacon's topical outline (and virtually all other outlines as well) and with the prevailing views on Matthew's concept of salvation-history. An analysis of the broad structure of the Gospel reveals that it divides itself neatly into three principal parts: (I) The Person of Jesus Messiah (1:1–4:16); (II) The Proclamation of Jesus Messiah (4:17–16:20); and (III) The Suffering, Death, and Resurrection of Jesus Messiah (16:21–28:20). Moreover, attendant to this topical outline is a scheme of salvation-history in two epochs which corresponds to the categories of prophecy and fulfillment: there is the "time of Israel (OT)" and the "time of Jesus (earthly–exalted)." The overall function of the structure of the Gospel is to set forth the theological claim that the person of Jesus Messiah, his ministry and death and resurrection (topical outline), is of ultimate significance for Israel and the Gentiles alike (concept of salvation-history).

This understanding of the broad structure of Matthew's Gospel opens the way to a proper understanding of his christology. For Matthew, Jesus is preeminently the Messiah, the Son of God. This is clear, to begin with, from the fact that Matthew devotes the first main part of his Gospel to the person of Jesus, presenting him above all as the Messiah, the Son of God (1:1–4:16). But this is also clear from the circumstance that the controlling factor in Matthew's concept of salvation-history is the confessional truth that in the person of Jesus Messiah, the Son of God, God has drawn near to dwell with his people to the end of the age, thus inaugurating the eschatological time of salvation (1:23; 18:20; 28:20). Third, this is furthermore clear from the manner in which Matthew works with the many christological terms one encounters in his Gospel: the title Son of God is made "superior" to all others (although at one point it does coalesce with that of Son of Man). Last, this is likewise clear from the way in which Matthew develops the primary theological concept of his Gospel, "the Kingdom of Heaven," because at the center of this concept stands Jesus depicted precisely as the Messiah, the Son of God.

One additional word is in order about the analysis of the structure of the Gospel. Because both the immense number of topical outlines advanced through the years and the several theories regarding Matthew's concept of salvation-history are so diverse and conflicting, I have seen it as my task in Chapter I merely to attempt to specify what I believe the basic approach to these two aspects of the first Gospel must be. Consequently, while I have treated some of the subunits of the Gospel, I have not endeavored to arrange all its major and minor subdivisions and pericopes into a comprehensive topical outline. I hope, however, to do this in a subsequent publication.

The second major reason why students of the first Gospel have thus far achieved no agreement as to how to approach the christology of Matthew is that the ending of the Gospel (28:16–20) has, I believe, been almost uniformly misinterpreted. In the last century commentators have, almost without exception, explicated the ending of the Gospel in terms of a Kyrios or Son-of-Man christology. The evidence, however, seems to suggest that Matthew has imbued this text with a Son-of-God christology. If this is in fact the case, then Matthew can be seen to apply the title Son of God not only to the "earthly Jesus" but to the "exalted Jesus" as well. What this reveals, in turn, is that "Son of God" is easily the most comprehensive title Matthew employs: it embraces every facet of the "life of Jesus" from conception, birth, infancy, and ministry to death and resurrection and exaltation.

The intended goal of this book is to initiate a more focused discussion of especially the structure and christology of Matthew. Approximately half of it has appeared in articles published in various journals. At the same time, none of these articles has been incorporated into the book simply as written. All have been completely revised and, except for one, considerably expanded. Accordingly, should anyone wish to discuss the matters treated in these articles, I should prefer that this be done on the basis of the views enunciated here. The following is a list of the articles in question: "The Structure of Matthew's Gospel and His Concept of Salvation-History," *CBQ* 35 (1973). 451–74; "Form and Message of Matthew," *Int* 29 (1975): 13–23; "The Title 'Son of God' in Matthew's Gospel," *BibTB* 5 (1975): 3–31; "The Title 'Son of Man' in Matthew's Gospel," *CBQ* 37 (1975): 193–202; and "The Title 'Kyrios' in Matthew's Gospel," *JBL* 94 (1975): 246–55. The one article that is more complete in its journal form than in this book is "The Composition and Christology of Matt 28:16–20," *JBL* 93 (1974): 573–84.

With permission granted Fortress Press I have made use in this book of the Revised Standard Version of the Bible (copyright 1946 and 1952, and published by Thomas Nelson & Sons), although in particular instances I have modified this in the interest of stressing some point of exegesis.

It is now my great privilege to express my gratitude to all of the following: to President Lloyd Svendsbye and the administration of Luther Theological Seminary, for granting me a sabbatical in which to complete the manuscript; to Norman Perrin of Chicago and George MacRae of Harvard, who read the manuscript and offered valuable suggestions for improving it; to Günther Bornkamm of Heidelberg, who took time from his schedule to discuss at length with me Matthaean theology; to Aid Association for Lutherans of Appleton, Wisconsin, for the generous Fellowship Award that enabled me to consult with professors both in this country and in Europe about the book; to Norman Wente and the library staff at Luther Seminary and to Jennings Mergenthal in the Seminary Book Store, for their ready help in securing materials for research; and to my students at Luther Seminary, for their patience during the countless hours in which I have tested my ideas on them. Finally, I declare my greatest debt of gratitude of course to my wife, to whom this volume is dedicated.

J.D.K.

*Luther Theological Seminary, St. Paul*
*Trinity, 1975*

# Abbreviations

| | |
|---|---|
| AB | Anchor Bible |
| AnBib | Analecta Biblica |
| ATANT | Abhandlungen zur Theologie des Alten und Neuen Testaments |
| BEvT | Beiträge zur Evangelischen Theologie |
| *Bib* | *Biblica* |
| *BibTB* | *Biblical Theology Bulletin* |
| BKAT | Biblischer Kommentar: Altes Testament |
| BWANT | Beiträge zur Wissenschaft vom Alten und Neuen Testament |
| *BZ* | *Biblische Zeitschrift* |
| BZNW | Beihefte zur ZNW |
| *CBQ* | *Catholic Biblical Quarterly* |
| CNT | Commentaire du Nouveau Testament |
| ConNT | Coniectanea neotestamentica |
| *CTM* | *Concordia Theological Monthly* |
| *EvT* | *Evangelische Theologie* |
| FRLANT | Forschungen zur Religion und Literatur des Alten und Neuen Testaments |
| HKNT | Handkommentar zum Neuen Testament |
| HNT | Handbuch zum Neuen Testament |
| ICC | International Critical Commentary |
| *Int* | *Interpretation* |
| *JBC* | *The Jerome Biblical Commentary* |
| *JBL* | *Journal of Biblical Literature* |

| | |
|---|---|
| *JTS* | *Journal of Theological Studies* |
| KNT | Kommentar zum Neuen Testament |
| LUA | Lunds universitets årsskrift |
| LXX | Septuagint |
| Meyer | H. A. W. Meyer, Kritisch-exegetischer Kommentar über das Neue Testament |
| Moffatt | The Moffatt New Testament Commentary |
| *NovT* | *Novum Testamentum* |
| NovTSup | Novum Testamentum Supplements |
| NT | New Testament |
| NTAbh | Neutestamentliche Abhandlungen |
| NTD | Das Neue Testament Deutsch |
| *NTS* | *New Testament Studies* |
| NTSMS | New Testament Studies Monograph Series |
| OT | Old Testament |
| *PCB* | *Peake's Commentary on the Bible* |
| *RB* | *Revue biblique* |
| RNT | Regensburger Neues Testament |
| RSV | Revised Standard Version |
| *RGG* | *Religion in Geschichte und Gegenwart* |
| SBJ | La sainte bible de Jérusalem |
| SBLMS | Society of Biblical Literature Monograph Series |
| SBM | Stuttgarter Biblische Monographien |
| SBS | Stuttgarter Bibelstudien |
| SBT | Studies in Biblical Theology |
| *SE* | *Studia evangelica* |
| StANT | Studien zum Alten und Neuen Testament |
| StudNeot | Studia neotestamentica |
| Str-B | H. Strack and P. Billerbeck, *Kommentar zum Neuen Testament* |
| *TDNT* | G. Kittel and G. Friedrich (eds.), *Theological Dictionary of the New Testament* |
| *TLZ* | *Theologische Literaturzeitung* |
| TU | Texte und Untersuchungen |
| WMANT | Wissenschaftliche Monographien zum Alten und Neuen Testament |
| ZNW | *Zeitschrift für die neutestamentliche Wissenschaft* |
| ZThK | *Zeitschrift für Theologie und Kirche* |

Chapter I

# The Structure of Matthew's Gospel and His Concept of Salvation-History

Matthaean research has thus far achieved no consensus of opinion on either the broad structure of the first Gospel or on the Evangelist's concept of the history of salvation. Moreover, little attention has been given to the problem of how these relate to each other. This general situation has produced two negative results. The first is that there has been only a handful of commentators in the last decades who have attempted to ascertain the nature or the purpose of Matthew's Gospel from its structure or scheme of salvation-history. And the second is that there are fewer still who have endeavored to let the structure of the Gospel be their guide as they determine its portrait of Jesus. The objective of this chapter is to delineate both the structure of Matthew's Gospel and his concept of the history of salvation, relating the one to the other, so that the structure of the Gospel may show us the way to a viable approach, in Chapters II and III, to the christology of the Gospel. Then, in Chapter IV, we can attempt to place the christology of Matthew within the context of his wider thought, as represented by his concept of the Kingdom of Heaven. Our procedure, therefore, is analytical in character.

### A. THE STRUCTURE OF THE GOSPEL

Attempts to solve the problem of the structure of the first Gospel are legion, but by and large they may be divided into three categories. Two of these categories have to do with topical outlines, and the third covers various explications of Matthew's view of the history of salvation.

The first category need not detain us. It comprises topical outlines that

1

commentators have drafted where there is no clear indication as to how any given outline enables one to comprehend better the nature or the purpose of Matthew's Gospel as a whole. This is the case with the outlines advanced by A. Schlatter,[1] M.-J. Lagrange,[2] E. Lohmeyer,[3] Albright–Mann,[4] and E. Schweizer,[5] among others.[6] But it is also true of the two-part outline proposed by X. Léon-Defour[7] and the chiastic divisions suggested by J. C. Fenton[8] and H. B. Green.[9]

The second category of scholarly attempts to come to grips with the structure of the first Gospel comprises variations of a single outline. But here each proposal does reflect to a great degree the respective commentator's conception of the nature or the purpose of the Gospel. The one responsible for the basic outline that countless others have adopted is B. W. Bacon.[10] His position is that the first Gospel contains five "books" which culminate in discourses of Jesus and are supplemented by preamble (chs. 1–2) and epilogue (chs. 26–28).[11] The Evangelist was a converted rabbi, a Christian legalist, who, as a member of a church threatened by lawlessness, met this heresy by providing a systematic compend of the commendments of Jesus in five parts after the fashion of the Mo-

---

1. *Der Evangelist Matthäus* (5th ed.; Stuttgart: Calwer, 1959), passim.

2. *Évangile selon Saint Matthieu* (7th ed.; Paris: J. Gabalda, 1948), XXV, XXX.

3. *Das Evangelium des Matthäus* (Meyer; Göttingen: Vandenhoeck & Ruprecht, 1956), 7*–10.*

4. W. F. Albright and C. S. Mann, *Matthew* (AB; Garden City, New York: Doubleday, 1971), LXII–LXXIII.

5. *Das Evangelium nach Matthäus* (NTD 2; Göttingen: Vandenhoeck & Ruprecht, 1973), 369.

6. Cf. also W. C. Allen, *Gospel according to S. Matthew* (ICC; 3d ed.; Edinburgh: T. & T. Clark, 1912), lxiii, 1, 22, 33, 167, 201, 219; A. H. M'Neile, *The Gospel according to St. Matthew* (London: Macmillan, 1915), xii; T. H. Robinson, *The Gospel of Matthew* (Moffatt; London: Hodder & Stoughton, 1928), xix; E. Klostermann, *Das Matthäusevangelium* (HNT 4; 2d ed.; Tübingen: J. C. B. Mohr, 1927), "Inhaltsübersicht"; J. Schniewind, *Das Evangelium nach Matthäus* (NTD 2; Göttingen: Vandenhoeck & Ruprecht, 1936), 8; K. Staab, *Das Evangelium nach Matthäus* (Echter-Bibel; Würzburg: Echter, 1951), passim; J. Schmid, *Das Evangelium nach Matthäus* (RNT 1; Regensburg: F. Pustet, 1959), 34, 69, 231, 298, 378; A. W. Argyle, *The Gospel according to Matthew* (The Cambridge Bible Commentary; Cambridge: Cambridge University, 1963), 2–4; H. C. Kee, "The Gospel according to Matthew," *The Interpreter's One-Volume Commentary on the Bible* (Nashville: Abingdon, 1971), 610, 612, 640.

7. "The Synoptic Gospels," *Introduction to the New Testament*, ed. A. Robert and A. Feuillet; trans. P. W. Skehan, et al. (New York: Desclée, 1965), 169–73.

8. *The Gospel of St. Matthew* (Pelican Gospel Commentaries; Harmondsworth, Middlesex: Penguin Books, 1963), 16–17.

9. "The Structure of St. Matthew's Gospel," *SE IV* (TU 102; Berlin: Akademie, 1968), 57–59.

10. Cf. *Studies in Matthew* (London: Constable, 1930); idem, "The 'Five Books' of Matthew against the Jews," *The Expositor* 15 (1918): 56–66.

11. Bacon, *Matthew*, 82, 265–335.

saic Pentateuch.[12] Structural evidence of Matthew's intention is the five-fold, stereotyped formula found throughout the Gospel, which reads: *kai egeneto hote etelesen ho Iēsous* . . . ("And it happened when Jesus finished . . ."; cf. 7:28; 11:1; 13:53; 19:1; 26:1).

The influence of Bacon's hypothesis upon Matthaean studies has been immense. Today yet there are any number of commentators who sub-scribe to at least the nub of his contention concerning the structure of the first Gospel.[13] Concerning its nature and purpose, however, several com-mentators have drawn other inferences from his outline.

G. D. Kilpatrick, for example, asserts that Matthew has modeled his Gospel after the Pentateuch in such a way as to contrast Jesus and the law and to shape it to function as a lectionary for his church's services of worship.[14] K. Stendahl maintains that this fivefold Gospel, the product of a school, presents Jesus as the Wisdom of God[15] and assumes the form of a manual for teaching and administration within the church.[16] Still other scholars, such as P. Benoit,[17] P. Bonnard,[18] and D. Hill,[19] also claim

12. Ibid., 29, 40–41, 47, 81–82.

13. Cf., e.g., Lagrange, *Matthieu*, LXXXV; Schlatter, *Matthäus*, 125–28; F. W. Green, *The Gospel according to Saint Matthew* (reprinted; Oxford: Clarendon, 1950), 4–5; G. D. Kilpatrick, *The Origins of the Gospel according to St. Matthew* (Oxford: Clarendon, 1946), 107–108, 135–36; S. E. Johnson, "The Gospel according to St. Matthew," *The Interpreter's Bible* (Nashville: Abingdon, 1951), VII, 235; K. Stendahl, *The School of St. Matthew* (reprinted; Philadelphia: Fortress, 1968), 21–22, 24–27; N. A. Dahl, "Die Passionsgeschichte bei Matthäus," *NTS* 2 (1955/56): 29; P. Benoit, *L' évangile selon Saint Matthieu* (SBJ; 3d ed.; Paris: Cerf, 1961), 7–12; H. Milton, "The Structure of the Prologue to St. Matthew's Gospel," *JBL* 81 (1962): 175, 180; P. Bonnard, *L' évangile selon Saint Matthieu* (CNT 1; Neuchâtel: Delachaux & Niestlé, 1963), 7, 110; P. Gaechter, *Das Matthäusevangelium* (Innsbruck: Tyrolia, 1963), 16–17; F. Hahn, *The Titles of Jesus in Christology*, trans. H. Knight and G. Ogg (London: Lutterworth, 1969), 385–86; R. M. Grant, *A Historical Introduction to the New Testament* (London: Collins, 1963), 128; Fenton, *Matthew*, 14–15; A. Jones, *The Gospel according to Matthew* (New York: Sheed & Ward, 1965), 20–21; J. L. McKenzie, "The Gospel according to Matthew," *JBC* (Englewood Cliffs: Prentice Hall, 1968), II, 62, 64–65; R. A. Spivey and D. M. Smith, Jr., *Anatomy of the New Testament* (London: Macmillan, 1969), 96–97; Kee, "Matthew," 609–10; D. J. Selby, *Introduction to the New Testament* (New York: Macmillan, 1971), 110–13; D. Hill, *The Gospel of Matthew* (New Century Bible; London: Oliphants, 1972), 44–48.

14. Cf. Kilpatrick, *Origins*, 135–37.

15. On the question of the influence of Jewish wisdom traditions upon the christology of Matthew, cf., e.g., the recent study by M. J. Suggs (*Wisdom, Christology, and Law in Matthew's Gospel* [Cambridge: Harvard University, 1970]), the critical analysis of Suggs's position by M. D. Johnson ("Reflections on a Wisdom Approach to Matthew's Christology," *CBQ* 36 [1974]: 44–64), and the more general comments by K. Berger ("Die königlichen Messiastraditionen des Neuen Testaments," *NTS* 20 [1973/74]: 28–37).

16. Cf. Stendahl, *School*, 24–27, 29, 35.

17. Cf. *Matthieu*, 7–11.

18. Cf. *Matthieu*, 7, 10.

19. Cf. *Matthew*, 43–48, 63.

Bacon's outline for the first Gospel but view it as underlining the apologetic and especially the didactic[20] character Matthew intended to give it. And W. Marxsen, who follows Bacon to the extent that he, too, finds the heart of the first Gospel in the so-called five great discourses, avers that this structural feature shows the document to be, not a "gospel" per se, as is Mark, but a "book,"[21] which highlights "sermons" mediated by (the risen) Jesus to the church of Matthew.[22]

Because the number of commentators who have found in Bacon's outline the key to the structure of the first Gospel is so large, it is clear that any fresh approach to the problem of structure must necessarily begin with a careful appraisal of Bacon's position. The critique of his views is scattered but massive. Thus, some have pointed out that it is inappropriate to designate the infancy narratives of Matthew as a "preamble" and the passion and resurrection narratives as an "epilogue." To do this is to place these narratives outside the main structure of the Gospel[23] and hence to overlook both the climactic nature of the cross and resurrection in the gospel-story[24] and the fact that Matthew is not without a concept of history.[25]

A second objection has to do with the number five in relation to the great discourses of Matthew. Owing to the complete change of setting between ch. 23 and chs. 24–25, to be consistent must not one speak of six

20. Cf. also G. Schille, "Bemerkungen zur Formgeschichte des Evangeliums. II. Das Evangelium des Matthäus als Katechismus," *NTS* 4 (1957/58): 113; Fenton, *Matthew*, 23, 26–27; McKenzie, "Matthew," 62–64; Key, "Matthew," 610.

21. N. Perrin (*The New Testament: An Introduction* [New York: Harcourt Brace Jovanovich, 1974], 176–77) follows Marxsen to the extent that he, too, terms Matthew's Gospel a "book." But whereas Marxsen (*Introduction to the New Testament,* trans. G. Buswell [Philadelphia: Fortress, 1968], 151–52) understands by "book" that the first Gospel represents Matthew's attempt to "historicize" the past in a way that will enable it to speak to the church of his day, Perrin (cf. *Introduction,* 174–77) understands by "book" that the first Gospel represents Matthew's attempt to set forth for his church, in opposition to Jamnia, the new "verbal revelation" of the law which Jesus Messiah has delivered to it and which it must interpret further as it carries out its mission to the nations.

22. Cf. Marxsen, *Introduction,* 151–52.

23. Cf. W. D. Davies, *The Setting of the Sermon on the Mount* (Cambridge: Cambridge University, 1964), 25.

24. Cf. Green, "Structure," 49.

25. Cf. G. Strecker, *Der Weg der Gerechtigkeit* (FRLANT 82; Göttingen: Vandenhoeck & Ruprecht, 1962), 147 n. 2; W. Trilling, *Das wahre Israel* (StANT X; 3d ed.; München: Kösel, 1964), 217–18.

26. Cf. E. J. Goodspeed, *Matthew, Apostle and Evangelist* (Philadelphia: John C. Winston, 1959), 27, 134; A. Wikenhauser, *New Testament Introduction,* trans. J. Cunningham (New York: Herder & Herder, 1958), 182–83; Schmid, *Matthäus,* 24; R. Walker, *Die Heilsgeschichte im ersten Evangelium* (FRLANT 91; Göttingen: Vandenhoeck & Ruprecht, 1967), 146 n. 112.

great discourses[26] or of a "Matthaean Hexateuch"?[27] Indeed, the logia-character of ch. 11 has prompted one commentator to suggest that the first Gospel in reality contains seven great discourses.[28]

Still other telling criticisms of Bacon's position relate to his division of each of the "books" of Matthew into a narrative section and a discourse section allegedly in accordance with the Pentateuch, to the architechtonic emphasis he places on the five stereotyped formulas, and to his contention that Matthew has operated with a "new Moses" typology. With respect to the first point, since a glance at Genesis, Leviticus, and Numbers shows that they do not admit of any neat division between narrative and legal materials, there is good reason to deny that Matthew has made the structure of his Gospel rigidly parallel to the books of the Pentateuch.[29] As for the second matter, if it cannot be demonstrated that Matthew has consciously patterned his Gospel after the Pentateuch, what evidence is there that one is to attribute basic structural, as opposed to perhaps transitional, significance to the five stereotyped formulas?[30] And as far as the "new Moses" typology is concerned, while Matthew may in instances have permitted this to color his Gospel, it is not so dominant a trait as to render Bacon's proposal credible.[31]

These arguments make it plain that Bacon's outline and the concomitant views as to the nature and purpose of the first Gospel are unable to stand the test of critical scrutiny. By the same token, neither do the inferences others have drawn from this outline, which we have noted above, survive the fall of Bacon's hypothesis. Whether Matthew's document is described as "liturgical," "apologetic," "catechetical," "didactic," a "manual," or even a "book," the term either tends to be onesidedly paraenetic in connotation or does not do justice to Matthew's own summary of the contents of his work as "the Gospel of the Kingdom" (26:13; 24:14; cf. also 4:23; 9:35),[32] an expression that will occupy our attention in Chapter IV.

Consequently, Bacon's outline of the first Gospel will not do. On the other hand, it does pose the question as to the significance of the fivefold

27. Cf. A. Farrer, *St Matthew and St Mark* (London: Dacre, 1954), 177–97.

28. Cf. Green, "Structure," 18.

29. Cf. Davies, *Setting*, 19–20.

30. Cf. M'Neile, *Matthew*, 99; B. H. Streeter, *The Four Gospels* (revised; London: Macmillan, 1930), 262.

31. Cf. G. Barth, "Matthew's Understanding of the Law," *Tradition and Interpretation in Matthew*, trans. P. Scott (Philadelphia: Westminster, 1963), 157–59; Davies, *Setting*, 92–93; Trilling, *Israel*, 38, 186, 217.

32. Contrary to W. Marxsen (*Mark the Evangelist*, trans. R. Harrisville [Nashville: Abingdon, 1969], 141), J. Schniewind (*Matthäus*, 241) is correct in making this observation.

stereotyped formula *kai egeneto hote etelesen ho Iēsous* . . . (7:28; 11:1; 13:53; 19:1; 26:1). In our opinion, this formula is literarily and theologically significant, and also stresses the element of historical movement.

In style, the fivefold formula is not Matthaean but Lucan (*egeneto* + finite verb). Because of this, Sir John Hawkins[33] and others[34] have traced it to the document Q. Regardless of its origin, however, this formula is found five times in the first Gospel and, except for Luke 7:1 in D, exclusively here. For this reason, it can properly be construed as a thoroughly Matthaean idiom.

To consider the use of this formula, four observations are of interest: (a) it is not, in fact, employed to separate narrative material from discourse material (this is true in the strictest sense only of 7:28);[35] (b) it is regularly appended to discourses of Jesus (Sermon on the Mount, Missionary Discourse, Parable Discourse, Ecclesiological Discourse, Eschatological Discourse); (c) save for 13:53, it is never made to sound the theme of any given discourse; and (d) it is of the nature of a subordinate clause and is therefore always dependent upon the primary clause it modifies (cf. 7:28b; 11:1b; 13:53b; 19:1b; 26:1b). In regard to the latter, aside from 7:28b, the independent clause upon which the formula in each case depends points forward. By contrast, the formula itself, with its emphasis on "finishing," necessarily points in each case to the discourse preceding it. Hence, from its repeated use we conclude that the basic literary function of the fivefold formula in Matthew's Gospel is simply to mark each of five discourses of Jesus as terminated.

Theologically, other aspects of the formula stand out. For one thing, the name "Jesus" is a constituent feature. For another, the formula refers back to the discourses it characterizes as terminated by means of such phrases as "these words" of Jesus (7:28; 19:1; 26:1) or "these parables" (13:53) or Jesus' "instructing his twelve disciples" (11:1). Now when we recall that it is a major objective of Matthew to depict Jesus as the promised Messiah[36] through whose words and deeds God reveals himself to his people (cf. 11:25–30; 12:28; 17:5; 28:18–20), we recognize that the theological function of this formula is to undergird the twin truths that specifically Jesus Messiah is the one who presents each discourse demar-

33. Cf. *Horae Synopticae* (revised; Oxford: Clarendon, 1909), 165.
34. Cf. M'Neile, *Matthew*, 99; Streeter, *Four Gospels*, 262; Davies, *Setting*, 22–23; W. Grundmann, *Das Evangelium nach Matthäus* (HKNT I; Berlin: Evangelische Verlagsanstalt, 1968), 244.
35. Cf. also Davies, *Setting*, 19–20.
36. Cf. 1:1, 16–18; 11:2–6; 16:16, 20–21; 26:63–64.

cated by the formula and that these "words" or "parables" or "instructions" of his have the status of divine revelation.

As for the element of historical movement, the fivefold formula shares in this both directly and indirectly: directly, by making reference to Jesus as, again, "finishing" any given discourse; and indirectly, by preparing for or modifying clauses that record that Jesus "descended from the mountain" (8:1) or "went on from there" (11:1) or "went away from there" (13:53; 19:1) or "spoke" anew to his disciples (26:1). This emphasis on historical movement is important, because it indicates that the formula is, ultimately, part of a larger pattern that we shall analyze below, namely, Matthew's concept of the history of salvation.

Accordingly, the significance of the fivefold formula, upon which Bacon and others have placed so much stress in their approach to the structure of Matthew's Gospel, is indeed multiple. It is a thoroughly Matthaean idiom; it serves to signal the termination of five discourses; it calls attention to Jesus, the Messiah, whose words are of the status of divine revelation; and it points beyond itself to Matthew's concept of the history of salvation. But for all this the formula cannot be pressed thematically, and neither literarily nor theologically is there sufficient cause for regarding it as the principle by which the Gospel is to be organized into five parts with prologue and epilogue. We shall have occasion later to return to this formula; but for now, since we have ruled against the viability of Bacon's outline for ascertaining the broad structure of Matthew's Gospel, we must ask whether there is not another outline that will commend itself better.

## B. THE STRUCTURE OF THE GOSPEL RECONSIDERED

At 4:17 and 16:21 Matthew writes: "From that time on Jesus began (*Apo tote ērxato [ho] Iēsous*). . . ." Already at the turn of the century Sir John Hawkins classified this expression as a "formula peculiar to Matthew."[37] Since then, occasional commentators have taken note of it,[38] but the general rule has been to attribute it little importance.

Exceptions to the rule were E. Lohmeyer and N. B. Stonehouse. The former utilized this formula to demarcate what he considered to be

---

37. Cf. Hawkins, *Horae Synopticae*, 168.
38. Cf. Allen, *Matthew*, 35, 180; M'Neile, *Matthew*, 45, 244; F. V. Filson, *The Gospel according to St. Matthew* (Harper's New Testament Commentaries; New York: Harper, 1960), 73, 188; Grundmann, *Matthäus*, 397. G. Strecker (*Weg*, 91–92) discusses this expression but states that it denotes merely the "fact of the time-line" and possesses no structural significance for the Gospel whatever.

larger sections of the Gospel (1:1–4:16; 4:17–9:34; 16:21–20:34),[39] and the latter suggested almost in passing that it is pivotal to the broad outline of the whole of the Gospel.[40] The best recent discussion of it is that of E. Krentz, who, like Lohmeyer, used it to determine the extent of Matthew's prologue.[41] Our study picks up on the suggestion of Stonehouse and attempts to prove the truth of it. In line with this, it is our thesis that Matthew did in fact intend that this formula should indicate the broadest divisions of the Gospel.

From a literary standpoint, the formula itself is distinctive. The phrase *apo tote* ("from that time on"), for example, which combines a preposition with an adverb, is the kind of expression that first occurs with increasing frequency in the Hellenistic period.[42] In the entire NT it is found but four times, once in Luke (16:16) and three times in Matthew (cf. also 26:16). Only at 4:17 and 16:21, however, does it appear as part of a fixed formula.[43] Its function is to mark the beginning of a new period of time.[44]

In a detailed analysis of *archomai* ("begin"), J. W. Hunkin concludes that, of the twelve instances in which Matthew employs this verb with the infinitive, in five cases it "distinctively or even emphatically equals 'begin,' "[45] and, unlike Marcan usage,[46] in no case has it become altogether pleonastic.[47] Accordingly, we see that Matthew, by combining the phrase *apo tote* with the verb *archomai*, has succeeded in creating an expression that strongly denotes the beginning of a new phase in the "life of Jesus."[48]

39. Cf. Lohmeyer, *Matthäus*, 1, 64, 264.
40. Cf. N. B. Stonehouse, *The Witness of Matthew and Mark to Christ* (London: Tyndale, 1944), 129–31.
41. Cf. E. Krentz, "The Extent of Matthew's Prologue," *JBL* 83 (1964): 409–414.
42. Cf. J. H. Moulton, *A Grammar of New Testament Greek* (3d ed.; Edinburgh: T. & T. Clark, 1908), I, 99.
43. H. Frankemölle (*Jahwebund und Kirche Christi* [NTAbh 10; Münster: Aschendorff, 1974], 344) ignores the fact that Matthew employs the phrase *apo tote* differently in 4:17 and in 16:21 than in 26:16 (*kai apo tote*), and even goes so far as to contend that its purpose is to point backward, to events recorded, respectively in 4:12 and in 16:13–20.
44. In 26:16, *apo tote* denotes a new turn of events in the life of Judas; in Luke 16:16, it contrasts the new time in which the Kingdom is proclaimed from the preceding time of the law and the prophets; and in Ps 92:2 (LXX), it points to the very beginning of the age. Cf. also Krentz, "Prologue," 410 n. 13.
45. Cf. 4:17; 14:30; 18:24; 26:22, 37.
46. Cf., e.g., Mark 6:7; 10:32; 13:5.
47. Cf. J. W. Hunkin, " 'Pleonastic' *archomai* in the New Testament," *JTS* 25 (1924): 391–93, 395.
48. Cf. also Allen, *Matthew*, 180; E. Klostermann, *Matthäus*, 141; Gaechter, *Matthäus*, 549, 552. We cannot prove but strongly suspect that Matthew has created this

In the content of this formula just as with the fivefold formula the name "Jesus" stands out prominently, and the references to time ("from that time on") and movement ("Jesus began") possess a historical dimension that likewise points to Matthew's concept of the history of salvation. Still, in one respect there is the sharpest contrast between the fivefold formula and this one. Whereas that formula, as we saw, resists the attempt to press it thematically, this one introduces sentences that serve as veritable superscriptions for whole sections of the Gospel. Thus, 4:17 describes Jesus as publicly presenting himself to Israel and summoning it to the Kingdom of Heaven. By the same token, 16:21 describes him as revealing to his disciples that it is God's will that he go to Jerusalem to suffer, die, and be raised. If, therefore, we utilize this formula to arrange Matthew's Gospel according to topic, the following outline readily emerges: (I) The Person of Jesus Messiah (1:1–4:16); (II) The Proclamation of Jesus Messiah (4:17–16:20); and (III) The Suffering, Death, and Resurrection of Jesus Messiah (16:21–28:20).

Our present task is to show that the materials of the Gospel do indeed organize themselves in accordance with this outline. But before we undertake this task, we must give attention to the structural status of a verse we have not as yet discussed, viz., 1:1. The implication of our outline is that 1:1, in analogy to 4:17 and 16:21, functions as the "superscription" of the first main part of the Gospel (1:1–4:16). By contrast, other commentators hold that 1:1 serves either as the heading of the genealogy (vss. 2–17[49] or vss. 2–25[50]) or as the title of the entire Gospel[51] or both.[52] What, then, is the structural status of 1:1?

There are good reasons for believing that Matthew did not intend 1:1

formula (cf. 16:21 with Mark 8:31). In any case, Hawkins was correct when he designated it as a formula that is peculiarly Matthaean (cf. above, n. 37); cf. also Krentz, "Prologue," 411.

49. Cf. e.g., M'Neile, *Matthew*, 1; G. Schrenk, *TDNT*, I, 616; M. Lambertz, "Die Toledoth in MT 1, 1–17 und LC 3, 23bff.," *Festschrift Franz Dornseiff*, ed. H. Kusch (Leipzig: VEB Bibliographisches Institut, 1953), 201; Lohmeyer, *Matthäus*, 4; Schmid, *Matthäus*, 35; Schweizer, *Matthäus*, 8; M. D. Johnson, *The Purpose of the Biblical Genealogies* (NTSMS 8; Cambridge: University Press, 1969), 146.

50. Cf. A. Vögtle, "Die Genealogie Mt 1, 2–16 und die matthäische Kindheitsgeschichte," *Das Evangelium und die Evangelien* (Kommentare und Beiträge zum Alten und Neuen Testament; Düsseldorf: Patmos, 1971), 65, 73.

51. Cf. T. Zahn, *Das Evangelium des Matthäus* (KNT I; 3d ed.; Leipzig: A. Deichert, 1910), 39–44; Robinson, *Matthew*, 2; Klostermann, *Matthäus*, 1; Schniewind, *Matthäus*, 9; W. Marxsen, "Bemerkungen zur 'Form' des sogenannten synoptischen Evangelien," *TLZ* 81 (1956): 348; Davies, *Setting*, 67–70; Frankemölle, *Jahwebund*, 364.

52. Cf. Bonnard, *Matthieu*, 16; Gaechter, *Matthäus*, 34–35; Grundmann, *Matthäus*, 61.

to serve as the title for the entire Gospel.[53] To begin with, if Matthew applies any designation to the contents of his work, it is not that of "book" (*biblos*) but, as mentioned, that of "the Gospel of the Kingdom" (4:23; 9:35; 24:14; 26:13), an expression that enables him to summarize in the same terms both the pre-Easter message of Jesus and the post-Easter message of his church.

In the second place, the great majority of the commentators who look upon 1:1 as the title of the Gospel follow T. Zahn and render *geneseōs* as "history," translating *biblos geneseōs Iēsou Christou* as "Book of the history of Jesus Messiah."[54] The problem with this, however, is that the word *geneseōs* occurs again in 1:18, a verse that Matthew has so formulated that it relates directly to 1:1 by means of 1:17c (*"Christou"*) and especially 1:16b (*"egennēthē Iēsous . . . Christou"*).[55] The result is that *genesis* should not be translated in two different ways in 1:1 and 1:18.[56] In vs. 18 it means "origin."[57] Should this translation be employed in vs. 1 ("Book of the origin of Jesus Messiah"), we see at once that Matthew does not intend vs. 1 to function as the title for the entire Gospel.

W. D. Davies, who likewise considers 1:1 to be the title of the Gospel, attempts to overcome the latter argument by suggesting that *genesis* in 1:18 is to be emended to read *gennēsis* ("birth").[58] But the evidence does not support this emendation, neither on the grounds of intrinsic probability, as A. Vögtle's analysis of ch. 1 proves,[59] nor on the grounds of the external witness of the manuscripts. Nevertheless, Davies' proposal is that the opening words of 1:1 be rendered as "The book of the 'New' Creation being wrought by Jesus Christ."[60] Still, this translation, too, is not without difficulty: first, the context in which Matthew speaks of the new creation per se is not that of the coming of the Messiah but that of the parousia of the Son of Man (cf. 19:28); and second, while Matthew clearly places 1:1 in the service of his christology, we cannot see from the way in which he further develops the latter that the thought that

53. Cf. also Allen, *Matthew*, 2; Lohmeyer, *Matthäus*, 4; Schweizer, *Matthäus*, 8; Vögtle, "Genealogie," *Evangelium*, 73.
54. Zahn, *Matthäus*, 42; cf. also Klostermann, *Matthäus*, 1; Schniewind, *Matthäus*, 9; Grundmann, *Matthäus*, 61; Frankemölle, *Jahwebund*, 365.
55. Cf. K. Stendahl, "Quis et Unde? An Analysis of Mt 1–2," *Judentum, Urchristentum, Kirche*, ed. W. Eltester, (BZNW 26 [Festschrift J. Jeremias]; Berlin: A. Töpelmann, 1960), 101–102; Vögtle, "Genealogie," *Evangelium*, 70.
56. Cf. Lambertz, "Toledoth," 203.
57. Cf. Stendahl, "Quis," 101.
58. Davies, *Setting*, 68–69.
59. Cf. Vögtle, "Genealogie," *Evangelium*, 65–66.
60. Davies, *Setting*, 70.

Jesus Messiah is the one who effects the new creation is the theme that is uppermost in his mind.

In other respects, H. Frankemölle contends that one reason 1:1 must be regarded as the title of Matthew's Gospel is that the word *biblos* ("book"), where it appears in the superscription of such documents as are associated with Jewish apocalyptic or the community of Qumran, regularly refers to a writing in its entirety.[61] But this observation, valid as it may be, contributes little, for we are at a loss to know to what extent Matthew's use of *biblos* was influenced by this alleged literary convention. Moreover, should it be true, as virtually every exegete including Frankemölle[62] asserts, that Matthew was influenced in his use of *biblos* by Gen 2:4a or 5:1a (LXX), then, as O. Eissfeldt[63] has remarked, Matthew knew of a use of the word *biblos* that connects it with only a portion of a document. And finally, as T. Zahn[64] and W. Grundmann[65] acknowledge, 1:1 can function as the title of the whole of the Gospel only so long as one is able to maintain successfully that Matthew does not operate with any verses that can be construed as "superscriptions" of sections of his Gospel. It is exactly this claim, however, that the twofold formula at 4:17 and 16:21 challenges.

If 1:1 does not serve as the title for the whole of Matthew's Gospel, is it to be restricted in application to the genealogy alone (1:2–17) or, at most, to ch. 1? The expression *biblos geneseōs* almost certainly has been taken, as we just noted, from the Septuagint, where it occurs at Gen 2:4a and 5:1a. In both cases, "book of the origin" is made to apply, not merely to what may be termed a genealogy, but to narrative material as well (cf. Gen. 2:4–4:26; 5:1–6:8).[66] Consequently, what these two examples show is that "book of the origin" is an elastic expression that can introduce at once a genealogy and the narration of circumstances attendant to that genealogy. With reference to Matthew, in that he utilizes, as we hope to demonstrate presently, the section 1:1–4:16 of his Gospel to bring the reader to a proper understanding of the person of Jesus Messiah, we see that 1:1 serves admirably as the superscription of this section: more immediately, it introduces the genealogy of ch. 1 and, more broadly, the whole of 1:1–4:16.

61. Cf. Frankemölle, *Jahwebund*, 363.
62. Ibid., 364.
63. "Biblos geneseōs," *Gott und die Götter* (Festschrift E. Fascher; Berlin: Evangelische Verlagsanstalt, 1958), 34–36.
64. *Matthäus*, 39.
65. *Matthäus*, 61.
66. Cf. also Zahn, *Matthäus*, 42; Allen, *Matthew*, 1.

*The Person of Jesus Messiah (1:1–4:16)*

The first main part of the Gospel (1:1–4:16) concentrates, we stated, on the person of Jesus Messiah. Ch. 1, for example, informs the reader by means of the genealogy that Jesus is to be sure the Messiah. He is the "Son of Abraham," for God has directed the whole of Israelite history, which began with Abraham and bears promise also for the Gentiles (Gen 12:3; 18:18; 22:18; 26:4), to the end that it might issue climactically in him (1:1–17). He is the "Son of David," for Joseph son of David gives him his name, adopting him (1:1, 16, 20, 25). But above all he is the Son of God, for he is conceived "by (*ek*) the Holy Spirit" (1:18, 20) and through the prophet God himself says that he will be called "Emmanuel" (1:23), a name that attests to the confessional truth that his origin is in God and that in him God dwells with his own.

Ch. 2 continues to treat of the person of Jesus by presenting him as the ruler of the eschatological people of God: he is the "King of the Jews" (vs. 2), "the Messiah" (vs. 4) who "will shepherd by people Israel" (vs. 6). Significant is the circumstance that from vs. 7 on, Matthew consistently designates Jesus the new-born King as "the child" (*to paidion;* cf. vss. 8–9, 11, 13–14, 20–21). In vs. 15, however, which is a formula quotation, Matthew breaks this otherwise consistent pattern and in this way explains how he would further define this term: "the child" Jesus is in fact "my Son," that is to say, the Son of God. Therefore Jesus Son of God, in analogy to Moses[67] and in fulfillment of OT prophecy (vss. 15, 18, 23), miraculously (vss. 12–13; cf. vss. 19, 22) escapes death at the hands of an evil sovereign and finds refuge in a foreign land until, upon the death of his adversary, he can return again to his homeland. Indicative of ch. 2, then, is the assertion that the messianic King who will shepherd the people of God is in reality the Son of God as well as the correlation of Moses typology with Jesus as the Son of God.

Ch. 3 appears to disrupt the internal unity of 1:1–4:16. The break is ostensibly caused by the shift in time from the infancy of Jesus to the years of his adulthood (3:13), and by the public nature both of the appearance of John (3:5) and, as some allege, of the baptism of Jesus

---

67. There is considerable debate as to whether the narratives in ch. 2 concerning the infant Jesus make allusion to Moses or to Jacob. Each hypothesis has its strengths and weaknesses, but we are inclined to agree with A. Vögtle (*Messias und Gottessohn* [Theologische Perspektiven; Düsseldorf: Patmos, 1971], 32–88) that the Moses-hypothesis is the stronger of the two. For a presentation of the Jacob-hypothesis, cf. D. Daube, "The Earliest Structure of the Gospels," *NTS* 5 (1958/59): 184–86; C. H. Cave, "St. Matthew's Infancy Narrative," *NTS* 9 (1962/63): 382–90; and especially M. M. Bourke, "The Literary Genus of Matthew 1–2," *CBQ* 22 (1960): 167–73.

(3:13, 17). For these reasons, many commentators hold that with ch. 3 the public ministry not only of John but also of Jesus begins.[68]

The shift in time is obviously an important factor, and we shall discuss it when we analyze Matthew's concept of the history of salvation. At this juncture, we shall simply assert that it is not so important as to compel us to mark ch. 3, in outlining the Gospel, with a Roman numeral. Ch. 3 is closely related to chs. 1–2, and a structural sign of this, which is virtually ignored by commentators, is the particle *de* ("now," "then") in 3:1, which serves to link ch. 3 with the preceding. The fact that some manuscripts omit *de* is, on internal grounds, to be understood as a scribal attempt precisely to disassociate ch. 3 from chs. 1–2.

The appearance of John the Baptist (3:1–12) is indeed a public one. But whatever merit this argument may have for determining the broad outline of the Gospel is of little consequence when measured against the recognition that this pericope on John is of a piece with the materials of 1:1–4:16 in that they all have to do with events that are *preliminary* to the public ministry of Jesus. It is commonly known that the role of John in Matthew's Gospel is chiefly that of forerunner (3:3). John is the eschatological Elijah (3:4; 11:14; 17:12–13), who readies Israel for its Messiah (3:2, 5–6, 11) and reflects in his own person and work the person and work of the Mightier One, whose coming means salvation and judgment (3:11–12).[69]

And what of the view that Matthew presents the baptism of Jesus (3:13–17) as an act in public and therefore as the beginning of Jesus' ministry?[70] On the one hand, we readily acknowledge that Matthew has bound the pericope on the Baptism of Jesus closely to the one on John. Stylistically, he has assimilated 3:13 to 3:1 ([a] temporal reference, [b] *paraginetai*, [c] name, [d] place, and [e] articular infinitive, vs. 13 / participle, vs. 1); and he employs to the same end the catchwords "John,"[71]

68. Cf. Green, *Matthew*, 114; Schlatter, *Matthäus*, 50; Benoit, *Matthieu*, 47; Jones, *Matthew*, 59; Walker, *Heilsgeschichte*, 115; Grundmann, *Matthäus*, 89; Hill, *Matthew*, 88. Cf. also W. Trilling, "Die Täufertradition bei Matthäus," *BZ* 3 (1959); 285–86.

69. Cf. Trilling, "Täufertradition," 271–89; W. Wink, *John the Baptist in the Gospel Tradition* (NTSMS 7; Cambridge: University Press, 1968), 27–41.

70. Concerning the view that the Baptism marks the beginning of the public ministry of Jesus, cf. Johnson, "Matthew," 266. Concerning the view that the Baptism of Jesus in Matthew's Gospel should be construed as an act in public, cf. Allen, *Matthew*, 28–30; Lagrange, *Matthieu*, 55–56; Klostermann, *Matthäus*, 25; Green, *Matthew*, 117; Johnson, "Matthew," 268; Benoit, *Matthieu*, 50; Fenton, *Matthew*, 59–60; Jones, *Matthew*, 63; Albright–Mann, *Matthew*, 31; Hill, *Matthew*, 97.

71. Cf. 3:13 to 3:1, 4.

"baptize,"[72] "Jordan," (cf. vs. 13 to vs. 6), and "Spirit" (cf. vs. 16 to vs. 11). In addition, the words of John regarding the "Mightier One" also create anticipation of Jesus in the mind of the reader.

But one misreads the data if one concludes from them that the baptism of Jesus is therefore portrayed as a "public affair." Matthew utilizes *tote* ("then") in 3:13, as he does in 4:1, to point out that the baptism of Jesus is, however imprecisely, chronologically removed from the preceding public scenes surrounding John. Moreover, no reference whatever is made in 3:13–17 either to the great crowds or to the "Pharisees and Sadducees" (cf. 3:5, 7). When Jesus does finally present himself to Israel, Matthew highlights this with a massive summary-passage (4:23–25). On the contrary, the baptism of Jesus is portrayed as an eminently "private affair," involving solely Jesus, John, and the voice from heaven. Indeed, when Matthew depicts the descent of the Spirit, he is more explicit still than Mark in restricting sight of it to Jesus alone (*Iēsous . . . eiden*, 3:16; cf. Mark 1:10). And not even do the words *houtos estin* ("this is," 3:17), as opposed to Mark's *sy ei* ("you are," 1:11), demonstrate that the voice was addressing a public gathering. Matthew uses this turn of phrase in order to assimilate his account of the Baptism to that of the Transfiguration: here Jesus is declared the Son of God in the private company of one human witness; there he is declared the Son of God in the equally private company of three human witnesses (17:1, 5).

Accordingly, we find no compelling reason for disassociating ch. 3 from chs. 1–2 (as though the latter constitute the prologue of the Gospel), and have discovered two factors that indicate they belong together as constituent parts of a more comprehensive unit: the connective *de* at 3:1; and the circumstance that all of the narratives in these chapters describe events that are *preliminary* to the public ministry of Jesus. Is there other evidence of unity between chs. 1–2 and ch. 3?

The answer lies in the verse with which ch. 3 reaches its culmination, which, we should note, has to do with the overall theme we have claimed for 1:1–4:16, namely, the person of Jesus Messiah. We have already delineated the central thought of the pericope on John the Baptist (3:1–12). The central thought of the pericope on the Baptism of Jesus (3:13–17) is the following: Jesus is baptized by John in order to fulfill all righteousness (vs. 15); unlike John, however, Jesus is furthermore declared by the voice from heaven to be the Son of God (vs. 17).

It is precisely this recurrent theme of the Son of God, sounded in 3:17

72. Cf. 3:13–14, 16 to 3:[1], 6, [7], 11a and d.

with unparalleled force thus far, that further compels us to regard ch. 3 as internally related to chs. 1–2. In chs. 1–2, Matthew graphically portrays Jesus as the Son of God, but this truth is never openly asserted. Once, to be sure, it is stated directly (2:15), but even then only in the words of the ancient prophet. At 3:17, on the other hand, Matthew brings just such an open assertion of the divine sonship of Jesus, and this by none other than God himself. What these factors show, therefore, is that in Matthew's eyes it is not only ch. 3 that reaches its culmination in vs. 17, but chs. 1–2 as well: what is essentially implicit there becomes explicit here. And that in averring this we have in fact captured the mind of Matthew is evident from his use throughout chs. 1–3 of such related idioms as "his people" (1:21), "my people" (2:6), and "my Son" (2:15; 3:17), for with these idioms in particular Matthew succeeds in binding the contents of chs. 1–2 to the climactic verse 3:17.

Consequently, the conclusion stands: ch. 3 is part and parcel of the first main section of Matthew's Gospel. In addition, a review of the subsection 4:1–16 indicates that it, too, finds its place with chs. 1–3. The story of the Temptation (4:1–11), for example, displays all of the following traits: it is structurally bound to the story of the Baptism (cf. the assimilation of 4:1 to 3:13: [a] temporal reference, [b] name, [c] place, [d] agent, [e] aorist passive infinitive); it is preliminary to the public ministry of Jesus; it portrays action that takes place in private; and it concentrates on the person of Jesus Messiah, designating him specifically as the Son of God. Two of these traits stand out in the central thought:[73] Jesus Messiah, the Son of God, is led by the Spirit (4:1; cf. 3:16) into the desert and tempted by Satan (4:3, 5–6, 8–9) even as Israel, son of God, had been tempted; but whereas Israel failed its test, Jesus does not (4:4, 7, 10), and so he successfully recapitulates this history of Israel and gives proof of his divine sonship.

This brings us to 4:12–16, the final pericope in the section 1:1–4:16. Since it tells of the resettlement of Jesus in Capernaum of Galilee, a number of commentators hold that with 4:12 Jesus commences his public ministry.[74] That this cannot be the case is evident from vs. 12 itself: the

73. Cf. J. A. T. Robinson, "The Temptations," *Twelve New Testament Studies* (London: SCM, 1962), 53–60; B. Gerhardsson, *The Testing of God's Son* (ConNT 2:1; Lund: Gleerup, 1966); J. Dupont, *Les tentations de Jésus au désert* (StudNeot 4; Tournai; Desclée, 1968), 9–42.
74. Cf. Allen, *Matthew*, 33; M'Neile, *Matthew*, 42; Lagrange, *Matthieu*, 66; Klostermann, *Matthäus*, "Inhaltsübersicht"; Schmid, *Matthäus*, 69; Filson, *Matthew*, 71; Bonnard, *Matthieu*, 47; Gaechter, *Matthäus*, 81; Léon-Dufour, "Synoptic Gospels,"

subject ("Jesus") is left to be inferred from 4:1–11;[75] *de* ties vss. 12–16 to the preceding narrative;[76] and the statement concerning John's arrest presupposes his earlier conflict with the "Pharisees and Sadducees" (3:7–10).

The function of 4:12–16 likewise reveals that these verses belong to 1:1–4:11. Vs. 13, complemented as it is by the formula quotation in vss. 15–16, is directly associated both formally and materially with 2:23, which also contains a formula quotation.[77] We can observe how flawlessly the one passage picks up on the other: "... *and he came and dwelled in a city which is called Nazareth,* in order that what was spoken by the prophets might be fulfilled ..." (2:23); "... *and he left Nazareth and came and dwelled in Capernaum beside the sea,* in the regions of Zebulun and Naphtali, in order that what was spoken by Isaiah the prophet might be fulfilled ..." (4:13–14). From this we learn that the "divinely ordained" travels of Jesus, which began in ch. 2, do not, as Matthew tells it, come to an end until Jesus settles in Galilee, which is the region in which God has decreed he should embark upon his public ministry to Israel. To signal the termination of these travels and to ready Jesus for the beginning of his public ministry is the dual purpose of 4:12–16.

Before we conclude our examination of 1:1–4:16, there is a final matter pertaining to structure we must consider. J. C. Fenton contends that 3:2 and 4:17b, which are identical in wording ("Repent, for the Kingdom of Heaven is at hand"), form an inclusion, with the result that 4:17 should be aligned structurally with the materials that precede it instead of with those that follow.[78] However one may assess the implications of inclusion for determining structure, there are weighty reasons that speak against aligning 4:17 with 4:12–16. Stylistically, had Matthew desired to associate 4:17 with 4:12–16, he almost certainly would have begun the verse with *kai* to make it read *kai apo tote* ... ("*And from that time on* Jesus began to proclaim ..."), for this is the exact manner in which he has proceeded at 26:16. Linguistically, 4:17 is not of the same character as the materials comprising 1:1–4:16, because, again, whereas they tell of

169; W. G. Thompson, *Matthew's Advice to a Divided Community. Mt. 17, 22–18, 35* (AnBib 44; Rome: Biblical Institute Press, 1970), 19–25; Albright—Mann, *Matthew,* 38.

75. Cf. Lohmeyer, *Matthäus,* 62.

76. Cf. Krentz, "Prologue," 411.

77. Cf. also Lohmeyer, *Matthäus,* 62; C. T. Davis, "Tradition and Redaction in Matthew 1:18–2:23," *JBL* 90 (1971): 407–409.

78. Fenton, *Matthew,* 51–52.

events that are preliminary to the public ministry of Jesus, 4:17 portrays Jesus as beginning this public ministry. Third, 4:17 is literarily parallel to 16:21; but there can be no question that Matthew uses the latter, not to signal the end of a section, but to alert the reader to what is coming. Finally, when Fenton argues that 3:1–4:17 must be construed as one of the great divisions of the first Gospel because it represents Matthew's revision of Mark 1:2–15, he measurably weakens his own case since he makes himself guilty methodologically of reading one Evangelist in the light of another. Hence, for these four reasons we are unable to concur in Fenton's judgment that 4:17 belongs structurally with 4:12–16, and instead maintain that its fundamental disposition is with the materials that follow, that is, the second main part of the Gospel (4:17–16:20).

In sum, therefore, the section 1:1–4:16 proves itself to be the first main part of Matthew's Gospel. The subsections 1:1–2:23 and 3:1–4:16 are intimately related to each other by virtue of structure and content: the particle *de* at 3:1 connects the pericope on John the Baptist (3:1–12) with preceding narrative; the "divinely ordained" travels of Jesus prior to his public presentation of himself to the Jews bind ch. 2 to ch. 4 (cf. 2:22–23 to 4:12–16); all the pericopes in 1:1–4:16 describe events in the "life of Jesus (John)" which are preliminary to the Galilean ministry (4:17); and the theme of the divine sonship of Jesus pervades all four chapters. With reference to the latter, Jesus Messiah is, to be sure, Son of Abraham, Son of David, and King, but foremost he is the Son of God, for his origin can be traced to God. The conjecture is surely correct that the title "Son of God" is absent from 1:1 because Matthew intends that God himself should be the first to make this pronouncement.[79] However this may be, the theme of the divine sonship of Jesus runs like an unbroken thread through 1:1–4:16, becoming ever more visible and thus alerting the reader to the manner in which Matthew would have him comprehend the person of Jesus.

### The Proclamation of Jesus Messiah (4:17 16:20)

Now that we have argued the case for understanding 1:1–4:16 as the first main part of Matthew's Gospel, we shall endeavor to demonstrate that 4:17–16:20 constitutes the second main part of the Gospel. This part focuses on the proclamation of Jesus Messiah in the sense that Jesus publicly presents himself to Israel and summons it to the Kingdom of Heaven

79. Cf. R. Pesch, "Der Gottessohn im matthäischen Evangelienprolog (Mt 1–2)," *Bib* 48 (1967): 416.

(4:17). An investigation of the materials in this part proves that they develop this central thought.

To begin with, Jesus is portrayed as discharging throughout Galilee a ministry of teaching, preaching, and healing (4:23–25; 9:35; 11:1). His initial act in public is to call his first disciples (4:18–22). Followed by them and attracting huge crowds (4:20, 22–25; 5:1), Jesus presents himself to his disciples and Israel as the Messiah of Word (5:2–7:29).[80] Wandering in the area of Capernaum and traveling across the Sea of Galilee and back, Jesus performs ten mighty acts of deliverance, in so doing setting forth the nature and the cost of discipleship.[81] At the height of his ministry, in order to gather the crowds, driven and harassed as sheep without a shepherd (9:36), Jesus commissions the twelve disciples (10:1, 5) to a ministry modeled on his own, one of preaching and healing though not of teaching (10:1, 7–8). Although the ministry of the disciples to the "lost sheep" from the house of Israel (10:6) is motivated by the compassion of the Messiah for his people (9:36), the anticipated results are sketched in negative terms (10:5b–11:1).

As adumbrated by the Missionary Discourse (ch. 10), the next subsection of the Gospel tells of the rejection of Jesus Messiah by all segments of Israel (11:2–12:50). John the Baptist questions whether Jesus is the Messiah who is to come (cf. 11:2–3, 6). "This generation" looks upon him as a glutton and drunkard, the friend of tax-collectors and sinners (11:19). The cities of Chorazin, Bethsaida, and Capernaum, in which Jesus did his mightiest miracles, refuse to be moved to repentance (11:20–24). In explanation of such rejection, Jesus invokes the will of his Father (11:25–26). Following this, the leaders of the people attack Jesus: they charge first the disciples and then him with breaking the law (12:2, 10); they plot his death (12:14); they accuse him of carrying out his ministry on the authority of Beelzebul, the prince of demons (12:24); and they demand from him a sign (12:38). At the close of ch. 12, even the family of Jesus appears to desert him, so that his disciples alone remain as those who do the will of the Heavenly Father (12:46–50).

The response of Jesus to his total rejection by Israel is pictured as being a duel one. On the one hand, he declares that Israel has become

---

80. Schniewind, *Matthäus*, 37.
81. Cf. the insightful article by C. Burger ("Jesu Taten nach Matthäus 8 and 9," *ZThK* 70 [1973]: 272–86), who shows that it is not enough to construe Matt 8–9 simply as a section containing a cycle of ten miracles that present Jesus as the "Messiah of Deed." Cf. also W. G. Thompson, "Reflections on the Composition of Mt 8:1–9:34," *CBQ* 33 (1971): 365–88.

hard of heart, and gives public demonstration of this by addressing the crowds in "parables," that is to say, in speech they cannot comprehend (13:2–3, 10–13).[82] On the other hand, he turns his attention to his disciples (13:16–17, 36–52), interpreting his parables for them (13:18–23, 36–43) and, in general, revealing to them the mysteries of the Kingdom of Heaven (13:11).[83]

By the close of the Parable Discourse, there is no longer any doubt in the first Gospel as to the course Jesus' ministry will take, and an analysis of the subsection 13:53b–16:20 confirms this. Jesus continues, for example, to show himself to be Israel's Messiah, through his miracles (14:15–21; 15:32–39) and, what Matthew particularly emphasizes, through his ministry of healing among the people (14:13–14, 34–36; 15:29–31). But though the "crowds" (*ochloi*) per se are not said to reject him,[84] neither do they accept him, and in his home village of Nazareth the townspeople take offense at him (13:53–58). As for the leaders, the encounters of Jesus with them do not rise above the level of acrimonious debate (15:1–14; 16:1–4). Indeed, in the face of their propensity for violence against him (cf. 12:14), which is true of Herod Antipas as well (cf. 14:1–12), Jesus "withdraws" (*anachōreō*) to a deserted place (14:13) or into the regions of Tyre and Sidon (15:21) and hence momentarily "goes away" (*aperchomai*) from them (16:4). Among those in Israel, only the disciples comprehend the person of Jesus (16:13–20), and even they can be men of "little faith" (14:28–33; 16:5–12) and in need of clarification (15:15–20). Finally, in that Jesus heals the Canaanite woman's daughter (15:21–28), the note of "universalism," which crops up throughout the Gospel, is sounded anew.

This brief review of 4:17–16:20 thus documents the claim that the materials of this broad section are controlled by the central thought expressed in 4:17. What is more, Matthew can even be seen to have proceeded "logically" in that he treats in turn such themes as the salvation Jesus proffers Israel in word and deed (4:18–11:1), the rejection of Jesus by all segments of Israel (11:2–12:50), the negative response of Jesus to Israel which the people themselves prompted (13:1–35), the concentration of Jesus on his disciples (13:36–53a), and the periodic withdrawal of Jesus from his opponents (14:13; 15:21; 16:4). As regards the latter portion of 4:17–16:20, since, beginning with 13:53b, Matthew adheres

82. For a detailed analysis of 13:1–35, cf. J. D. Kingsbury, *The Parables of Jesus in Matthew 13* (London and Richmond, Va.: S.P.C.K. and John Knox, 1969), 22–91.
83. For a detailed analysis of 13:36–52, cf. ibid., 92–129.
84. On Matthew's understanding of the term *ochlos*, cf. ibid., 24–28.

virtually point by point to the outline of Mark's Gospel,[85] one understands why there is a certain interweaving throughout 13:53b–16:20 of the themes set forth in the chapters immediately preceding.

Striking evidence of the internal unity of 4:17–16:20 can also be found in further examination of the "superscription" 4:17 and of the summary-passages 4:23–25, 9:35, and 11:1. For one thing, the very location of these summary-passages, namely, that they occur solely in the block of material 4:18–11:1, confirms the truth of the observations we made above: in 4:18–11:1, Matthew is predominately concerned to portray Jesus Messiah as proffering salvation to Israel in word and deed; in 11:2–12:50, Matthew is predominately concerned to portray the complete rejection of Jesus Messiah by Israel.

In the second place, one of the key terms in 4:17 is the verb "proclaim" (*kēryssein*), and this is reported in each of the summary-passages.[86] A study of this verb in the Gospel reveals that only in the subsection 4:18–11:1 does Matthew speak of there being "proclamation" in any positive sense to Israel. After 11:1, "proclamation" takes place only in conjunction with the worldwide mission of the church (24:14; 26:13). Consequently, Matthew's use of the term "proclaim" corresponds exactly to the overall pattern we discovered in 4:17–16:20: Jesus summons Israel to the Kingdom (4:18–11:1), but its response is one of rejection (11:2–12:50; cf. 12:41), with the result that Jesus turns from the people (13:1–35) and toward his disciples (13:36–53a), withdrawing at times from his opponents (chs. 14–16).

In the summary-passages, a parallel stress is placed on the verbs "teaching" (*didaskein*, 4:23; 9:35; 11:1) and "healing" (*therapeuein*, 4:23; 9:35). Interestingly, Matthew employs the combination *didaskein-didachē* in complete harmony with his use of *kēryssein*. In 4:18–11:1, Matthew presents Jesus in a positive light as the teacher of Israel.[87] Following 11:1, Jesus is still pictured as "teaching" the people, but now this activity is colored by the motif of rejection.[88] Thus, Jesus' teaching is in principle diametrically opposed to that of the leaders of Israel (15:1–9; 16:12). His reputation as a teacher or his engaging in teaching simply provides occasion for them to challenge his authority (21:23–27) or to

---

85. Cf. 13:53b–16:20 to Mark 6:1–8:30.
86. Cf. 4:23; 9:35; 11:1; also 10:7, 27.
87. Cf. 4:23; 5:1–2; 7:28–29; 9:35; 11:1.
88. For a discussion of the manner in which the motif of rejection enters into Matthew's description of Jesus' "teaching" and "preaching" on the one hand and of his "speaking" in parables on the other (cf. 13:1–3a with Mark 4:1–2), cf. Kingsbury, *Matthew 13*, 28–31.

attempt to entrap him in his speech (22:15–22). Amazement at his teaching, far from signaling its acceptance, only indicates that he has had the last word in doctrinal debate with the Sadducees (22:23–33). In point of fact Jesus' teaching in the synagogue at Nazareth merely causes the townspeople to take offense at him (13:53–58), and his teaching in the temple is acquitted by the crowds with his arrest (26:55). So again, the same pattern prevails for *didaskein–didachē* as for *kēryssein*.

The verb *therapeuein* does not fully conform to the usage of *kēryssein–didaskein*, for Matthew gives it almost exclusively a positive ring throughout his Gospel.[89] Indeed, the one expansive summary-passage Matthew builds in 11:2–16:20 is devoted singularly to Jesus' activity of healing (15:29–31; cf. also 21:14). Do these findings invalidate our conclusions on *kēryssein–didaskein*?

The answer is that they rather support these conclusions. For although Matthew presents the rejection of Jesus by Israel as, to all intents and purposes, bringing his preaching and teaching (4:18–11:1) to a close, he is still interested in revealing Jesus as Israel's Messiah. This he effectively does, almost to the end (cf. 21:14), by portraying Jesus as the Messiah who continues to heal the very people who have "long ago" showed themselves obdurate to his word. Furthermore, if Matthew does operate with *kēryssein–didaskein* on the one hand and *therapeuein* on the other in the manner we have stipulated, we can then understand how it happens that, following 11:1, Matthew in two cases prefers to speak of Jesus as "healing" the crowds whereas Mark, in parallel passages, speaks of him as "teaching" them.[90] At any rate, it is now clear why Matthew's use of *therapeuein* both conforms to and differs from that of *kēryssein–didaskein*.

The analysis, then, of the "superscription" 4:17, of the summary-passages, and, in general, of the material comprising 4:17–16:20 goes to prove that the large central section of the Gospel does indeed form a basic unit. We turn, therefore, to a discussion of the third main section of the Gospel, 16:21–28:20.

*The Suffering, Death, and Resurrection of Jesus Messiah (16:21–28:20)*

The "superscription" 16:21 alerts us to the theme of this section: the suffering, death, and resurrection of Jesus Messiah. In the development

89. Cf. 4:23–25; 8:16; 9:35; 10:1, 8; 12:15; 14:13–14; 15:29–31; 19:2; 21:14.
90. Cf. 14:14 with Mark 6:34; 19:2 with Mark 10:1.

of this theme, Matthew is dependent upon the outline of Mark's Gospel,[91] supplementing it at prescribed points with logia, parables, and an occasional narrative.[92]

Matthew writes in 16:21 that Jesus began to show "his disciples" that suffering, death, and resurrection lay before him in Jerusalem Such concentration on the disciples is in accordance with the flow of events established already in 4:17–16:20. To be sure, following his repudiation by all Israel (11:2–12:50), Jesus continues to appear in public, withdrawing for the last time only two days before the passover and crucifixion (26:2). As far as Israel is concerned, however, from chs. 11–12 onward Jesus has become the rejected Messiah, and he remains so also throughout 16:21–28:20. Accordingly, this latter part of the ministry of Jesus is not at all punctuated with summary-passages of a positive nature with respect to the preaching and teaching of Jesus before the people (cf. 4:23–25; 9:35; 11:1). Beginning with 16:21, the summaries we encounter are the three passion-predictions (16:21; 17:22–23; 20:17–19); the single positive bond still existing between Jesus and Israel is, as we stated above, Jesus' activity among the people of healing.[93]

In regard to the words and deeds of Jesus, only the disciples truly comprehend them.[94] Even when Jesus rides into Jerusalem and is saluted by the crowds with shouts of "Hosanna to the Son of David . . . who comes in the name of the Lord" (21:9), the most this means to them is that Jesus is the "prophet" who hails "from Nazareth of Galilee" (21:11).[95] Indeed, from 16:21 on, Jesus has proportionately less to do with the crowds and more to do with his disciples on the one hand and the leaders of the people on the other. To his disciples Jesus imparts paraenesis[96] and an epiphany of himself (17:1–8). Over against the leaders, he engages in debate,[97] enunciates his so-called parables against Israel (21:28–22:14), and delivers his scathing apology against the scribes and Pharisees (ch. 23). So again, in view of the flow of events as recorded by the Gospel, the reference to the "disciples" in 16:21 has its necessary place.

That such increasing concentration of Jesus on his disciples despite his

91. Cf. 16:21–28:20 to Mark 8:31–16:8.
92. Cf., e.g., 17:24–27; 27:3–10, 24–26, 62–66; 28:9–20.
93. Cf. [17:18]; 19:2; [20:34]; 21:14.
94. Concerning Matthew's portrait of the "disciples," cf. Kingsbury, *Matthew 13*, 40–42.
95. Cf. also Strecker, *Weg*, 106–107.
96. Cf. 16:21–28; 17:9–21; 19:10–30; 20:20–28; 21:18–22.
97. Cf. 19:3–9; 21:14–17; 21:23–27; 22:15–46.

continued appearance in public is an especially distinctive feature of the third main section is also evident from the five so-called great discourses of Jesus. Thus, the first three, which, significantly, are found in 4:17–16:20, are delivered, respectively, both to the crowds and the disciples (5:1–2; 7:28–29), to the disciples (10:5) but on behalf of the crowds (9:35–10:1, 6–8), and to the crowds in part (13:1–3a) and to the disciples in part (13:10–23, 36–52). By contrast, the final two discourses, which are embedded in this third section, are delivered exclusively to the disciples (cf. 17:22–18:35; 24:1–4a).

We had occasion above to make reference to the three passion-predictions. The very fact that each of the two sections 4:17–16:20 and 16:21–28:20 contain three principal summaries[98] attests to the internal unity of both.

There are some commentators who would make the term "Galilee" the basis for an outline of the Gospel and consequently designate the chs. 4:12–18:35 as the central section.[99] This position cannot be upheld: the pericope 4:12–16 is, as we have already demonstrated, an integral part of the material preceding it; and the first passion-prediction at 16:21, in which Matthew unlike Mark specifically mentions "Jerusalem," shows that the latter, geographically speaking, now supersedes Galilee as the focus of attention. Hence, while Jesus is not described as leaving the region of Galilee until 19:1, from 16:21 until the closing verses of the Gospel (cf. 28:16–20) Jerusalem is the place of prominence.

The arguments just advanced indicate that Matthew's primary interest in Galilee as a setting for the ministry of Jesus extends to what we have designated as the second main section of the Gospel, 4:17–16:20. How this interest is to be defined we discover in 4:12–16, the pericope that, again, stands outside this second section but serves as a transition to it. In the formula quotation 4:15–16, the text speaks of "Galilee of the Gentiles," where the "people who sat in darkness have seen a great light, and for those who sat in the region and shadow of death light has dawned."

Now Matthew's purpose in stressing the word "Gentiles" in his reference to Galilee in 4·15 is not only historical in nature but also theological: following the resurrection of Jesus, the disciples are described as

---

98. Cf. 4:23–25; 9:35; 11:1; and 16:21; 17:22–23; 20:17–19.
99. This division of the Gospel is advocated by Huck–Lietzmann (*Synopse der drei ersten Evangelien* [9th ed.; Tübingen: J. C. B. Mohr, 1950], 9, 143) and may be said to be supported also by K. Aland (*Synopsis Quattuor Evangeliorum* [5th ed.; Stuttgart: Württembergische Bibelanstalt, 1968], 44, 334). Thompson (*Matthew's Advice*, 16–25) presents what is perhaps the most detailed discussion of this position. Cf. also Grundmann, *Matthäus*, 426; Albright–Mann, *Matthew*, 227–28.

going "to Galilee" (*eis tēn Galilaian*, 28:16) where they are commissioned to make disciples of all "Gentiles," or nations (*ethnē*, 28:19). Consequently, in bringing the expression "Galilee of the Gentiles" as early as 4:15, Matthew is already preparing the reader at the close of the first main part of his Gospel for the narrative that will come at the end of his Gospel.

But before the disciples can go to Galilee to undertake their mission to the nations, Matthew contends that it is first necessary that Jesus go "to Galilee" (*eis tēn Galilaian*, 4:12) in order to undertake his mission, not to the Gentiles, but to Israel. Thus in 4:15–16, Matthew's primary interest in Galilee stems from his understanding of it as the region where Jesus Messiah proffers salvation to Israel. But again, Jesus is portrayed as fulfilling this expectation in 4:17–16:20 (or, more exactly, in 4:17–11:1), not in 16:21–28:20, where the passion-prediction sets the tone. Galilee has significance for Matthew, therefore, because of its divinely ordained place in the history of salvation; once Scripture has been fulfilled (4:14–16), Jesus can even remain in Galilee although, technically, Jerusalem has superseded it in importance (16:21–19:1). Accordingly, the way in which Matthew employs the term Galilee, far from challenging our conception of the structure of his Gospel, in reality supports it.

One additional reason why the broad division of Matthew's Gospel cannot be determined on the basis of the mere occurrence of the word Galilee in the text is the circumstance that Matthew is so christologically oriented that, in passages of all types having structural significance, he invariably places emphasis on the person of Jesus. To cite the chief examples, the name "Jesus" appears in all of the following key passages: in the opening verse of the Gospel, in the twofold formula (4:17; 16:21), in the summary-passages (4:23–25 [critical apparatus]; 9:35; 11:1), in the passion-predictions (16:21; 17:22–23; 20:17–19), and in the fivefold formula (7:28–29; 11:1; 13:53; 19:1; 26:1). Such emphasis on the person of Jesus precludes the notion that the word Galilee has structural relevance for Matthew.

This brings us to the final question of the present discussion: what is the relationship between the fivefold formula and the twofold formula? As is obvious from all we have said, the answer is that the fivefold formula is to be subsumed under the twofold formula. We stated that the literary and structural function of the fivefold formula is above all to signal the close of selected discourses of Jesus. The structural function of the twofold formula, we maintained, is to divide the Gospel into its three most comprehensive parts. Is there a simple way to test this hypothesis?

The reciprocal relationship between the three summary-passages in 4:17–16:20 and between the three passion-predictions in 16:21–28:20 is so strong that, however the Gospel is outlined, it should be done in such a fashion that classification leaves each grouping intact. Now if the Gospel is divided into sections according to the fivefold formula, we recognize at once that the groupings are broken: 7:28–29 separates 4:23–25 from 9:35, 11:1; and 19:1 separates 16:21, 17:22–23 from 20:17–19. By the same token, the unity of each grouping is respected when the Gospel is divided into sections according to the twofold formula.

In sum, our investigation of both the fivefold formula and the twofold formula proves that it is the latter that points to the most basic divisions of Matthew's Gospel. These have to do, in sequence, with the person of Jesus Messiah (1:1–4:16), the proclamation of Jesus Messiah (4:17–16:20), and the suffering, death, and resurrection of Jesus Messiah (16:21–28:20).

## C. THE EVANGELIST'S CONCEPT OF SALVATION-HISTORY

At the beginning of this chapter we stated that, by and large, scholarly attempts to solve the problem of the structure of Matthew's Gospel may be divided into three categories the first two of which have to do with topical outlines. In our analysis of the fivefold and twofold formulas, we pointed out that both, in describing Jesus as "finishing" a discourse or as "beginning" a new phase of his ministry, evince temporal movement and therefore direct attention to the chronological dimension of the Gospel. Within the last years, several commentators have devoted themselves to a study of precisely this facet of Matthew's Gospel. The upshot of their work is that each in his own way has advanced the thesis that Matthew's concept of the history of salvation, not the topical outline per se, is the chief principle by which he has organized the materials of his Gospel. Our present task, then, is to review the explanations these commentators give of Matthew's concept of salvation-history, if necessary propose our own, and, finally, show how Matthew relates the topical outline of the Gospel which we have established to his concept of the history of salvation.

As to the factor that has most determined the shape of the first Gospel, W. Trilling, for one, takes the position that it is Matthew's understanding of the church as the "true Israel." Basing his arguments in the main on the passages 28:18–20, 21:43, and 27:25, Trilling asserts that Matthew intends to portray the church as the "true Israel" which has replaced the

Jews, or "false Israel," who have forfeited their place in the history of salvation as the chosen people of God.[100] G. Strecker, for his part, holds that the delay of the parousia is this determining factor. In response to such a delay Matthew, contends Strecker, composes a "life of Jesus" with eschatological relevance and orders it as the "way of righteousness" in the history of salvation, which spans the "time of the fathers and of the prophets," the "time of Jesus," and the "time of the church."[101]

From another perspective, R. Walker believes that the factor that has most determined the strucure of he Gospel is Matthew's view of his own age as the age of the Gentile mission. Matthew, claims Walker, writes at once a "life of Jesus" and an "acts of the Apostles" in order to set forth in three epochs particularly the more recent history of salvation: the "pre-history of the Messiah," the "history of the call of Israel," and the "call of the Gentiles."[102] With yet a different approach, W. G. Thompson avers that the experience of Matthew's community of internal dissension and of external opposition, not from Jews but from the Gentile nations, is the factor that has most guided Matthew, if not in the composition of the whole of his Gospel, at least in that of particular sections (cf., e.g., chs. 5–7, 10, 24–25; 17:22–18:35; 28:16–20).[103]

All four of the men just cited see Matthew as dividing the history of salvation into three epochs. According to them, Matthew draws the lines of demarcation in such a way as to distinguish sharply among the times of Israel, of Jesus, and of Matthew, or of the church. Moreover, in emphasizing, respectively, the church as the true Israel, the delay of the parousia, the influx of the Gentiles into the church, or the circumstances of internal discord and of external opposition provoked by the Gentile mission, Trilling, Strecker, Walker, and Thompson reveal that, to their way of thinking, ecclesiology is the element that can be said to control Matthew's scheme of the history of salvation and therefore the structure of his Gospel.

In one respect we find this conclusion to be remarkable, because for all the differences of opinion on the structure of the first Gospel between these men on the one hand and Bacon and those who advocate his topical outline on the other, in the last analysis both groups can be seen to agree on one matter of fundamental importance, namely, that the structure of

100. Cf. Trilling, *Israel*, 95–96, 162, 213.
101. Cf. Strecker, *Weg*, 45–49, 184–88.
102. Cf. Walker, *Heilsgeschichte*, 114–15.
103. Cf. W. G. Thompson, "An Historical Perspective in the Gospel of Matthew," *JBL* 93 (1974): 244, 252–54, 262.

the first Gospel has been decisively molded by the ecclesiology of Matthew. This, however, is a point we should like to contest.

That Matthew has given mature consideration to the problem of time goes without saying. But is it accurate to argue that he divides the history of salvation into three epochs? This is the initial question we must pose, and only after answering it can we then broach the further questions as to the relationship Matthew establishes between the topical outline of his Gospel and his concept of salvation-history and as to the factor that has influenced him most in giving shape to his Gospel.

## Temporal Expressions in the Gospel

If we take the Gospel according to Mark for purposes of comparison, we may say that Matthew has "historicized" the evangelical tradition to a greater extent than has Mark. Although, proportionately, the second Gospel contains more narrative than the first, the fact of the matter is that whereas Mark employs such temporal terms as *aiōn* ("age"), *hēmera* ("day"), *kairos* ("time"), *synteleia* ("consummation"), *telos* ("end"), *chronos* ("time"), and *hōra* ("hour") a total of fifty-three times, Matthew employs them no less than ninety-eight times, and in more variegated expression. What do these terms connote in Matthew's Gospel?

To begin with, Matthew often utilizes temporal phrases simply to designate some point in time that otherwise remains indistinct. This is the case with phrases like "at that time,"[104] "at that hour,"[105] "from that hour,"[106] "on that day,"[107] and "from that day."[108] Vague though they are, these contribute considerable chronological movement to the text.

Still, not all of these phrases or their constituent terms are bland. On the contrary, Matthew can follow the lead of the tradition[109] and combine the terms "day" and "hour" to form a vivid eschatological expression denoting the parousia of the Son of Man (25:13; cf. 24:37). Similarly, the phrase "on that day" is used by Matthew as the equivalent of the eschatological Day of the Lord to refer to the time of the Final Judgment (7:21).

Accordingly, Matthew operates with temporal terms also on a second level, investing them with eschatological significance in the strictest

104. *en ekeinō tō kairō;* cf. 11:25; 12:1; 14:1.
105. *en ekeinē tē hōra;* cf. 8:13; 10:19; 18:1; 26:55.
106. *apo tēs hōras ekeinēs;* cf. 9:22; 15:28; 17:18.
107. *en ekeinē tē hēmera;* cf. 13:1; 22:23.
108. *ap' ekeinēs tēs hēmeras;* cf. 22:46.
109. Cf. 24:36, 44, 50 to Mark 13:32; Luke 12:40, 46.

sense. When evoking the image of the Day of the Lord, for example, he prefers the apocalyptic phrase "on the day of judgment"[110] to the phrase "on that day," probably because the former is less susceptible particularly to Gentile ears to the loss of its eschatological force. To stipulate the time when present history shall have run its course, Matthew draws on the term "end"[111] or the expression the "consummation of the age."[112] Finally, we should note that of the Synoptists, Matthew employs the term "end" in its absolute sense four times as compared with twice for Mark (13:7, 13) and once for Luke (21:9), and that it is only Matthew who brings the expressions "on the day of judgment" and the "consummation of the age." These statistics convey the intention of Matthew to remind the reader repeatedly that the direction of all time and history is squarely toward the Latter Day.

There is one temporal phrase  e have thus far ignored, namely, "in those days" (*en tais hēmerais ekeinais = bayyāmîm hāhēm*). In the books of the OT explicitly quoted by Matthew, this phrase refers to a period of time that is either indicative of present history[113] or is eschatologically qualified.[114] If we peruse the first main section of Matthew's Gospel, we discover that, with the exception of 1:1, 18, which have been stylistically assimilated to each other (cf. also 1:16), Matthew begins each pericope in one of only two ways: with a circumstantial participle of time (2:1, 13, 19; 4:12), or with the adverb *tote* ("then," 2:16; 3:13; 4:1). Because the phrase "in those days" disrupts this double pattern at 3:1, it stands out so prominently that it evokes the question as to whether it possesses special significance.[115]

In all, this phrase appears only five times in Matthew's Gospel, here

110. *en hēmera kriseōs;* cf. 10:15; 11:22, 24; 12:36.

111. *telos;* cf. 10:22; 24:6, 13–14.

112. *hē synteleia [tou] aiōnos;* cf. 13:39–40, 49; 24:3; 28:20.

113. Cf. Gen 6:4; Deut 17:9, 12 (LXX); 19:17; 26:3 (LXX); Dan 10:2.

114. Cf. Jer 3:16, 18; 31:33 [LXX 38:33]; 50:4, 20 [LXX 27:4, 20]; Zech 8:23.

115. In discussing the significance of this phrase at 3:1, Krentz ("Prologue," 412) speaks the mind of several commentators (e.g., Allen, Plummer, Klostermann, Schmid, Bonnard, Fenton, Jones) when he describes it as being "vague and colorless." Other commentators give it a "historical" reference, but one that has no basis in the text: M'Neile (*Matthew,* 24) opines that its point is that "the reader is assumed by Matthew to know the period to which the events belong . . ."; Green (*Matthew,* 114) states that "there is no clear note of time, but 'by these days' [sic!] the writer clearly refers to a well-known period when the Christian movement first began . . ."; and Filson (*Matthew,* 63) avers that "*in those days* indicate that *John the Baptist* appeared while Jesus was still living at Nazareth . . . ." Strecker (*Weg,* 91) tentatively suggests that "in those days" (3:1) refers to the "time of revelation" that began with John.

at 3:1 and in ch. 24.[116] Since in ch. 24 Matthew regularly appropriates it from Mark,[117] we can assume that it comes to him from the tradition.

Still, there is evidence that Matthew has also worked with this phrase. For one thing, he has standardized it. Mark, with apparently no sacrifice of meaning, renders it in ch. 13 both with the demonstrative pronoun (vss. 17, 19, 24) and without it (vs. 20a, c). Matthew, however, consistently renders it with the demonstrative (24:19, 22a and c, 29).

As to its meaning, Mark employs it both with and without eschatological qualification. At 8:1, it merely denotes an indistinct period of time within the ministry of Jesus. In ch. 13, on the other hand, if Mark has composed vs. 4b with the consummation of all things in mind,[118] it is eschatological in tenor and denotes the period of time leading up to the end of the age.

In the first Gospel, Matthew avoids any such dual usage of the phrase and leaves no uncertainty as to his understanding of it. At 24:3b–c, Matthew follows Mark 13:4 word for word through the first part but departs from it radically in the second part. As a result, Matthew makes it clear that in his Gospel the Eschatological Discourse is related, not to the destruction of the temple (cf. 24:3b), but to the parousia of Jesus and the consummation of the age.[119] Indeed, historically the destruction of the temple lies behind Matthew (cf. 22:7), and while he expends no word throughout chs. 24–25 on this event, his text is replete with instruction and exhortation aimed at strengthening the church in the tribulations it encounters.[120]

Now in line with vs. 3, the phrase "(in) those days" in ch. 24 can be seen to possess a thoroughly eschatological connotation and to refer to that period of time which precedes the consummation of the age and the

116. It must be discounted in 24:38 as textually uncertain; on the basis of the external evidence, it is probably to be omitted.

117. Cf. 24:19, 22a and c, 29 to Mark 13:17, 20a and c, 24.

118. Cf. R. Pesch, *Naherwartungen* (Kommentare und Beiträge zum Alten und Neuen Testament; Düsseldorf: Patmos, 1968), 101–106.

119. A. Feuillet ("le sens du mot Parousie dans l' Évangile de Matthieu. Comparaison entre Matth. xxiv. et Jac. v, 1–11," *The Background of the New Testament and its Eschatology,* ed. W. D. Davies and D. Daube [Cambridge: Cambridge University, 1956], 268–69) argues that the whole of Matth. 24:3 must be interpreted as referring to the destruction of Jerusalem. The weakness of this position, however, is that the expression *synteleia tou aiōnos* must therefore be supposed to have two fundamentally different significations in Matthew's Gospel, one here in ch. 24 and another in ch. 13. But it cannot be demonstrated that the text of the Gospel demands this. Against Feuillet, cf. also D. R. A. Hare, *The Theme of Jewish Persecution of Christians in the Gospel according to St Matthew* (NTSMS 6; Cambridge: Cambridge University, 1967), 178–79.

120. Cf. Hare, *Persecution,* 178–79.

return of Jesus Son of Man (cf. 24:19, 22a and c, 29, 37, 39). The question is: does Matthew indicate when he believes this eschatological period began? We contend that he does by placing this very phrase at 3:1, which signals the inauguration of the ministry of John the Baptist. The following, then, is the importance of this phrase in the Gospel and why Matthew at 3:1 deliberately alters the manner in which he otherwise begins the pericopes of the first main section of his Gospel: "in those days" designates that eschatological period of time that breaks upon Israel with the public ministry of John the Baptist and will continue until the parousia of Jesus Son of Man.

There are two additional points to make. It is not apparent from the synopsis, but Matthew is indebted to Mark for this phrase also at 3:1. In his Gospel, Mark employs it in 1:9 to call attention to the beginning of the ministry of Jesus. Matthew, by contrast, guided by his understanding of John the Baptist as the eschatological Elijah who is himself privileged by God to inaugurate the last times (cf. 3:2; 11:13–14; 17:10–13),[121] has "relocated" this phrase forward to underline just this truth. Such an editorial revision by Matthew corresponds fully with the manner in which he assimilates the person and work of John to the person and work of Jesus.

Finally, the objection might be raised that the phrase "in those days" in Matt 3:1 could just as well be given a noneschatological interpretation. There is one piece of evidence, however, that meets the objection. As we stated above, in 8:1 Mark plainly employs this phrase in a conventional historical sense. Although Matthew takes up the Marcan pericope introduced by 8:1, he does not follow suit with the phrase "in those days." The explanation for this is that Matthew hereby discloses that he is intent on preserving for this phrase throughout his Gospel a uniformly eschatological meaning.

Accordingly, the upshot of our investigation of the temporal expressions found in the first Gospel is that Matthew operates with them according to plan and design. Thus, the phrase "on that day" can, on the one hand, simply be the equivalent of the indistinct chronological phrases "at that time," "at that hour," or "from that hour." The purpose of these is to give historical movement to the text. At the same time, "on that day" can also be the equivalent of the eschatological phrase the "day of judgment." This phrase is a precise one, and finds its proper place with similar phrases such as the "end" and the "consummation of

121. Cf. Trilling, "Täufertradition," 275–82; Wink, *John the Baptist,* 28–35.

the age." Equally precise in meaning is the phrase "in those days." Like those just mentioned it denotes the period of the "last times," which begins with the appearance of John and of Jesus and leads up to the end of present history.

*Salvation-History in Two Epochs*

To apply now the results of our investigation of these temporal expressions to the question of Matthew's concept of the history of salvation, we conclude inescapably that Matthew does not divide this history into three epochs but into two. It has long been recognized that especially the formula quotations reveal that Matthew has theological affinity for the categories of "prophecy and fulfillment." These two terms aptly characterize Matthew's view of the history of salvation. There is the "time of Israel (OT)," which is preparatory to and prophetic of the coming of the Messiah. And there is the "time of Jesus" (Messiah), in which the time of Israel finds its fulfillment and which, from the vantage point of Matthew's day, extends from the beginning of the ministry of John and of Jesus (past) through post-Easter times (present) to the coming consummation of the age (future).

Still, this definition of the "time of Jesus" raises a question. If in accordance with the phrase "in those days" (3:1) the ministry of John marks the beginning of the time of Jesus, how is one to regard those years immediately preceding John's appearance, the time between the birth of Jesus and the beginning of John's ministry (chs. 1–2)? In two strategically placed passages which refer to each other, one at the beginning of the Gospel (1:23) and one at the end (28:20), Matthew informs us that what is constitutive of the time of Jesus is his abiding presence in the world as the earthly and then the exalted One, for it is in his person that God dwells with his people. The passage 1:23, however, has to do with the birth of Jesus. In other words, what the related passages 1:23 and 28:20 reveal is that, in reality, Matthew conceives of the "time of Jesus" as extending from his birth to his parousia. Does this mean, consequently, that we have misconstrued the significance of the phrase "in those days" (3:1)? Not at all, because the phrase "in those days" points to the "public manifestation" of the time of fulfillment, or "time of Jesus." Hence, Matthew's overall understanding of the "time of Jesus" is that it extends from birth to parousia but does not "burst into public" until John the Baptist "in those days" (3:1) begins his ministry to Israel.

Should this line of reasoning be correct, another question poses itself: in what way does Matthew integrate his own age, the so-called time of the church, into his concept of the history of salvation? It appears that Matthew looks upon his own age, not after the manner of Luke, who reputedly views the time of the church as an epoch that is virtually on a par with the "time of Israel" and the "time of Jesus,"[122] but as an extension of the time of Jesus. In Matthew's scheme of things, the alleged time of the church is to be construed as of the nature of a subcategory of the time of Jesus; it is to be subsumed under the "last days" inaugurated by John and Jesus.

This formal subsumption of the alleged time of the church under the time of Jesus has its material counterpart in Matthew's treatment of his subject matter. We cannot pursue this in great detail here, but perhaps two or three examples will suffice for purposes of demonstration.

To begin with the obvious, Matthew, unlike Luke, brings no narrative of the ascension of Jesus. Neither does Matthew, as does Luke, develop an expansive theology of the Holy Spirit. The reason for these two circumstances is that, in Matthew's view, the earthly Jesus who lived in the company of his disciples continues to reside in and preside over the church and the world as the exalted One (13:37–38; 18:20; 28:18–20). Hence, we see that the subsumption of the so-called time of the church under the time of Jesus in the theology of Matthew is, ultimately, christologically motivated and has its roots in the pre-Easter–post-Easter continuity of the person of Jesus: the earthly Jesus and the exalted Jesus are one.

To elaborate on this last point, the very fact that Matthew depicts Jesus throughout his Gospel after the fashion in which his church "knows" him is evidence, at least in Matthew's case, of material correspondence to the formal category of the time of Jesus. Scholars have frequently asserted that Matthew's Gospel reflects a heightened "reverence" for the person of Jesus,[123] and this is sometimes attributed to a deepening of Christian piety.[124] Be that as it may, the truth of the matter is that Matthew's august portrait of Jesus is, again, christologically

---

122. H. Conzelmann, *The Theology of St. Luke,* trans. G. Buswell (New York: Harper, 1960).

123. Cf., e.g., Allen, *Matthew,* xxxi-xxxiii; Klostermann, *Matthäus,* 20–21; Johnson, "Matthew," 235; G. Bornkamm, "End-Expectation and Church in Matthew," *Tradition and Interpretation in Matthew,* trans. P. Scott (Philadelphia: Westminster, 1963), 41–43; Filson, *Matthew,* 27–28; Strecker, *Weg,* 123–26; Grundmann, *Matthäus,* 26; Albright–Mann, *Matthew,* CLIV–CLV.

124. Cf., e.g., Allen, *Matthew,* xxxviii.

based: the exalted Jesus addresses his community following Easter in the words of the earthly Jesus, and the earthly Jesus appears in the course of his ministry in the effulgence of the exalted Jesus. So it is that, throughout the Gospel, the earthly Jesus is "worshiped" (cf. *proskynein*), and if strangers, enemies, and Judas Iscariot always greet him with "teacher" or "rabbi" but never with the equally respectful title of *"kyrie"* ("sir," 27:62–63), the disciples and those who believe he can heal and save never accost him with "teacher" or "rabbi" but always with *"kyrie"* (not "sir," but "Lord!").[125]

Not only Jesus but the disciples, too, are portrayed by Matthew in a manner that is consistent with his comprehensive understanding of the time of Jesus as extending from birth to parousia. Matthew makes of the disciples the representatives of the Christians of his church. Many commentators would disagree, claiming that Matthew either "idealizes" them[126] or "historicizes" them.[127] The evidence, however, shows that Matthew's procedure is to attribute to the disciples of Jesus insights that were not attained, historically speaking, until after Easter by the church. In so doing, Matthew does not "idealize" the disciples, for he does not exonerate them from spiritual foibles. According to him, the disciples doubt (14:31; 28:17), can be reluctant to accept one of Jesus' precepts (19:10), are weak of faith (6:30; 8:26; 14:31; 16:8), fearful (14:26, 30), cowardly (8:26), indignant (20:24; cf. 26:8), and there is also Peter's massive affront against Jesus (16:22–23), which incidentally, takes on a sharper profile in the first Gospel than in the second (cf. Mark 8:32–33).

On the other hand, Matthew does permit the disciples to rise far above that level of comprehension that historical research postulates for them during the days of Jesus' ministry. One searches in vain, for example, for a notice in Matthew's Gospel such as one finds in those of Mark, Luke, and John to the effect that the disciples did not attain to true understanding until after the resurrection.[128] An essential part of Matthew's characterization of the disciples of Jesus is to set forth what it means to be an "enlightened Christian": they are blessed because they have eyes that do see and ears that do hear (13:16), they have been given by God to know the mysteries of the Kingdom of Heaven, and,

125. Cf. Bornkamm, "End-Expectation," 41.
126. Cf. W. Wrede, *Das Messiasgeheimnis in den Evangelien* (3d ed.; Göttingen: Vandenhoeck & Ruprecht, 1963), 157–60; Allen, *Matthew*, xxxi; Klostermann, *Matthäus*, 21; Johnson, "Matthew," 236; Strecker, *Weg*, 193–94.
127. Cf. Walker, *Heilsgeschichte*, 25–26, 37, 61–63, 67, 77, 82–83, 109, 115, 117–18.
128. Cf. Mark, passim; Luke 18:34; ch. 24; John 2:22; 12:16; 16:4.

what is more, they grasp them (13:11, 51); and they both know and do the will of the heavenly Father (12:49-50).[129] Consequently, Matthew's portrait of the disciples is, again, a further example of material correspondence to the formal category of the time of Jesus.

A final argument for our thesis is negative in nature. If Matthew intended to construe the so-called time of the church as an epoch on a par with the time of Jesus, we should expect that the text of his Gospel would give pointed indication of this. But such is not the case. In the eyes of Matthew, did this time of the church begin already during the ministry of Jesus (10:1-9; 13:11-17; 21:43),[130] at its end (23:39), at the crucifixion (27:51-54),[131] after the resurrection (28:18-20),[132] or after the destruction of Jerusalem?[133] Strecker concedes outright that the exact time of its inauguration cannot be determined, but declares somewhat vaguely that, in any event, it began at the "end of the life of Jesus."[134] J. P. Meier, on the other hand, is emphatic: associated with the death–resurrection of Jesus in Matthew's Gospel is not merely the inauguration of the time of the church but, indeed, *"die Wende der Zeit . . .* the earthshaking beginning of the new aeon. . . ."[135] The difficulty with this view, however, is that it places the days of Jesus, the time following Easter, and the consummation, respectively, on a graduated scale whereby each period is regarded as more intensely eschatological than the previous one, a schema that does not fit the relationship Matthew establishes between the days of Jesus and the time following Easter.[136] Our contention is that

129. Cf. J. D. Kingsbury, "The 'Jesus of History' and the 'Christ of Faith,' " *CTM* 37 (1966): 504–506; idem, *Matthew 13*, 40–42. Cf. also G. Barth, "Law," 118–21; E. P. Blair, *Jesus in the Gospel of Matthew* (Nashville: Abingdon, 1960), 102–109; J. Gnilka, *Die Verstockung Israels* (StANT 3; München: Kösel, 1961), 94–96.

130. Cf. the remarks of Lagrange (*Matthieu*, 418) to the effect that during his ministry Jesus "prepared" his apostles to replace their Jewish predecessors. Cf. also Bornkamm, "End-Expectation," 48.

131. Cf. M'Neile, *Matthew*, 312; Schlatter, *Matthäus*, 632; Schmid, *Matthäus*, 306; Gaechter, *Matthäus*, 688; Hare, Persecution, 155.

132. Cf. Bornkamm, "End-Expectation," 34. Strecker (*Weg*, 117) only reckons with this option. Cf. in this connection also the remarks of Trilling, *Israel*, 162.

133. Cf. Johnson, "Matthew," 514; W. Trilling, "Zur Ueberlieferungsgeschichte des Gleichnisses vom Hochzeitsmahl Mt 22, 1–14," *BZ* 4 (1960): 255; Walker, *Heilsgeschichte*, 96–97, 112, 114–17; Grundmann, *Matthäus*, 464.

134. Strecker, *Weg*, 117. Cf. also the comments of O. H. Steck (*Israel und das gewaltsame Geschick der Propheten* [WMAMT 23; Neukirchen: Neukirchener Verlag, 1967], 304–12) and of R. Hummel (*Die Auseinandersetzung zwischen Kirche und Judentum im Matthäusevangelium* [BEvT 33; München: Chr. Kaiser, 1963], 90).

135. J. P. Meier, "Salvation History in Matthew: In Search of a Starting Point," *CBQ* 37 (1975); 207; cf. also 208–10, 212–14.

136. R. Kratz (*Auferweckung als Befreiung* [SBS 65; Stuttgart: Katholisches Bibelwerk, 1973], 43–44) takes the position that, owing to the Matthaean notation concerning the raising of the saints (27:52), it is the death of Jesus in the first Gospel

the absence from Matthew's text of any specific indication as to the inauguration of a "time of the church" is further proof that Matthew does not operate with the latter as an independent category.

Accordingly, Matthew understands the history of salvation as divided into two epochs: the "time of Israel (OT)" and the "time of Jesus (earthly–exalted)." The former is inaugurated by Abraham (1:1–2); the latter is inaugurated by the birth of Jesus and is first publicly heralded by the ministry of John, which marks the beginning of "those days" that lead up to the consummation of the age. Specifically, the time of Jesus comprehends the ministries of John and of Jesus, and that of the disciples as well, which Matthew construes broadly as beginning with the mission of the original disciples (10:1–9) and continuing with that of their successors until the parousia (24:14; 26:13; 28:18–20). That Matthew does indeed view the ministry of the disciples in "past and present" as one is seen from the fact that he "contradicts" himself by attributing a "universal" dimension to the mission of the Twelve which, allegedly, was to be restricted to "Israel" (cf. 10:5b–6 with 10:18).[137]

This brings us at last to the question of the controlling element in Matthew's concept of the history of salvation. We recall from previous discussion that Trilling, Strecker, Walker, and Thompson show that they identify some aspect of the ecclesiology of Matthew as this controlling element. In contrast to them, we have argued that what is constitutive of Matthew's concept of the history of salvation, which finds its center in the "time of Jesus" covering the entire period from birth to parousia,

---

that inaugurates the "end-time." This position, however, flies in the face of the eschatological implications of a passage such as 1:23 and also ignores the fact that already in 11:5 Matthew writes of Jesus that "dead are raised" (cf. also 9:18–19, 23–26).

137. Thompson ("Historical Perspective," 253) argues that 10:18 refers to the fact that the disciples will, in the words of Jesus, stand before governors and kings, that is to say, non-Jewish officials in Palestine, and give testimony to their faith not only to them but also to other non-Jews at their trial. This interpretation, however, does not do justice to the "double horizon" of ch. 10. The one horizon, which Thompson envisages, has to do with the Matthaean emphasis that the pre-Easter disciples of Jesus, like Jesus himself, are sent to Israel (cf. 10:5b–6). The second horizon, which Thompson does not acknowledge, has to do with the fact that ch. 10, like every other portion of the Gospel, is likewise intended by Matthew to address the members of his church. We see this, for example, in the "timeless" nature of the injunctions Jesus gives throughout ch. 10 (cf. vss. 8–42), and, more specifically, in the circumstance that there are striking parallels between certain verses of ch. 10 and verses of ch. 24, which without doubt tell of conditions in the days of Matthew: cf. (a) 10:18 to 24:14a; (b) 10:21 to 24:10; (c) 10:22a to 24:9b; (d) 10:22b to 24:13; (e) 10:23d to 24:42b, 44b; 25:31a; and (f) 10:28a to 24:9a Cf. also the related remarks of the following: F. Hahn, *Mission in the New Testament*, trans. F. Clarke (SBT 47; London: SCM, 1965), 124–25; Steck, *Propheten*, 314–15; Grundmann, *Matthäus*, 284; F. W. Beare, "The Mission of the Disciples and the Mission Charge: Matthew 10 and Parallels," *JBL* 89 (1970): 1–13; Frankemölle, *Jahwebund*, 269.

is the abiding presence of Jesus with his disciples, both "then" and "now." Hence, the christology of Matthew, not his ecclesiology, more than anything else has molded his concept of the history of salvation.

In other respects, we will likewise recall that, as far as the topical arrangement of the first Gospel is concerned, we discovered that Bacon and others dependent upon his proposal reveal that they, too, regard the ecclesiology of Matthew as being normative for the structure of the Gospel. Over against them, we claimed for Matthew a topical outline that, focusing as it does on the person, ministry, and death and resurrection of Jesus Messiah, is thoroughly christological in tenor.

If, therefore, the question is asked as to the general character of the first Gospel, our position is that two separate lines of inquiry, the one having to do with the topical arrangement of the Gospel and the other with Matthew's concept of the history of salvation, converge in their results to prove that, although Matthew certainly occupies himself extensively in his document with ecclesiological concerns, it is his christological orientation that has most influenced the shape of his work. As we see it, Matthew's Gospel is principally christological in nature, a statement that, seemingly, is no truism.

### D.  SUMMARY

The time has come to specify the relationship between the topical outline we have advanced and the historical categories that can be uncovered. From our discussion it is clear that we cannot concur with those redaction-critics who disavow a basic topical outline and postulate the linear time-line as the chief principle by which the Gospel has been organized. The key to understanding the relationship between the topical outline and the time-line is Matthew's christology. Thus, Matthew arranges his materials to fall into three main sections that are demarcated by "superscriptions" (4:17; 16:21; cf. also 1:1) that he himself has composed in order to inform the reader that the major purpose of his Gospel is to set forth (a) the genesis and significance of the person of Jesus (1:1–4:16), (b) the nature and effect of his proclamation (4:17–16:20), and (c) the reason and finality of his suffering, death, and resurrection (16:21–28:20). The events surrounding Jesus are, in the eyes of Matthew, of ultimate meaning for Israel and for all humankind. Therefore to place Jesus within the proper context in history, directed as it is by God, and to delineate the ultimate implications he holds for the destiny of Israel and the Gentiles alike, Matthew employs a chronological scheme that

divides history into two epochs after the fashion of prophecy and fulfillment. To call attention in varying degrees to this chronological scheme
and consequently to the cosmic (*kosmos*)-historical significance of Jesus,
Matthew makes use throughout his Gospel of temporal expressions of
several kinds. The grand result in the first Gospel is the penetration of a
carefully developed topical outline by a precise conception of history,
and both, to say it again, are rooted in Matthew's christology.

## EXCURSUS

As the finishing touches were being put on this manuscript for publication,
H. Frankemölle's study on Matthew's Gospel (*Jahwebund und Kirche Christi*
[NTAbh 10; Münster: Aschendorff, 1974]) became available. Since much of
what he says is related to the theme of this chapter, we should like to speak
briefly to selected aspects of his position.

According to Frankemölle, Matthew and his community are Gentile Christian in orientation and universal in outlook. Nevertheless, in the situation that
calls forth the first Gospel there is a question, owing to Israel's rejection of
Jesus as the Messiah and the resultant destruction of Jerusalem, as to God's
faithfulness to his people in history and the validity of his OT promises. To
meet this situation, Matthew does "covenant theology" (*Bundestheologie*), that
is to say, he develops a theology of God's activity in history after the fashion of
the Deuteronomist and Chronicler. With the latter as his models, Matthew is
concerned to show his church that throughout the OT and in the person of
Jesus there has been continuity to God's activity in history. What has happened
is not that God has been unfaithful to Israel but that Israel has been unfaithful
to God. As a result, Israel has ceased to be God's chosen people, and the
church has taken its place. In short, God has come to be with his own in the
person of Jesus and to renew his covenant, but he has made neither Israel nor
a remnant of Israel his partner but the church. The church, then, is henceforth
called to respond to God by doing his will as set forth by Jesus.

Frankemölle's understanding of Matthew's Gospel leads him to take sharp
issue with G. Strecker and R. Walker. He contends that both misconstrue the
intention of Matthew, for both hold that his objective is to write a "life of
Jesus" (Strecker: "*Bios Jesu*"; Walker: "*Vita Jesu*").[138] In claiming this objective for Matthew, Strecker and Walker distort Matthew's concept of time and
history.[139] The truth is that Matthew is not interested in the "*bruta facta*" of
the immediate past; his interest is singularly in the present.[140] For him history
is of the nature of "prophecy and fulfillment" and has nothing to do with the
linear time-line that can be divided into segments.[141] Indeed, concerning the
brute facts and the linear time-line, Matthew can be seen consistently to "de-

---

138. Cf. Frankemölle, *Jahwebund*, 366, 371, 375.
139. Cf. ibid., 366–73.
140. Cf. ibid., 377, 386.
141. Cf. ibid., 366–69, 377, 388.

historicize" both his narrative (cf. the miracle-stories) and discourse (cf. the speeches of Jesus) traditions.[142] In reality, Matthew composes a "fictional" literary document the function of which is to address the members of his community in their own time and place on the authority of the exalted Lord who is one with the earthly Jesus.[143]

In consideration of Frankemölle's position, we heartily agree that central to Matthew's concept of history is the schema of prophecy and fulfillment, that Matthew is not interested in the time-line purely for its own sake, that he intends for the whole of his Gospel to address the members of his community, and that it is misleading to suggest that Matthew writes a life of Jesus which may be called a *"Bios Jesu"* or *"Vita Jesu."* On the other hand, we demur when Frankemölle goes on to characterize Matthew's theology as "covenant theology" and argues that the faithfulness of God throughout history and the validity of his promises are matters that have become problematic in the situation in which Matthew finds himself. On the contrary, on the basis of Matthew's use of the OT, the faithfulness of God an dthe continued validity of his promises are exactly what Matthew accounts as certain. Moreover, were Matthew doing "covenant theology" in the strict sense in which Frankemölle seems to be using the term, surely it would be incumbent upon him to depict the church as the "new Israel" or the "true Israel," terms he does not use.

Matthew's central concern is decidedly more christological in nature than Frankemölle is willing to concede. The very outline of the Gospel proves this to be the case, especially the circumstance that Matthew devotes the entire initial part to the person of Jesus and begins with a genealogy that is designed to inform the reader that specifically Jesus, the son of Mary, and no other is the long awaited Messiah.[144] In addition, in stipulating in 1:23 that it is precisely in the person of Jesus, who is the Son of God, that God draws near to dwell with his people, Matthew prepares for the decisive christological modification of the principal theological concept of his Gospel, the Kingdom of Heaven. And in line with this, the expression "the Gospel of the Kingdom," which Matthew employs to summarize the contents of his document, is, as we shall see in Chapter IV, thoroughly christological in tenor.

Nor is this all. If the first main part of Matthew's outline has to do with the person of Jesus Messiah, the Son of God, it is noteworthy that the second and third main parts have to do with his public ministry and his suffering, death, and resurrection. It is within this protracted christological framework, which embraces the whole of the Gospel, that Matthew speaks to questions pertaining to Israel or to the church or to the nations. In other words, what we find in the first Gospel is that Matthew deals christologically with matters both theological and ecclesiological.

As for the character of Matthew's Gospel, Frankemölle, who is inclined to designate it as a "kerygmatic portrait of history,"[145] seems to place the empha-

---

142. Cf. ibid., 377.
143. Cf. ibid., 143, 190, 203–204, 257–58, 268, 351, 398.
144. Cf. Vögtle, "Genealogie," *Evangelium*, 73.
145. Cf. Frankemölle, *Jahwebund*, 399.

sis almost exclusively on the term "kerygmatic," the fact, namely, that Matthew intends for his document to address his church in the present. When it comes to the term "history," Frankemölle maintains that Matthew operates "fictionally": he dispenses completely with the immediate past (the historical-temporal days of Jesus and of the church behind Matthew); in reality, all is present (the time of Matthew). What this means christologically and ecclesiologically, for example, is that Matthew's picture of Jesus and of the disciples contains no temporal distinction whatever between an earthly Jesus and his disciples "then" and an exalted Lord and his church "now." The earthly Jesus or the disciples are merely a cipher for the exalted Lord or the church.

While there certainly is a high degree of assimilation between past and present in the first Gospel, it does not follow that the document is consequently devoid of any sense of the immediate past. Matthew does not, as is well known, draft a chronicle of the life and times of Jesus. He has, variously, arranged, reformulated, abridged, or expanded upon the narrative and discourse traditions which have been handed down to him so that the resultant writing will "speak" to the present and be relevant in its entirety to the members of the church to which he belongs.

At the same time, Matthew and his community do indeed distinguish between "then" and "now," between the Jesus and the disciples who once walked on earth and the exalted One who henceforth resides in the midst of his church. Matthew's notion of the flow of time comes to the fore in his concept of the history of salvation. This concept is not without a linear-temporal dimension involving the sequence of events. Its contours are readily apparent, for instance, in the genealogy or in the so-called parables against Israel (21:28–22:14). Its overall pattern is in truth that of "prophecy and fulfillment." More particularly, the time of prophecy is the time of the OT, and the time of fulfillment is the eschatological time of Jesus. But within the overarching time of Jesus there is, successively, the ministry of John, of the earthly Jesus, of the pre-Easter and of the post-Easter disciples, to the end of the age. In harmony with the schema of first Israel and then the nations, the goal of these ministries is to make of people disciples of Jesus and sons of God. Thus, whether one be Israelite or Gentile, Matthew's concept of the history of salvation shows Jesus to be of ultimate significance for the destiny of all humankind. For the church to know precisely "now" what it means to live under God's Rule exercised as it is by the exalted Son of God and hence to know who this Son of God is, what it means to follow him, why it is that the Jews in the "synagogue across the street"[146] do not confess his name, and what the task of the church is to be to the close of the age, Matthew imbues the traditions relating to Jesus and his disciples "then" with the concerns of his own day. Although he does this, the evidence does not support the contention that in the document he writes he has, in effect, reduced his sense of history to the single point of the present.

---

146. Stendahl, *School*, xi.

Chapter II

# The Christology of Matthew:
# The Title Son of God

From our investigation thus far we have concluded that fundamental to
the first Gospel is a topical outline that treats of the person of Jesus
Messiah (1:1–4:16), of his proclamation, or public ministry (4:17–
16:20), and of his suffering, death, and resurrection (16:21–28:20). In
the second place, Matthew also operates with a carefully devised concept
of the history of salvation in two epochs, which features, in accordance
with the schema of "prophecy and fulfillment," the "time of Israel (OT)"
and the "time of Jesus (earthly–exalted)." The result is that even as Matthew tells of the person, ministry, and passion and resurrection of Jesus
Messiah, he is setting forth the salvation-historical meaning he has for
both Israel and the Gentiles. This is one of the ingenious characteristics
of the gospel genre and a reason why exegetes dare not be too hasty in
positing for Matthew a "time of the church" that is on a par with the
"time of Jesus."

In our analysis of the topical outline that Matthew fashions and of his
concept of the history of salvation, we pointed out that both show themselves to be thoroughly christological in nature. Hence, the first Gospel,
we maintained, is to be seen primarily, not as an ecclesiological, but as
a christological document. If this judgment is sound, it follows that the
topical outline of the Gospel should give an indication as to how we are
to approach Matthew's christology. This is all the more so because the
first main part of this outline has to do, we know, with the person of
Jesus Messiah (1:1–4:16). In this chapter, we propose to argue that a
careful examination, first of the initial part (1:1–4:16) and then of the

40

remainder of the first Gospel (4:17–28:20), will indeed prove the truth of our earlier assertion that "Son of God" is the central christological title of Matthew.

Christology is one area in which students of Matthew have not as yet achieved anything like a consensus of opinion. The most one can say is that a survey of monographs written in the last twenty years on this question reveals some tendency to regard certain titles as normative.

Thus, G. Bornkamm, in emphasizing the tension he discovers in the first Gospel between history and eschatology, finds such titles as "Son of David," "Son of God," "Kyrios," and "Son of Man" to be of major importance.[1] G. Barth[2] and H. J. Held,[3] pupils of Bornkamm, take the same position, as does R. Hummel,[4] although the latter is interested to stress "Son of David" as the foremost title for the earthly Jesus. G. Strecker, on the other hand, holds that "Son of David" and "Kyrios" are the principal christological titles of the Gospel, the one relating to Jesus' historical mission to Israel and the other to Jesus as the "eschatological Lord" in the time of Matthew himself.[5] W. Trilling,[6] interpreting the Gospel from the standpoint of its conclusion, indicates that he considers "Kyrios" to be the chief christological title of Matthew, and H. Frankemölle[7] agrees, provided that the earthly Jesus and the exalted Lord be understood as one and the same. From a different perspective, E. P. Blair, whose opinion is shared by J. Lange,[8] states that the "dominant category in the Gospel of Matthew is unquestionably that of the Son of Man,"[9] and R. Walker, while ascribing importance to this title, believes that it is secondary to the general category of the "earthly Messiah."[10] For his part,

---

1. Cf. G. Bornkamm, "End-Expectation and Church in Matthew," *Tradition and Interpretation in Matthew*, trans. P. Scott (Philadelphia: Westminster, 1963), 32–33.
2. Cf. "Matthew's Understanding of the Law," *Tradition and Interpretation in Matthew*, trans. P. Scott (Philadelphia: Westminster, 1963), 125–37.
3. Cf. "Matthew as Interpreter of the Miracle Stories," *Tradition and Interpretation in Matthew*, trans. P. Scott (Philadelphia: Westminster, 1963), 259–70.
4. Cf. *Die Auseinandersetzung zwischen Kirche und Judentum im Matthäusevangelium* (BEvT 33; München: Chr. Kaiser, 1963), 116–22.
5. Cf. G. Strecker, *Der Weg der Gerechtigkeit* (FRLANT 82; Göttingen: Vandenhoeck & Ruprecht, 1962), 118–20, 123–26.
6. Cf. *Das wahre Israel* (StANT X; 3d ed.; München: Kösel, 1964), 21–51.
7. Cf. *Jahwebund und Kirche Christi* (NTAbh 10; Münster: Aschendorff, 1974), 80, 85, 89, 144, 377, 398.
8. Cf. *Das Erscheinen des Auferstandenen im Evangelium nach Matthäus* (Forschung zur Bibel 11; Würzburg: Echter, 1973), 238–41, 245–46, 487–98.
9. Cf. E. P. Blair, *Jesus in the Gospel of Matthew* (Nashville: Abingdon, .960), 83.
10. Cf. R. Walker, *Die Heilsgeschichte im ersten Evangelium* (FRLANT 91; Göttingen: Vandenhoeck & Ruprecht, 1967), 116, 128–30.

W. D. Davies views the titles "Lord" and "Son of Man" as being primary for Matthew.[11]

In the face of this panoply of opinion, none of which recognizes in "Son of God" an exceptionally prominent christological strain in Matthew's Gospel, the potential significance of our thesis, if correct, would appear to be considerable.

## A.  THE TITLE "SON OF GOD" IN 1:1–4:16

As we discovered in the previous chapter, the first main part of Matthew's Gospel (1:1–4:16) concentrates on the origin and consequently on the person of Jesus Messiah, as 1:1, the "superscription," informs us. In this verse, Matthew refers to Jesus Messiah as the "Son of David" and the "Son of Abraham." Still, his primary objective in 1:1–4:16, we established provisionally, is to trace the origin of Jesus to God himself. But this means we can expect that an investigation of the christology of 1:1–4:16 will to a great extent be an investigation of Matthew's presentation of Jesus Messiah as the Son of God.

Before we begin our analysis of 1:1–4:16, one additional observation is pertinent to our study of the title Son of God throughout the whole of Matthew's Gospel. It is generally recognized that, whatever their separate origins, such terms as "my [his] Son" (2:15; 3:17; 17:5; 21:37), "the Son" (11:27; 21:38; 24:36; 28:19), and "Son of God" (8:29) are understood by Matthew to be variant expressions of the more comprehensive term "the Son of God."[12] In fact, we shall discover that even the word "son" (1:21, 23, 25) can be synonymous with the fuller designation. And that the term Son of God has not become a mere vacuous appellation for Jesus, simply appropriated by Matthew from the tradition, is apparent from the circumstance that of the twenty-three times it occurs in the first Gospel, eleven times it is redactional in nature.[13]

11. Cf. W. D. Davies, *The Setting of the Sermon on the Mount* (Cambridge: Cambridge University, 1964), 96–99.
12. Cf., e.g., Th. De Kruijf, *Der Sohn des lebendigen Gottes* (AnBib 16; Rome: Pontifical Biblical Institute, 1962), passim. E. C. Colwell ("A Definite Rule for the Use of the Article in the Greek New Testament," *JBL* 52 [1933]: 13–14, 20–21) has shown that "the Son of God" is the proper translation of the Greek of this title in such passages as Matt 4:3, 6; 14:33; 27:40, 54 (cf. to these 16:16; 26:63); cf. also M. Zerwick, *Biblical Greek*, trans. J. Smith (Scripta Pontificii Instituti Biblici 114; Rome: Biblical Institute Press, 1963), 56.
13. Cf. 1:21, 23, 25; 2:15; 14:33; 16:16; 21:38; 26:63; 27:40, 43; 28:19. Concerning the redactional character of "son" at 1:21, 25, cf. R. Pesch, "Eine alttestamentliche Ausführungsformel im Matthäus-Evangelium," *BZ* 11 (1967): 84–87.

*The Origin of Jesus (1:16, 18–25)*

Recent scholarship has devoted a great deal of attention to Matthew's opening chapter.[14] As far as the origin of Jesus Messiah is concerned, Matthew treats this topic within the context of "sonship" (cf. the genealogy, 1:1–17).

On the one hand, Matthew is intent upon showing that Mary's child can legitimately be called the Son of David: his birth fulfills a promise to the house of David (Isa 7:13–14), and Joseph son of David (1:20), on divine command (1:21), gives him his name, adopting him (1:25). On the other hand, Matthew is equally intent upon showing that Mary's child can be called the Son of God: he is conceived by the Holy Spirit (mentioned twice: 1:18, 20); he is not the product of the union of any man with Mary (cf. 1:18, 20, 24) because she is a "virgin" when she bears him (1:23) and Joseph, for his part, scrupulously refrains from having marital relations with her until after she has had her son (1:25); his mission is to save his people from their sins (1:21);[15] and God himself, albeit through the prophet (1:22),[16] is the one who discloses the true significance of his person ("God with us," 1:22–23). When these several factors are combined, they compel the following conclusion about the sonship of Jesus Messiah: Jesus Messiah, born to Mary, is without question the Son of David, but beyond this, by reason of his unique origin, he is the Son of God.[17]

Although Matthew makes direct reference to the Davidic sonship of Jesus Messiah in the genealogy that precedes 1:18–25 (cf. 1:1) but not to his divine sonship, it seems that he does allude to the latter in the genealogy. In 1:16b, he employs the passive voice in connection with the verb *egennēthē*, which may well be indicative of a circumlocution for divine activity ("Jesus *was born* [by a special act of God]").[18] This passive verb, in turn, points the reader forward, to the passive participle *gennēthen* ("that which *is conceived*") in 1:20, which is also suggestive

---

14. For a listing of the more recent literature on Matt 1–2, cf. R. Pesch, "Der Gottessohn im matthäischen Evangelienprolog (Mt 1–2). Beobachtungen zu den Zitationsformeln der Reflexionszitate," *Bib* 48 (1967): 395 nn. 1–2; A. Vögtle, *Messias und Gottessohn* (Theologische Perspektiven; Düsseldorf: Patmos, 1971), 15 n. 1. Cf. also C. T. Davis, "Tradition and Redaction in Matthew 1:18–2:23," *JBL* 90 (1971): 404–421; M. Hengel and H. Merkel, "Die Magier aus dem Osten und die Flucht nach Aegypten (Mt 2) im Rahmen der antiken Religionsgeschichte und der Theologie des Matthäus," *Orientierung an Jesus*, ed. P. Hoffmann (Festschrift J. Schmid; Freiburg: Herder, 1973), 139–69.

15. As we shall see, it is as the Son of God that Jesus accomplishes this.

16. Cf. Pesch, "Evangelienprolog," 410–11.

17. Cf. also ibid., 409–410.

18. Cf. ibid., 410.

of divine activity. But why Matthew should merely allude to the divine sonship of Jesus in the genealogy and not place the title "Son of God" beside the title "Son of David" in 1:1 is a matter we touched on briefly last chapter and will take up again when we discuss the story of the Baptism of Jesus.

In 1:18–25, then, Matthew stipulates concerning the person of "Jesus who is called the Messiah" (1:16) that, adopted into the line of David, he has his origin in God. As an index of the christology of Matthew, what is the peculiar importance of 1:18–25? To get at this, we note three things about this pericope: (a) tradition-critically, the thought that one who bears the predication Son of God should be described as coming from the house of David and therefore as also being a son of David is not original with Matthew but can be found in the OT (cf. 2 Sam 7:14; Pss 2:7; 89:26–27; 1 Chr 17:12–13; 22:10); (b) titularly, in terms of the relationship between the predications Son of David and Son of God, Son of God "outranks" Son of David in the same way as adoption by Joseph son of David cannot compare to conception by the Holy Spirit; (c) and exegetically, OT Scripture that is associated with the house of David is portrayed as attaining its fulfillment in Jesus as seen especially as the Son of God (1:23; cf. also 2:6; 3:17; 4:15–16; 17:5). These observations tell us at least the following: that the christology of Matthew has deep roots in the OT;[19] and that Matthew does not hesitate to subsume the christological category of Son of David under that of Son of God, thereby serving notice as early as his first chapter that it is Jesus precisely as the Son of God (in the line of David to be sure) who by and large assumes the office of Messiah in his Gospel.

The theological dimension of the title Son of God in ch. 1 comes to the fore in vss. 21–23. Here we learn initially what it means for Matthew to designate Jesus as the Son of God: he whose origin is in God (1:16b, 18, 20) is the one in whose person God comes to dwell with his people,[20] thus inaugurating the eschatological age of salvation.

### Narratives about the Magi and the Child (2:1–23)

Matthew begins ch. 2 by referring back, through word-association, to

19. On this point, cf. the tradition-critical remarks of Frankemölle, *Jahwebund*, 19–21.

20. The "people" (*ton laon*) to whom God in the person of his Son Jesus grants his saving presence and who confess Jesus to be "Emmanuel" (cf. *kalesousin*, 1:23) are, as 1:21 shows, the people whom Jesus saves from their sins, that is, the church (cf. A. Vögtle, "Das Schicksal des Messiaskindes," *Bibel und Leben* 6 [1965]: 273; Frankemölle, *Jahwebund*, 16–19).

the notation in his genealogy that David was "the king" (1:6) in order to shed further light on the person of Jesus. The Magi, writes Matthew, arrive in Jerusalem and ask where the newborn "King of the Jews" is to be found (2:2). Herod responds by designating this king as "the Messiah" (2:4), that is to say, the one whom he anticipates will lay claim to his throne, as is evident from his secret desire "to destroy" Jesus (2:13). By means of a formula quotation that cites the words of God to king David, Matthew sets forth a proper understanding of the royal Messiah: in reality, he is the eschatological Shepherd of "my people Israel" (2:5b–6).

But Matthew has yet more to say in ch. 2 about the person of the newborn, royal Messiah. Relative to this, and highly significant, after 2:6 Matthew never once refers to Jesus in his second chapter as "king" or "ruler," even though 2:2 ("Where is he who has been *born king* of the Jews? . . . we have come to worship him") raises every expectation that, once the Magi have found Jesus, Matthew would write at 2:11: "And when they entered the house, they saw the *one born king,* and they fell down and worshiped him. . . ." Instead, after 2:6 Matthew consistently refers to Jesus as "the child" (*to paidion*) and repeatedly employs the expression "the child and [with] his mother" (cf. 2:11, 13–14, 20–21).

The remarkable thing about this expression is that it is at once appropriate to the narrative and a means by which Matthew can speak of Jesus without giving the impression that he is the son of Joseph[21] and hence, we should like to add, solely the Son of David (cf. 1:20, 25). Indeed, in that Matthew makes reference to Jesus and Mary exclusive of Joseph, he alludes to the situation of ch. 1: the virgin Mary gives birth to a son who has been conceived apart from Joseph son of David by the Holy Spirit.[22] If this is understood, it immediately becomes clear that the purpose of the expression "the child and [with] his mother" is to remind the reader that the son of Mary is at the same time the Son of God. But this, in turn, reveals that the designation "the child" in ch. 2 functions as a surrogate for "Son of God."[23] Appeal for the accuracy of this observation can even be made to Matthew himself: at 2:15, a formula quotation, Matthew breaks his otherwise consistent use through-

---

21. Cf. Pesch, "Evangelienprolog," 413; E. Nellessen, *Das Kind und seine Mutter* (SBS 39; Stuttgart: Katholisches Bibelwerk, 1969), 95.
22. Cf. F. Hahn, *The Titles of Jesus in Christology,* trans. H. Knight and G. Ogg (London: Lutterworth, 1969), 264; Pesch, "Evangelienprolog," 413–14; Vögtle, *Gottessohn,* 22, 87.
23. Cf. also Davis, "Matthew 1:18–2:23," 414.

out 2:7–23 of the expression "the child and [with] his mother" so that none other than God (through the prophet) might call "the child" Jesus "my Son." In the final analysis, therefore, we see that "the child" whom the Magi come to Bethlehem to "worship" (*proskyneō*, 2:11) is in truth the "Son of God,"[24] just as "the child" whom Herod plots to kill is no political throne-pretender but likewise the "Son of God."

In sum, our argument runs as follows. From Matthew's perspective, Jesus, the newborn child of Mary who has been adopted by Joseph, is indeed the King of the Jews. As such, he is Israel's royal Messiah. Still, he is most assuredly not a political figure, as Herod mistakenly assumes. Instead, he is, as God says through the prophet, the eschatological Shepherd of "my people Israel," the one who comes in fulfillment of the divine promise given to king David of old. This eschatological Shepherd, however, is more in origin than simply the scion of David. He is, as God again says through the prophet, "my Son." Accordingly, asserts Matthew, what God makes known through the prophets is that the royal scion of David who will shepherd "my people Israel" is, like none other, "my Son."

Before we leave this argument, it is of advantage to draw out the wider implications it holds for the christology of Matthew. In ch. 1, Matthew describes Jesus Messiah as the Son of Abraham (vs. 1), the Son of David (vss. 1, 20, 25), and above all as the Son of God (vss. 18, 20, 22–23). Here in ch. 2, the imagery Matthew employs ostensibly suggests that he continues to work with these same three titles, but what happens in reality is that he permits the title Son of God to supersede the other two. Thus, in that Jesus "the Messiah" (vs. 4) is said to be "the King of the Jews," the eschatological Shepherd of God's people whose birth takes place in "Bethlehem" (vss. 1–2, 5–6),[25] Matthew appears to be alluding to Jesus as the Son of David. And in that the "Magi," who are Gentiles, are made to journey to "Jerusalem" (and subsequently to Bethlehem) in order to "worship" Jesus the child (vss. 1–2, 11), Matthew appears to be alluding to Jesus as the Son of Abraham, the one in whom the nations of the earth find blessing (cf. Gen 12:3; 18:18; 22:18; 26:4).

But Matthew does not use at all the titles Son of David and Son of Abraham in ch. 2. The one title he uses is Son of God ("my Son," vs. 15).

---

24. Cf. H. Greeven, *TDNT*, VI, 763-64; Pesch, "Evangelienprolog," 414–15.

25. C. Burger (*Jesus als Davidssohn* [FRLANT 98; Göttingen: Vandenhoeck & Ruprecht, 1970], 104–105) shrewdly observes that for Matthew, unlike Luke (cf. 2:4, 11), Bethlehem is not the "city of David" per se but simply the place where Jesus was born. In Matt 2, therefore, the birth of Jesus in Bethlehem does not of itself point to Jesus as the Son of David.

Moreover, in that the term "the child" is a surrogate for the title Son of God, and in that Matthew identifies both "the King of the Jews" for whom the Magi search (vss. 2) and "the Messiah" born in Bethlehem whom Herod seeks to kill (vss. 4–6) as "the child" (cf. vss. 11, 13), it is evident that what Matthew does in ch. 2 is to attribute to Jesus exactly as the Son of God messianic expectations otherwise more narrowly associated with him as the Son of David or the Son of Abraham.

Matthew's procedure in ch. 2, therefore, is analogous to that in ch. 1: he in concerned to enlarge the concept Son of God by infusing it with messianic significance on a broad scale, to the point where Jesus Messiah as the Son of God fulfills, as a matter of course, expectations relating more particularly to David or to Abraham. The guiding principle for this Matthew found, we believe, in the OT. For in several passages we cited in connection with our study of ch. 1 (2 Sam 7:14; Pss 2:7–8; 89:26–27; 1 Chr 17:12–13; 22:10), the composite description of the one given the designation son of God ("my son," "first-born") is that he is a king from the house of David who will rule in the name of Jahweh over Israel and the nations. But this is the very picture that Matthew sketches of Jesus Messiah here in ch. 2: Jesus Messiah, the Son of God, is the Davidic King born in Bethlehem who is chosen to shepherd the eschatological people of God and to whom the Gentiles (Magi) come to pay their homage. Hence, we see once more that Matthew's basic understanding of Jesus Messiah is as the Son of God, a concept that, again, not only does not discount messianic expectations associated with either David (Israel) or Abraham (nations), but is expansive enough to embrace them. Consequently, in looking ahead we can expect that it will be primarily as the Son of God that Jesus Messiah will confront Israel in his public ministry (4:17–16:20) and preside over the church of Jewish and Gentile Christians (28:16–20).

A. Vögtle contends on the basis of his insightful analysis of the sources underlying ch. 2, as have others as well, that these sources show that a Christian narrator prior to Matthew had it in mind to portray Jesus, the promised Messiah, as the new Moses.[26] Vögtle is seemingly correct in this judgment, but, in regard to the Evangelist Matthew, whatever the analogy between Jesus and Moses in ch. 2, Jesus stands out not as a new Moses but, to repeat, as the Son of God. In the next chapter we shall consider in more detail the question of the presence of new-Moses typology in the first Gospel.

26. Cf. Vögtle, *Gottessohn*, 62.

Several comments will conclude our investigation of ch. 2. Matthew writes of the leaders of Israel ("all the chief priests and scribes of the people," vs. 4) that they take their place beside Herod in the manner in which they receive the news of the birth of their King, and of the people that "all Jerusalem" becomes "terrified" on hearing of him (vs. 3). This reaction on the part of the leaders and people adumbrates Israel's later rejection of its Messiah.[27] In addition, the best explanation of the story of the Slaughter of the Innocents (vss. 16–18) is that it is an initial sign of the judgment that will befall Israel for having rejected its Messiah.[28] Hence, already in chs. 1–2 Matthew prefigures the passion and ressurrection–exaltation of Jesus. Because in chs. 27–28 Matthew, as we shall see, again associates with one another the several motifs we have discovered here: Israel's repudiation of its Messiah; the judgment that overtakes Israel; the forgiveness of sins; Jesus as the King of the Jews; and Jesus as the Son of God, rejected (in the cross) yet exalted to eschatological dominion (in the resurrection). This theological affinity between chs. 1–2 on the one hand and chs. 27–28 on the other, which rests in greatest measure on Matthew's Son-of-God christology, serves to corroborate further our understanding of ch. 2.

*The Baptism, the Temptation, and the Relocation of Jesus (3:13–4:16)*

The story of the Baptism of Jesus (3:13–17) is central to our study of the title Son of God throughout 1:1–4:16. Apart from the introduction (vs. 13), Matthew uses the literary technique of inclusion (vs. 13: *baptisthēnai;* vs. 16: *baptistheis*) to divide the text into two equal parts: vss. 14–15, and vss. 16–17. Vss. 14–15 are editorial in character, and emphasize that Jesus submits to baptism by John not because he, like the people, has need to repent of sin (cf. 3:14 with 3:5–6, 11) or because he would become a disciple of John,[29] but because "it is necessary" for him and John to "fulfill all righteousness" (3:15). As far as the figure of Jesus is concerned, his submission to baptism reflects, in Matthew's view, the fact that he is perfectly obedient to the will of God.[30]

The occurrence of *kai idou* ("and behold") at 3:16b and 3:17a indi-

---

27. Cf. Nellessen, *Kind,* 90; Vögtle, *Gottessohn,* 62, 67, 70; Hengel–Merkel, "Magier," 153, 165.
28. Cf. Vögtle, *Gottessohn,* 68–70.
29. Cf. Frankemölle, *Jahwebund,* 93–94.
30. Cf. O. Eissfeldt, *"Plērōsai pasan dikaiosynēn* in Matthäus 3, 15," ZNW 61 (1970): 209–215. Cf. also J. Bieneck, *Sohn Gottes als Christusbezeichnung der Synoptiker* (ATANT 21; Zürich: Zwingli, 1951), 62–63; De Kruijf, *Sohn,* 46, 54.

cates that in these verses, especially the latter, the story of the Baptism reaches its culmination. The purpose of the opening of the heavens is both to permit the Spirit to descend and to signal that divine revelation is about to take place (cf. Ezek 1:1).[31] The descent of the Spirit upon Jesus denotes the divine act whereby God empowers Jesus to discharge the messianic ministry he is shortly to begin (4:17), a ministry in which God himself will be at work in Jesus (1:23) and which will issue in salvation or damnation for people (1:21; 3:11d). Such "empowerment," however, is not to be interpreted as Jesus' initial endowment with the Spirit, for he was, to say it again, conceived by the Spirit. It is, however, to be construed as a commentary as to what it means for John to speak of Jesus as the "Mightier One" (3:11). The first to proclaim the Kingdom (3:2), John does so in such a way as to prepare for the coming of Jesus (3:11–12). But when Jesus proclaims the Kingdom (4:17), it is a present reality in him, rescuing men in the power of the Spirit from the dominion of Satan (12:28; cf. 3:11d).

At 3:17, the voice from heaven declares, "This is [cf. 17:5] my beloved Son, with whom I am well pleased." Although this announcement is made only in the presence of John and not before the crowds (cf. *tote* ["then"], 3:13), it occurs openly, and in this sense can be said to be "public" in nature. In substance, the announcement contains words taken from Ps 2:7 (a royal psalm) and Isa 42:1 (a Servant song). How did Matthew understand it?

The *Sitz im Leben* of Ps 2 in Israel is thought to be the coronation ceremony of kings who stood in the succession of David.[32] In the course of each such coronation, the new king asserted in the name of Jahweh that he reigned over all the nations (cf. Ps 2:7–8).[33] The early church, we know, interpreted Ps 2 in terms of the revelation of Jesus as the Messiah.[34] With respect to Isa 42:1–4, the early church applied this text to the revelation of Jesus as the chosen Servant of God.[35]

Since Matthew employs the OT with care, it is not inconceivable that he should have regarded his quotation of Ps 2 here at 3:17 as alluding

31. Cf. W. C. van Unnik, "Die 'geöffneten Himmel' in der Offenbarungsvision des Apokryphons des Johannes," *Apophoreta* (BZNW 30 [Festschrift E. Haenchen]; Berlin: A. Töpelmann, 1964), 273; L. E. Keck, "The Spirit and the Dove," *NTS* 17 (1970/71): 60.

32. Cf. H.–J. Kraus, *Psalmen* (BKAT XV; Neukirchen: Neukirchener Verlag, 1960), I, 18–19.

33. Ibid., 16–18.

34. Cf. B. Lindars, *New Testament Apologetic* (London: SCM, 1961), 141.

35. Ibid., 145.

to Jesus as the Messiah from the house of David. At the same time, the
idiom "my Son," in view of chs. 1–2, is unambiguous in meaning: for
Matthew, it identifies Jesus as the Son whose origin is in God. In the
light of these two factors, Matthew intended that the words "This is my
Son . . ." should proclaim the confessional truth we have already encountered, namely, that Jesus, scion of David, is the Son of God.

As for the expressions *agapētos* and *en hō eudokēsa*, they apply in this
context, not to Jesus as the Servant per se, but, again, to Jesus as the
Son of God. Following Mark, Matthew most likely construed *agapētos*
as designating Jesus as God's "only," or "unique," Son ( cf. 21:37 to Mark
12:6), and the verb *eudokēsa*, which connotes that God has "chosen"
Jesus,[36] Matthew certainly interpreted in terms of the conviction that
Jesus is the one in whom God brings his Rule to humankind ( cf. 1:23;
4:17, 23; 9:35; 12:18; 24:14; 28:18b–20). The latter thought, then, introduces the theme of dominion, which is prominent in Ps 2. If this exegesis
is correct, Matthew would therefore have understood the heavenly voice
of 3:17 as openly declaring in the company of John that Jesus, specifically
as the unique Son of God, is the Messiah from the house of David, the
one in whom God confronts people with his Rule.

As Matthew has shaped it, then, the story of the Baptism of Jesus
highlights his uniqueness. It presents him as the one who is perfectly
obedient to the will of God (3:15), the one whom God empowers for his
messianic ministry (3:16), and the one who is "publicly" proclaimed in
the presence of John to be the unique Son of God who stands in the line
of David, Israel's Messiah. Consequently, it only stands to reason that
with the declaration of the heavenly voice at 3:17, we should have
reached the apex, not only of the story of the Baptism of Jesus but,
indeed, of the entire first part of Matthew's Gospel (1:1–4:16). The
pericopes that follow (4:1–11, 12–16) flow from this declaration even as
the previous ones have tended toward it.

In 1:1–4:16, then, Matthew focuses on the person and origin of Jesus.
The overriding truth he desires to set forth is that Jesus, who is the royal
Messiah, is uniquely the Son of God. He does not state this truth in 1:1,
the heading of the first main part of his Gospel. For as something that can
be known solely by revelation (16:16–17), it must first be proclaimed,
not by any character in the gospel narrative and not even by himself, the
author of the Gospel, but only by God.[37] Accordingly, Matthew alludes

36. Cf. G. Schrenk, *TDNT*, II, 740–41.
37. Cf. also Pesch, "Evangelienprolog," 416.

to this truth with circumlocutions (1:16, 18, 20), with metaphors (2:8–9, 11, 13–14, 20–21; 3:11), or with a term ("son") that is susceptible of dual meaning (1:21, 23, 25), and he even permits it to sound softly as the word of the Lord spoken through the prophets (1:22–23; 2:15). Still, all remains adumbration until that climactic point following the baptism of Jesus when the voice from heaven "publicly" proclaims in the presence of John that Jesus is indeed the unique Son of God.

The story of the Temptation (4:1–11) develops in particular one aspect of the divine sonship of Jesus: as we observed already at the baptism, Jesus is perfectly obedient to the will of God. Three times Satan tempts Jesus in his capacity as the Son of God.[38] In that these temptations are antitypical to those experienced by the Israelites in their wanderings from Egypt to Canaan, Jesus is portrayed as recapitulating in his person this history of Israel, who had also been designated by God as his son (Exod 4:22–23). But whereas Israel son of God broke faith with God, Jesus Son of God renders to him perfect obedience. As we shall see, it is exactly as the one who is himself perfectly obedient to God, ideal Israelite, that Jesus atones for the sins of many (cf. ch. 27).

In our treatment of the structure of Matthew's Gospel, we demonstrated the formal relatedness of 4:12–16 to the pericopes preceding it. As we said there, this pericope is transitional in nature: its purpose is to place Jesus, now presented in full as the Messiah, Son of God, in Galilee, where he will begin his public ministry to Israel.

We can now attempt a summary of the argument we have been pursuing thus far. We stated that our immediate objective is to delineate the christology of Matthew by relating it to the Gospel's structure, yet to do so in such a way that the latter determines the former. Structurally, we noted that the first main part of the Gospel extends from 1:1 to 4:16. Materially, we discovered that Matthew, by sounding the theme of the person (origin) of Jesus in the heading of this first main part (1:1), indicates that this part is of paramount significance to him in the development of his christology.

In exploring the christology of 1:1–4:16, we were concerned to ascertain whether or not there was one strain that predominates. Our answer

---

38. The third temptation, too, has to do with the divine sonship of Jesus even though the term "Son of God" does not occur (cf. 4:8–10), for, as E. Lövestam (*Son and Saviour* [ConNt XVIII; Lund: C. W. K. Gleerup, 1961], 100) and others have pointed out, the devil would be depicted as openly contradicting himself were he to address Jesus as the Son of God on the one hand but request that Jesus fall down and worship him on the other; to have the devil address Jesus as the Son of God would mean that the devil should be doing obeisance to Jesus.

is in the affirmative, for while Matthew in 1:1–4:16 develops more than
one type of christology, he permits the title Son of God to surpass all
others (e.g., "Son of Abraham," "Son of David," "Messiah," "King").
This title sounds climactically in 3:17, but figures prominently in the
materials that both precede this verse and follow it. The development
of the structure of the first main part of Matthew's Gospel coincides
perfectly with the development of the christology. The one points to the
other, thus confirming our basic conclusions in both areas. And because
the "superscriptions" to the second and third main parts of the Gospel
reveal that the public ministry of Jesus in the one case (4:17) and his
suffering, death, and resurrection in the other (cf. 16:21) are, respectively, the major topics Matthew would hence develop, it is incumbent
upon us to show from here on, that Son of God, as Matthew's predominate christological predication, continues to be preeminent throughout
the Gospel.

In addition to establishing Son of God as the chief christological
predication of the first Gospel, the section 1:1–4:16 also provides us
with a representative, though not exhaustive, understanding of its meaning for Matthew. To our knowledge, commentators have overlooked the
circumstance that in 1:1–4:16 Matthew deftly operates in key passages
with a series of related idioms, namely, "his people" (1:21), "my people"
(2:6), "my Son" (2:15; 3:17), and "Son of God" (4:3, 6). The thing to
notice is that the contents of the passages in which these idioms occur
easily lend themselves to combination. What results is a brief sketch of
the christology of the first main part of the Gospel: Jesus, in the line of
David (1:21), is the Son of God (2:15; 3:17), that is to say, he has his
origin in God (1:20) and is the one chosen to shepherd the eschatological
people of God (2:6) for, empowered by God for messianic ministry
(3:16–17), he proves himself in confrontation with Satan to be perfectly
obedient to the will of God (4:3–4, 5–7, 8–10) and, as such a one, he
saves his (God's) people from their sins (1:21).

If this statement is in fact representative of the way in which Matthew
would have us define the predication Son of God, we can begin to
appreciate the absolute importance to his Son-of-God christology of yet
another passage, the so-called Emmanuel passage (1:23).[39] It requires
little effort to recognize that the words "God with us," applied to the

---

39. On the importance of 1:23 in the thought of Matthew, cf. K. Stendahl, "Quis et
Unde? An Analysis of Mt 1–2," *Judentum, Urchristentum, Kirche,* ed. W. Eltester
(BZNW 26 [Festschrift J. Jeremias]; Berlin: A. Töpelmann, 1960), 103; Trilling,
*Israel,* 41; Davis, "Matthew 1:18–2:23," 412–13.

person of Jesus, contain *in nuce* everything that Matthew otherwise says in 1:1–4:16 of Jesus Son of God. It is our contention, therefore, that 1:23 is Matthew's "thumbnail definition" of the predication Son of God, and that his entire Gospel may be seen as an attempt to elaborate on the implications of this passage and others that are similar to it (cf., e.g., 14:27; 18:20; 28:20). We must keep these comments in mind as we move to our study of the concept Son of God in the second and third main parts of the Gospel.

## B. THE TITLE "SON OF GOD" IN 4:17–28:20

At 4:17, Jesus Messiah is portrayed as embarking upon his public ministry to Israel. He does this as the one whom God has declared to be his Son and who has proved the truth of this declaration by resisting the temptations of Satan calculated to effect the loss of his sonship. In consequence of this, it is logical to assume that Matthew, having gone to great lengths in the first part of his Gospel to present Jesus Messiah as especially the Son of God, should continue to view him in this light. But it is just at this point that we ostensibly encounter a problem.

### The Title "Son of God" in 4:17–10:42

A glance at the narrative and discourse materials in the section 4:17–10:42 reveals that, except for 8:29 (// Mark 5:7), the title Son of God or its equivalent does not occur in the text at all. On what grounds, therefore, can we justify the claim that also in the chapters following 4:17 Jesus is to be seen preeminently as the Son of God? To answer this question, we need to make a number of random observations covering several topics before attempting a general description of Jesus in 4:17–10:42 as the Son of God.

One reason it is possible to maintain that Matthew regards Jesus Messiah in 4:17–10:42 predominately as the Son of God even though the title occurs only once in these chapters has to do with the nature of this term and its relationship to other titles. As for its nature, this term does not constitute for Matthew what might be called a "public" title. Thus, unbelievers and enemies address Jesus in the first Gospel never with "Son of God," unless it be in mockery or blasphemy (cf. 26:63, 65; 27:40, 43), but with "teacher" (cf. 8:19; 12:38; 19:16; 22:16, 24, 36) or "rabbi" (cf. 26:25, 49). Similarly, Jesus, in public or in the presence of a scribe, refers to himself not as the "Son of God" but, for example, as the "Son of Man" (cf. 8:20; 9:6). On the other hand, when disciples or people who approach Jesus in faith appeal to him, Matthew prefers to bring, not the title Son of God, but the vocative of the term *kyrios* ("Lord"; cf., e.g., 8:2, 6, 8, 21, 25; 9:28),[40] since the function of this word (which, as we shall see, is merely an auxiliary christological title in the first Gospel) is to attribute to Jesus the status and authority, for instance, to heal or save. Occasionally, with a view to his apology against Israel, Matthew describes persons who are not disciples but who search Jesus out in the belief he can heal as accosting him with "Son of David" (cf., e.g., 9:27 and Chapter III). In the last analysis it is a combination of peculiar but perfectly comprehensible factors which explains why it is that the title Son of God is, with one exception (8:29 // Mark 5:7), absent throughout 4:17–10:42: (a) Jesus being regularly pictured in these chapters as heavily engaged with the crowds and also their leaders, a context that in itself precludes the utilization of the title Son of God (cf. 4:23; 5:1; 7:28; 8:1, 16, 18–19, 34; 9:1, 8, 11, 23–25, 32–34, 35–36); (b) Matthew's penchant for employing the term *kyrios* as a surrogate for other christological titles, one of which, we shall learn, is Son of God; and (c) the apologetic purposes for which Matthew makes use of the title Son of David. Hence, the christological terminology of 4:17–10:42 does not contravene our argument that Matthew continues to regard Jesus in these chapters predominately as the Son of God.

Perhaps we should speak a preliminary word in this connection on the relationship between the titles "Messiah" and "Son of God." At 1:1, "Messiah" is for all intents and purposes a personal name. By contrast, in the mouth of Herod in ch. 2 it amounts to little more than a popular designation for that royal figure the Jews await as their national deliverer (cf. vss. 4, 13, 16, 23). But Matthew, we saw, quickly "corrects" the latter view with his formula quotation at 2:6: the Messiah is not a political throne-pretender but the eschatological Shepherd of God's people Israel. And who, specifically, is this Messiah? As Matthew declares in such passages as 2:15, 16:16, and 26:63, he is Jesus the Son of God. Hence, we discover that not only the title *kyrios* but also the title Messiah, except where it is pointedly political in connotation, can be a surrogate in the first Gospel for the title Son of God (cf., e.g., 11:2; 23:10). This is an important additional factor that supports our position that Matthew construes Jesus also after 4:17 as above all the Son of God.

There is one question that yet remains, the presence of the title Son

---

40. On Matthew's use of *kyrie* at 7:21–22, cf. the discussion of the title *kyrios* in Chapter III.

of God in 8:29. How is it, in light of our statement that unbelievers do not address Jesus with the title Son of God, that Matthew should portray two men in this verse as doing exactly this? The answer of course is that the contradiction is only apparent, for the two men in the narrative are said to be possessed of demons (8:28). But according to Matthew, once God has openly proclaimed the mystery of the person of Jesus, viz., that he is the Son of God, supernatural beings such as Satan and demons as a matter of course know this (cf. 3:17 to 4:3, 6; 8:29). On the basis of this observation and our previous discussion we can now formulate what will emerge as a cardinal principle in understanding Matthew's concept of Jesus as the Son of God: except for such transcendent personalities as God (3:17; 17:5), Satan (4:3, 6), and demons (8:29), only those who confess Jesus, never enemies or unbelievers (unless it be in blasphemy), assert the truth that Jesus is the Son of God.

*The Disciples as Sons of God*

Once Jesus Messiah has begun his public ministry to Israel, Matthew records that his initial act is to call his first disciples (4:18–22). Elsewhere in the Gospel, Matthew depicts Jesus as designating his disciples as "sons of God" (5:9), "sons of your heavenly Father" (5:45), and "the sons of the Kingdom" (13:38). By the same token, Matthew has Jesus, in addressing his disciples, refer to God as "your Father" nineteen times, fifteen or sixteen of which are without synoptic parallel (cf. also 6:9: "our Father"; 13:43: "their Father").[41] Moreover, in relation to himself, Jesus on one occasion, says Matthew, even stretches out his hand toward his disciples and remarks that they, in reality, are "my mother and my brothers" (12:49). Accordingly, when Jesus Messiah in 4:18–22 calls his first disciples to follow him, he does so, in Matthew's eyes, precisely as the Son of God. For inherent in the call of the disciples is the idea that through Jesus Messiah, who is the Son of God, they enter into a relationship of sonship with God.

Three other passages support this conclusion. The one is 12:50, where Matthew has Jesus speak of his relationship both to his Father and to his disciples in the following words: "For whoever does the will of *my Father* who is in heaven, he is *my brother and sister and mother*" (cf. also 18:35). The second is 23:8, where Matthew describes Jesus as telling

41. Cf. 5:16, 45, 48 (// Luke 6:36); 6:1, 4, 6b–c, 8, 14 (// Mark 11:25), 18a–b, 26, 32 (// Luke 12:30); 7:11; 10:20, 29; 18:14; 23:9. Textually, Mark 11:26 is an uncertain parallel to Matt 6:15.

his disciples that "all you are brothers" (cf. also 18:21). And the third
is 28:10, where the resurrected Jesus, whom Matthew thinks of as the
resurrected Son of God, commands the women to "go and tell my
brothers . . . ."

Further corroboration for the view that Matthew understands Jesus
to be the Son of God who makes of his disciples sons of God is H.
Frankemölle's analysis of the concept of the disciples' being "with
Jesus." Through addition,[42] omission,[43] and revision,[44] Frankemölle demonstrates that Matthew works not merely linguistically but theologically
as well with phrases that feature the preposition *meta* ("with": "with
Jesus [me, you, them]") and function to portray Jesus as being present
with his disciples.[45] The theological dimension of such "togetherness" is
that even as God the Father promises to be present with his own in the
person of Jesus his Son (cf. 1:23), so Jesus Son of God mediates this
divine presence to his disciples who are "with him," hereby revealing
them to be, again, sons of God.

### The Son of God on the Mountain

In the pericope on the Call of the Disciples (4:18–22), Matthew
therefore alludes to Jesus as the Son of God. Following this, he gives a
summary of the ministry of Jesus to Israel with the first of three parallel
passages (4:23; cf. 9:35; 11:1): it is one of teaching, preaching, and
healing. Then, at 5:1, the text states that Jesus ascends "the mountain."
A review of this setting in the Gospel proves that it, too, serves as a
means by which Matthew can allude to Jesus as the Son of God.

In making reference to the "Mount of Olives," Matthew draws upon
Mark (cf. 21:1; 24:3; 26:30 to Mark 11:1; 13:3; 14:26). On the other
hand, there are six instances in which Matthew simply refers to "a [the]
mountain" as a setting for some activity of Jesus (cf. 4:8; 5:1; 14:23;
15:29; 17:1; 28:16), and in four of these instances we have to do with
Matthaean redaction (4:8; 5:1; 15:29; 28:16). What transpires on the
unidentified mountain provides some insight as to the meaning this
setting holds for Matthew. Thus, the mountain is the place of eschato-

---

42. Cf., e.g., 26:29, 36, 38, 40; also 17:17.
43. Cf., e.g., 8:34 with Mark 5:18; 9:22 with Mark 5:37; 15:39 with Mark 8:10;
21:17 with Mark 11:11; 26:21 with Mark 14:18; 26:55 with Mark 14:49.
44. Cf., e.g., 26:51 with Mark 14:47; 26:71 with Mark 14:49; also 12:4 with Mark
2:26; 12:45 with Luke 11:26.
45. Cf. Frankemölle, *Jahwebund*, 10–12.

logical revelation (cf. 4:8; 5:1; 15:29; 17:1; 28:16)[46] and of solitude and nearness to God (cf. 14:23);[47] for these reasons, it also underlines the divine authority with which Jesus speaks there or heals (5:1; 7:28–29; 15:29; 28:16, 18; cf. also 17:1, 5).

The themes of eschatological revelation, of intimate fellowship with God, and of divine authority are integral to Matthew's portrait of Jesus as the Son of God. Consequently, it is not surprising that "Son of God" should be the only predication Matthew explicitly associates with the setting of the unidentified mountain. Jesus, for example, is tempted on a mountain as the Son of God (4:8).[48] Then, too, he retires to the mountain for prayer, yet the report of this falls within a pericope in which the disciples are said to worship him as the Son of God (14:23, 33). Again, on the mountain on which Jesus is transfigured, he is declared by the voice from the cloud to be God's Son (17:1, 5). Last, after his resurrection Jesus meets the eleven disciples on the mountain, and here the reference he makes to himself is as "the Son" (28:16, 19).

In view of this pattern, can we assume that Matthew, at 5:1 and 15:29, is likewise employing the mountain to point to Jesus as the Son of God? All indications are that this is indeed the case. We have already seen that Jesus in the first Gospel embarks upon his public ministry as, above all, the Son of God (4:17–22), and that Matthew characterizes this ministry as one of teaching and preaching on the one hand and of healing on the other (4:23). With the ministry of Jesus Son of God so characterized, it cannot be accidental that, at 5:1, Matthew has Jesus ascend the mountain specifically to teach (cf. 5:2; 7:28–29), and, at 15:29, specifically to heal (cf. 15:30–31). Now we have also seen that three times directly and once indirectly Matthew has utilized the mountain as a place where Jesus is revealed to be the Son of God. At the same time, Matthew shows in 16:16–17 that the height of Christian revelation is, in his eyes, that a person be enabled by God to confess Jesus to be the Messiah, the Son of God (cf. also 27:54).[49] Hence, that Matthew has Jesus teach and heal on the mountain indicates that Jesus is in the midst of Israel as the Messiah, the Son of God. But if this is so, why is it that

---

46. Cf. also W. Schmauch, *Orte der Offenbarung und der Offenbarungsort im Neuen Testament* (Göttingen: Vandenhoeck & Ruprecht, 1956), 76–77, 80.

47. Cf. ibid., 78–79; also J. Manek, "On the Mount—On the Plain (Mt. v 1—Lk. vi 17)," *NovT* 9 (1967): 127–28.

48. See above, n. 38.

49. Cf. A. Vögtle, "Messiasbekenntnis und Petrusverheissung. Zur Komposition Mt 16, 13–23 Par. (1 Teil)," *BZ* 1 (1957): 257–62, 264.

there is no mention of this title in chs. 5–7 and in the passage 15:29–31? Because in both places Jesus is in public, and here he is not properly recognized to be the Son of God.[50] Nevertheless, the fact remains: Matthew makes use of "a [the] mountain" as a setting that in itself alludes to Jesus as the Son of God.

### The Authority of the Son of God

Matthew presents Jesus mainly as the Son of God, not only in 1:1–4:16, but also as he discharges his public ministry to Israel: as he calls his first disciples and is surrounded by the crowds in the setting of the mountain. If we survey the whole of Jesus' ministry as sketched by Matthew, we discover that its distinguishing mark is the "authority" (*exousia*) with which he speaks and acts.[51] Matthew closely associates the authority of Jesus with his status as the Son of God.[52]

In 28:18–20, we have a clear example of this, for here the resurrected Jesus, to whom God has given "all authority in heaven and on earth," designates himself as "the Son." Still, there is also evidence of this in the forepart of the Gospel.

The first specific reference Matthew makes to the authority of Jesus is to describe as binding the Sermon on the Mount (cf. 7:28–29 to 5:1–2). To understand this authority in regard to the person of Jesus correctly, we dare not forget that the Jesus who delivers this sermon is the one who has ascended the mountain (5:1), who is "mightier" than John (3:11) in the sense that he has been conceived (1:18, 20) and empowered for messianic ministry by none other than the Spirit (3:16), and who has been proclaimed by the heavenly voice to be "my Son" (3:17), that is, "God with us" (1:23). Thus, we see that in Matthew's perspective

50. In our discussion of the title "Son of Man" in Chapter III, we endeavor to show in detail that in the first Gospel Jesus presents himself with this designation to the "public" (e.g., the crowds and his opponents). In comparison with the title Son of Man, the title Son of God may be termed "confessional" in character: although such supernatural beings as God (3:17; 17:5), Satan (4:3, 6), and demons (8:28–29) use it to address Jesus, in the world of humankind it can be uttered only by people of faith unless such utterance be accounted as blasphemy or mockery (cf. 26:63–66; 27:40, 43).

51. Cf. 7:29; 9:6, 8; 10:1; 11:27; 21:23–27; 28:18.

52. At 9:6, Matthew in the words of Jesus associates Jesus' "authority" with his status as the Son of Man. The reason for this has to do in large part with the setting: Matthew here depicts Jesus as speaking of himself in "public" (cf. 9:8), confronting his opponents ("some of the scribes," 9:3). As we stated in n. 50, one of the peculiar uses to which Matthew puts the title Son of Man is that, employed only by Jesus to refer to himself, it functions as the "public" counterpart to the "confessional" title Son of God. Since these two titles complement each other in this fashion, the passage 9:6 does not contradict the basic observation that Matthew closely associates the authority of Jesus with his status as the Son of God.

the authority of Jesus, like Jesus himself, is of divine derivation and is therefore directly related to the circumstance that he is the unique Son of God. In the passage 11:27a, which is the "pre-Easter" counterpart to the "post-Easter" passage 28:18b mentioned above, Matthew draws upon a Q logion to give expression to this very thought: "All things (*panta*) have been delivered to me by my Father . . . ."

The pericope on the Question about Authority (21:23–27) likewise associates the authority of Jesus with his divine sonship. The confrontation depicted here between Jesus and the members of the Sanhedrin is said to take place in the "temple" (vs. 23), and Matthew makes use of this setting to bind together into one subsection this pericope and the following so-called parables against Israel (cf. 21:28–32, 33–46; 22:1–14). The imagery of these parables is transparent to the reader of the Gospel. Matthew pictures Jesus as applying to himself such terms as "his Son" (21:37; 22:2), "my Son" (21:37), and "the Son" (21:38). Hence, Matthew leaves no doubt that the one whom the leaders of the Jews confront in the parables against Israel and consequently, as part of the same subsection, also in our pericope is Jesus the Son of God.

We stated that the confrontation between Jesus and the leaders of the Jews occurs in the temple, the dwelling place of God (21:23). The words of inquiry the chief priests and the elders put to Jesus as to the source of his authority to do "these things" are repeated three times (21:23–24, 27) and even form an inclusion (21:23, 27), all of which suggest that this inquiry, and not the talk of the baptism of John, are the heart of the matter. The counter-question of Jesus, "The baptism of John, whence was it; from heaven or from men?" (21:25), functions in the debate to identify Jesus with John in a manner that permits what is said of John to be accounted as applicable also to Jesus. The phrase "from heaven" is of course a circumlocution for "from God" (cf., e.g., 3:17). When, therefore, Jesus challenges the leaders of the Jews with the truth that John performed his baptism on the authority of God himself, the unmistakable implication is that like John he, too, is acting on the authority of God. The anticipated reply to the question "Who has given you this authority?" (21:23) is "God," which means, in turn, that Matthew's overall intention with this pericope is to assert that the one who confronts the members of the Sanhedrin in the house of God is none other than the Son of God, who wields the authority of God.

Should this reasoning be sound, why does Matthew leave it to the reader to infer this point? Why does he not have Jesus state it explicitly?

Because, as was said earlier, "Son of God" in the first Gospel is not a "public" title; the very partners of Jesus in debate, for example, rule out for Matthew the use in this pericope of the title Son of God.[53] Nevertheless, the conclusion stands: Matthew closely associates here, as elsewhere also, the authority of Jesus with his status as the Son of God.[54]

### The Son of God as One Who Teaches

The divine authority of Jesus Messiah, the Son of God, extends in the first Gospel particularly to his teaching (cf., e.g., 7:29) and to his ability to perform miracles, especially those of healing (cf., e.g., 10:1 to 4:23–25; 8:16–17; 9:35; 11:4–6; 12:15b). We recall, however, that the nature of Jesus' ministry to the Jews is that of teaching and preaching on the one hand and of healing on the other (4:23; cf. 9:35; 11:1–2). Accordingly, we should like to show that Matthew establishes a close connection between, respectively, the teaching and the healing of Jesus and his status as the Son of God.

We have already shown that, in terms of his teaching, Jesus Messiah delivers authoritative instruction in the Sermon on the Mount as the Son of God (5:1–2; 7:28–29). But this is not all. In the story of the Transfiguration, the voice from the cloud first designates Jesus as "my Son," and then exhorts the disciples to "hear him" (17:5). The obvious intention of this command is that the three disciples are to give heed to the teaching of Jesus Messiah, who is the Son of God. In 23:10, Jesus says to the disciples: "One is your teacher, the Christ" (cf. the inclusion, vss. 8–10). As we learned above, with one necessary exception (1:1), Matthew in other passages in his Gospel utilizes the title Son of God to explain his deepest understanding of the term "Christ" (cf. 16:16; 26:63; also 11:2 and 25–27). In the mind of Matthew, therefore, the point of 23:10 is that the one teacher of the disciples is Jesus Messiah, the Son of God. But again, if this is so, why is the title Son of God not found in the text? Because, according to Matthew, Jesus speaks these words to his disciples in public (cf. 23:1); hence, the setting itself precludes the use of this exalted title.[55] Finally, in 28:20, a passage that also falls within the sphere of Matthew's Son-of-God christology,[56] the resurrected Jesus

---

53. Concerning this statement, cf. n. 50.
54. Concerning the passage 9:6, cf. n. 52.
55. See above, n. 50.
56. Cf. our discussion of the passage 28:16–20 below; also J. D. Kingsbury, "The Composition and Christology of Matt 28:16–20," *JBL* 93 (1974): 573–84.

instructs his disciples to keep "all that I have commanded you"; so here, too, Matthew connects the teaching of Jesus to his status as the Son of God.

Apart from 28:18–20, the programmatic passage in which Matthew gives expression to the belief that the teaching activity of Jesus is a fundamental aspect of his divine sonship is, again, the pericope on the Question about Authority (21:23–27). Source-critically, Matthew has appropriated this text from Mark and, in general, follows the latter without great variation (cf. 21:23–27 to Mark 11:27–33). In the opening verse, however, Matthew has added the participle "teaching" (*didaskonti;* cf. 21:23 with Mark 11:27). What is noteworthy about this question is that it makes the word *tauta* in the query the members of the Sanhedrin put to Jesus ("By what authority are you doing *these things?*" vs. 23) relate not only to the miracles of healing Jesus performed the previous day in the temple (cf. 21:14–15), but also to the teaching in the temple in which he is presently engaged. Now we know from our earlier examination of this pericope that its central message is that Jesus the Son of God wields the authority of God. Still, this divine authority, says Matthew through his introduction at vs. 23 of the participle "*didaskonti,*" specifically covers the "teaching" of Jesus. Hence, the pericope 21:23–27 sets forth the same thought we adduced from the passages discussed in the last paragraph: the teaching ministry of Jesus Son of God is accomplished with the authority of God.

### The Son of God as One Who Heals

If Jesus Messiah, as the Son of God, teaches with the authority of God, so he, as the Son of God, also heals with the authority of God. Matthew gives indication of the latter both directly and indirectly. Directly, Matthew depicts Jesus Son of God as healing two men who are possessed of demons (8:28–34) and as having dominion over nature (14:22–33). Moreover, he likewise employs the now familiar pericope on the Question about Authority (21:23–27) to establish a direct relationship between the healing of Jesus and his divine sonship.

Thus, the verb *poieis* in 21:23b picks up on the verb *epoiēsen* in 21:15. The result is that the words *tauta poieis* in the query "By what authority *are you doing these things?*" (21:23b) embrace, as we stated above, both the healing and the teaching activity of Jesus in the temple (cf. 21:23 to 21:14–15). It follows, therefore, that even as this pericope underlines the truth that Jesus, as the Son of God, teaches with the authority of

God, so it advances with equal force the claim that Jesus, as the Son of God, heals with the authority of God.

Indirectly, the evidence is that Matthew understands all three of his great summaries of the healing ministry of Jesus to be setting forth the work of Jesus Son of God. The first great summary comes as early as 4:23–25. We have already explained, however, that up to this point in the Gospel Matthew's predominant characterization of Jesus has been that of Son of God. The third great summary is presented at 15:29–31. In this case, the fact that Jesus is made to ascend the mountain to heal alludes to him as the Son of God.

This leaves the second great summary, which is found at 11:4–5. In the immediate context, Jesus' acts of healing (and preaching) are termed the "works [*erga*] of the Christ" (11:2) and the "works" of wisdom (11:19), so that these twin references to "works" become the antecedents of "these things" (*tauta*) mentioned in 11:25.[57] In 11:25, however, Jesus renders thanks to his heavenly Father as "the Son" (cf. 11:27). Hence, Matthew shows that the acts of healing enumerated in the summary 11:5 are also to be construed as the activity of Jesus Son of God.

Yet another point begs for consideration. At 8:16–17 and 12:15–21, Matthew makes use of formula quotations taken, respectively, from Isa 53 and 42 in order to picture Jesus as filling the role of Servant through his healing ministry to Israel (cf. *pais*, 12:18a). In this connection, the affinity between 12:18 on the one hand and 3:16–17 and 17:5 on the other is so striking that it raises the question as to the relationship in the first Gospel between "Servant christology" and Son-of-God christology. For at least the following four reasons it seems clear that Matthew intends the "Servant christology" to be subsumed under his Son-of-God christology, not the reverse:[58] (a) the term *pais* ("Servant") occurs in Matthew's Gospel only here at 12:18; (b) in the mixed quotations at 3:17 and 17:5, which combine words taken from Ps 2 and the Servant song of Isa 42, Matthew employs the Servant song both times only in order to enhance his Son-of-God christology; (c) as we have seen, Matthew otherwise ascribes to Jesus Son of God a ministry of healing; and (d) we shall find that Matthew also associates both the forgiveness of sins and death on

---

57. Cf. also Davies, *Setting*, 207. Since *tauta* in 11:25 is an inclusive term, it should probably be understood to refer, regardless of the difference in gender, also to the expression *hai [pleistai] dynameis* found in 11:20–21.

58. Cf. also Strecker, *Weg*, 68, 70 n. 2; Pesch, "Evangelienprolog," 408; W. Rothfuchs, *Die Erfüllungszitate des Matthäus-Evangeliums* (BWANT 8; Stuttgart: W. Kohlhammer, 1969), 123.

the cross with Jesus, not as the Servant, but as the Son of God. In the last analysis, therefore, the passages 8:16–17 and 12:15 likewise serve to illustrate the healing ministry of Jesus Son of God.

### Jesus Son of God in 4:17–10:42

Keeping in mind our preceding discussion of the nature of the title Son of God, the disciples as sons of God, the setting of the mountain, and the authority of Jesus Son of God particularly as it extends to his messianic ministry of teaching and healing, we can at last attempt to trace in bold strokes the way in which Matthew develops his portrait of Jesus as the Son of God in the chapters immediately following 4:17.

In Galilee, Jesus Messiah, having been presented at his baptism (3:13–17) and temptations (4:1–11) as the Son of God, is described by Matthew as embarking upon his ministry to Israel, a ministry in which God confronts men with his gracious Rule (4:17). Jesus, the Son of God, calls his first disciples (4:18–22), who through him become sons of God (5:9, 45). Accompanied by them, he engages, says Matthew in summary fashion, in a ministry to Israel of teaching and preaching on the one hand and of healing on the other (4:23; cf. 9:35; 11:1–2). As for his teaching activity, Jesus Son of God ascends the mountain and there provides instruction for his disciples and all Israel (chs. 5–7). As for his healing activity, he goes about Galilee and performs ten mighty acts of deliverance (chs. 8–9). In the teaching and healing ministry to Israel of Jesus Son of God, the authority of God graciously manifests itself (7:28–29; 8:9). And finally, in order to widen the scope of his efforts on behalf of Israel, Jesus Son of God also authorizes his disciples to go throughout the land, entrusting them with a ministry of proclamation and healing patterned after his own (10:1, 5–8).

With this summary of Matthew's presentation of Jesus Messiah as the Son of God in 4:17–10:42, we can proceed to an investigation, in sequence, of other pertinent texts in the remainder of the Gospel which have a bearing on Matthew's portrait of the Son of God.

### Jesus' Thanksgiving to the Father (11:25–27)

Although Jesus Messiah, the Son of God, discharges in the midst of Israel his gracious ministry of teaching, preaching, and healing, Israel, Matthew continues in chs. 11–12, does not recognize that, in the person of Jesus his Son, God has drawn near to dwell with his people; the result is that Israel utterly rejects its Messiah. Located at the center of these chapters describing the rejection of Jesus is Matthew's pericope on Jesus' Thanksgiving to the Father (11:25–27), which ranks as one of the most elevated expressions of his Son-of-God christology in the entire Gospel.

The key words of the pericope sound the dominant themes. Thus, the antithetic parallelism that exists in vs. 25 reflects the importance in this pericope of the theme of "revelation." It features the verbs "hide" and "reveal," and the double use of the verb "reveal" (vss. 25, 27) forms an inclusion. Moreover, the fivefold use of the word "Father" coupled with the threefold use of the term "the Son" as well as the key position in vs. 27 of the verb "know," indicate that "knowledge" and the "personal relationship" of the Son with the Father are two other prominent themes. In addition, we will want to give attention to such words as *nēpiois* ("infants," vs. 25), *eudokia* ("good pleasure," vs. 26), *panta* ("all things," vs. 27), and *paredothē* ("have been given over," vs. 27), and we shall assume an *auton* ("him") as the object of *apokalypsai*[59] ("to reveal") at the end of vs. 27.

The immediate context of this pericope is, as we noted, chs. 11–12, in which Matthew provides, again, a résumé of the messianic ministry of Jesus: he has come to Israel and has been rejected, by "this generation" (11:16), by the cities of Galilee (11:21, 23), by the leaders of the people (12:14, 24, 38–39), and apparently by members of his own family (12:48–49). Situated as this pericope is at the heart of these chapters, Matthew gives the words of Jesus both a positive and a negative application: negatively, Jesus Son of God states that his rejection by Israel (the "wise and understanding") is in accordance with the will of God (11:25); positively, Jesus Son of God claims for himself a singular role in God's plan of salvation.

The singular role of Jesus Son of God in God's plan of salvation is grounded by our text in his unique relationship with God the Father. The use of "Father" in the vocative, of the idiom "my Father," and of such absolute terms as "the Father" and "the Son" is designed to stress the thought that this relationship finds expression in the act of "knowing" (*epignōskō*), a verb that connotes, among other things, that there exists total unity of will between the Father and the Son: the Father elects the Son and authorizes him to represent him in the world, and the Son

---

59. Cf. De Kruijf, *Sohn*, 75; M. J. Suggs, *Wisdom, Christology, and Law in Matthew's Gospel* (Cambridge: Harvard University, 1970), 71–77.

acknowledges this election by living in complete fellowship with the Father, rendering to him perfect obedience.[60]

In consequence of this unique relationship, the Father, "Lord of heaven and earth" (vs. 25), determines (*eudokia*, vs. 26)[61] to encounter men with his gracious Rule in the messianic ministry of the Son (*tauta* ["all things," vs. 25] = *ta erga tou Christou* ["the works of the Messiah," 11:2]). To this end he entrusts the Son with "all things" (*panta*, vs. 27). If, as seems most likely, the clause *edothē moi pasa exousia* ("all authority has been given to me") in 28:18 best explains the clause *panta moi paredothē* ("all things have been given over to me") in our text (vs. 27), fundamental to the expression "all things" is the divine "authority" the Father gives the Son (cf. also 21:23–27).[62] Since Matthew elsewhere in his Gospel associates the divine authority of Jesus Son of God with his messianic ministry of teaching and of healing, we may conclude that what Matthew has in mind in 11:27a, c is that, through his messianic ministry, the Son reveals the Father to whomever the Son will. Because Israel, as we have seen, has rejected the Son, the Son reveals the Father to the "infants" (vs. 25). These infants are the disciples of Jesus, as is plain from 12:49–50 (cf. also 13:16–17 with 13:10–11, 13). And what Matthew understands under "revealing the Father" we discover in other passages in his Gospel: in Jesus, the Son, God the Father draws near with his Rule (4:17) to forgive men their sins (1:21; 9:5–8;[63] 26:28) and make them his sons (5:9, 45; 13:38), whose distinguishing mark is the greater righteousness (5:20), that is, they do the will of God (6:10; 7:21; 12:50). Perhaps vss. 25–27 of our text can be summarized from Matthew's point of view as follows: Jesus Son of God, who alone knows the Father as the Father knows him, occupies a singular place in God's plan of salvation; namely, as the Father's exclusive representative among men, he has been entrusted by the Father with divine authority to reveal the Father to whomever he will, notably to those whom he makes his disciples.

60. Cf. Hahn, *Christology*, 310–12; E. Schweizer, *TDNT*, VIII, 372–73.
61. Cf. G. Schrenk, *TDNT*, II, 740–42, 747.
62. Cf., among others, E. Percy, *Die Botschaft Jesu* (LUA 49, 5; Lund: C. W. K. Gleerup, 1953), 263–66; A. Fueillet, "Jésus et la Sagesse divine d' après les Évangiles Synoptiques," *RB* 62 (1955): 188–89; Hahn, *Christology*, 310.
63. Matt 9:5–8 associates the forgiveness of sins with Jesus as the Son of Man. For one thing, as we stated in nn. 50 and 52, Matthew in the words of Jesus employs Son of Man in 9:6 because this is the title Jesus uses in the first Gospel to present himself to the "public" and to his opponents. In addition, Matthew also brings the title Son of Man into play in his Gospel when he has in mind the saving work of Jesus as it relates specifically to the "world" (cf., e.g., 13:37–38; 20:28).

*The Walking on the Water (14:22–33)*

In terms of the flow of his gospel-story, the basic point Matthew makes in chs. 11–12 is that Jesus Messiah, the Son of God, is rejected by his people. In response to this rejection, Matthew portrays Jesus in ch. 13 as addressing the crowds in parables, that is to say, in speech they cannot comprehend (cf. 13:1–17, 24–35).[64] Through Jesus' use of parabolic speech, Matthew signals that Jesus is now turning from Israel and will henceforth increasingly devote his attention to his disciples (cf. 13:36–52). For although Israel will not recognize that in the person of Jesus his Son God reveals himself and mediates to people his gracious presence, the disciples of Jesus do receive the grace to perceive this (cf. 13:11, 16–18, 36, 51). In order to illustrate the latter thought, Matthew narrates the story of the Walking on the Water (14:22–33).

Aside from the introduction (vss. 22–23), the text divides itself into two parts that are strikingly parallel in structure and content: vss. 24–27 and vss. 28–33. In each part, the description of the perilous situation on the sea is remarkably the same, and the language is replete with expressions denoting terror and dread (cf. vss. 24–26 to vss. 29–31). In addition, the saving act, whether of word or of deed, is in both parts reported as occurring swiftly (*euthys, eutheōs*), with fear and doubt giving way to faith (cf. vss. 27–28 to vss. 31–33).

Of special interest to us are the respective conclusions (vss. 27, 32–33), for the words "Truly you are the Son of God" disclose that the pronouncement *"egō eimi"* is properly to be understood, not as the kind of statement the words of Peter in vs. 28b suggest ("It is I [i.e., Jesus]"), but as a divine revelation-formula.[65] Now it has been noted that Matthew employs this pericope to address the situation of his community.[66] If the boat signifies the church,[67] the truth that the story divulges is that in time of vicissitude the church can rest assured that Jesus is ever near with his saving presence (vss. 27, 32). And who is this Jesus? He is the one who has dominion over chaos and evil,[68] the one whom the church confesses and worships as the Son of God, "God with us" (*egō eimi;* cf. 1:23). Consequently, from Matthew's standpoint this story of the Walking on the Water is a christophany, and the reader learns that the

64. For a detailed study of Matt 13, cf. J. D. Kingsbury, *The Parables of Jesus in Matthew 13* (London and Richmond, Va.: S.P.C.K. and John Knox, 1969).
65. Cf. Lövestam, *Son,* 105; Hahn, *Christology,* 303.
66. Cf. Held, "Miracle Stories," 265–68.
67. Cf. ibid.
68. Cf. Lövestam, *Son,* 106.

most exalted confession of Matthew's church is that Jesus is the Son of God.

### Peter's Confession (16:13–20)

Within the groundplan of his Gospel, Matthew employs the story of the Walking on the Water to prepare for the story of Peter's Confession (16:13–20). This pericope, in turn, is as pivotal to a proper grasp of Matthew's Son-of-God christology as is that of Jesus' Thanksgiving to the Father (11:25–27).

Uppermost in this story is the question of the true identity of Jesus, and the broad context in which it is placed is that of the history of salvation.[69] The concept of Jesus in vogue among "men" is that he is John the Baptist or one of the notable prophets come back to life (vss. 13b–14). Peter, however, proclaims the true identity of Jesus: he is the Messiah in the sense that he is the Son of the living God of history (16:16).[70]

In confessing Jesus as the Son of God, Peter reiterates the confession of the disciples in the boat (14:33). Still, at the point where that story leaves off this one continues, so that it possesses an added dimension: Matthew has Jesus respond to Peter's confession with a benediction in which he asserts that such insight into the identity of his person is beyond human attainment and can be known only by revelation of God (16:17). And when we take into account the rest of the text relating to the founding of the church (vss. 18–20), we recognize that Matthew's intent with this pericope is to put across the message that Jesus is the decisive figure in the history of salvation and that divine revelation, which is imparted by God to Jesus' disciples, is required in order to penetrate the mystery of his person. This message, in turn, confirms our previous observations that the most exalted confession of Matthew's church is that Jesus is the Son of God and that this title is one which is inaccessible to the "public."[71]

### The Transfiguration (17:1–8)

With the story of the Transfiguration (17:1–8), we have left behind the materials that comprise the second main part of the Gospel (4:17–

---

69. Cf. A. Vögtle, "Messiasbekenntnis und Petrusverheissung. Zur Komposition Mt 16, 13–23 Par. (2. Teil)," *BZ* 2 (1958): 95–96.

70. Cf. J. Schniewind, *Das Evangelium nach Matthäus* (NTD 2; Göttingen: Vandenhoeck & Ruprecht, 1936), 188.

71. See above, n. 50.

16:20) and have moved on to those comprising the third (16:21–28:20). As is evident from the "superscription" 16:21, the overriding topic of this third main part is the suffering, death, and resurrection of Jesus Messiah. The pericopes we treat will admirably reflect this change of emphasis.

The similarity of language between the Transfiguration (17:1–8) and the story of the Walking on the Water (14:22–33) indicates that Matthew regards the Transfiguration, too, as of the nature of a christophany.[72] The cloud and the voice terrify the disciples, and they fall to the ground (vss. 5–6). But the presence of Jesus overcomes their fear: he approaches them, touches them, and with his authoritative word dispels their fright and enables them to rise as from the dead (vs. 7).

As at the baptism, the voice declares Jesus to be the unique and chosen Son of God (17:5), which means in effect that he, the Son, is designated as the one in whom God draws near to people with his eschatological Rule. Indeed, the nearness of God to those who are on the mountain is underlined by the notation that it is from a "bright cloud" (vs. 5) that the voice calls forth. And since the voice is the voice of God, the solemn pronouncement it makes can further be seen as divine confirmation of the truth of the revelation that enabled Peter earlier to confess Jesus to be the Son of God (16:16–17).[73]

In contradistinction to the story of the Baptism, two things in particular are of interest to us in this text. The first is the transfiguration itself of Jesus (17:2). In speaking of his face as shining "like the sun" and of his garments as being white "like the light" (vs. 2), Matthew, to a greater degree even than Mark (cf. 9:3), pictures the transfigured Jesus in the full radiance of heavenly splendor (cf., e.g., 13:43; Ps 104:2). This, in turn, serves to reinforce the cardinal Matthaean dogma that it is in the person of his Son Jesus that God is present.[74] The second thing is that the voice from the cloud also enjoins the disciples to "hear him" (17:5). Such an injunction stresses the circumstance that the teaching of Jesus is not without divine authority. And whereas this injunction is absolute in character and so points in the last analysis to the whole of Jesus' teaching (". . . all that I have commanded you," 28:20),[75] it refers most

---

72. Cf. also E. Lohmeyer, *Das Evangelium des Matthäus* (Meyer; Göttingen: Vandenhoeck & Ruprecht, 1956), 268; W. Grundmann, *Das Evangelium nach Matthäus* (HKNT I; Berlin: Evangelische Verlagsanstalt, 1968), 402–404; R. Kratz, *Auferweckung als Befreiung* (SBS 65; Stuttgart: Katholisches Bibelwerk, 1973), 22–24.

73. Cf. Grundmann, *Matthäus*, 402.

74. Cf. ibid., 403–404.

75. Cf. E. Schweizer, *Das Evangelium nach Matthäus* (NTD 2; Göttingen: Vandenhoeck & Ruprecht, 1973), 227.

immediately to Jesus' instruction to his disciples concerning his approaching passion (cf. 17:12; also 16:21; 17:22–23; 20:17–19).

*Jesus "in the Midst of Them" (18:20)*

The logion 18:20 contains no christological title, yet a discussion of it is pertinent to the larger argument because, along with 1:23 and 28:20, it is one of the key passages that provide direct insight into the peculiar character of Matthew's christology.

That the passages 1:23, 18:20, and 28:20 are in substance related to one another is generally acknowledged by students of Matthew.[76] W. Trilling, on the other hand, contests this opinion, asserting that the adverbial phrase *en mesō autōn* ("in the midst of them") in 18:20 is dissimilar in content from the prepositional phrase *meth' hēmōn [hymōn]* ("with us [you]") in 1:23 and 28:20. His contention is that whereas the former phrase is "static" and has reference to the presence of the exalted One in the assembly of the community gathered for worship and prayer (18:20), the latter phrase is "dynamic" and has reference to the presence of the exalted One with his community as it moves out to undertake its mission to the world (28:20).[77]

In a test of Trilling's thesis, H. Frankemölle has investigated the use of these two phrases in the OT (Hebrew and LXX) and in the literature of Qumran. He concludes on the basis of his analysis that Trilling's distinction is ill-founded, citing instances where the two phrases are even used interchangeably with no apparent difference in meaning.[78]

Accordingly, the prevailing view obtains: the three passages 1:23, 18:20, and 28:20 are indeed essentially related to one another, and they connote the presence, respectively, of God with his people in the person of Jesus (1:23) and of the exalted Jesus with his disciples, that is, the church (18:20; 28:20). But to say this is not to exhaust the matter, for there is still the question as to how Matthew construes the person of Jesus in 18:20. In answer to this, it is simply not enough for commentators to speak of Jesus in some vague fashion as the "exalted One."[79] Recognizing

76. Cf., e.g., Barth, "Law," 135; Strecker, *Weg*, 210, 213; Grundmann, *Matthäus*, 420; Schweizer, *Matthäus*, 244; Frankemölle, *Jahwebund*, 8, 36.
77. Cf. Trilling, *Israel*, 42.
78. Cf. Frankemölle, *Jahwebund*, 32–34.
79. Cf., e.g., Barth, "Law," 134–36; P. Bonnard, *L' évangile selon Saint Matthieu* (CNT 1; Neuchâtel: Delachaux & Nestlé, 1963), 275; Grundmann, *Matthäus*, 420; Schweizer, *Matthäus*, 244; Frankemölle, *Jahwebund*, 34–36.

this, G. Strecker,[80] W. Trilling, [81] and G. Bornkamm[82] identify Jesus more explicitly as *"kyrios,"* the exalted Lord of the church. In our view, however, this does not square with the intention of Matthew.

From a negative standpoint, we show in our examination of *"kyrios"* in Chapter III that this term in the first Gospel is of the nature, not of a primary, but of an auxiliary christological title: it regularly refers beyond itself to some other, more definitive, christological designation. Should this assessment be accurate, it goes without saying that Matthew necessarily thinks of Jesus in 18:20 in some other capacity than as *kyrios.*

The christological title that admirably commends itself as far as 18:20 is concerned is Son of God. Three considerations support this conclusion. The essential relatedness of 18:20 to 1:23 and 28:20 suggests this title, because, as we argue elsewhere in this chapter, it is a Son-of-God christology that informs both of these passages. In the second place, the context, too, points to the title Son of God for 18:20. Thus, the theme of "binding and loosing" in 18:18 calls to mind this same theme in 16:19, which in turn is embedded in the pericope (16:13–20) that highlights Peter's confession of Jesus as the Son of God (cf. 16:16). And the references to "prayer" and to God as "Father" in 18:19 evoke the thoroughly Matthaean concept that through Jesus, the Son of God, the disciples of Jesus know God as Father and can address him as such in prayer (cf. 4:18–22; 5:9, 45; 6:9, 14–15, 18, 26, 32; 7:7–11).

Consequently, the content-associations of 18:20 and its context prove that in this verse Matthew conceives of Jesus, the exalted One, more specifically as Jesus, the exalted Son of God. The thrust of 18:20 is that this Jesus resides in the circle of his disciples, or church. Because this thought occurs, despite variation of form, in 1:23 and 28:20, passages which are foundational to the christology of Matthew, we can see the central importance also of 18:20 to Matthew's portrait of Jesus.

*The Parables of the Wicked Husbandmen (21:33–46) and of the Great Supper (22:1–10)*

We mentioned that in the scene following the story of the Transfiguration (17:9–12) the Matthaean Jesus touches on the idea of suffering. In the parables of the Wicked Husbandmen (21:33–46) and of the Great

---

80. *Weg*, 213.
81. *Israel*, 40–42.
82. "The Authority to 'Bind' and 'Loose' in the Church in Matthew's Gospel: The Problem of Sources in Matthew's Gospel," *Jesus and Man's Hope*, ed. D. G. Buttrick (Pittsburgh: Pittsburgh Theological Seminary, 1970), I, 44.

Supper (22:1–10), Matthew develops this idea further. We remember from previous discussion that these two parables, together with that of the Two Sons (21:28–32), make up a group commonly called the parables against Israel. The significance of the two parables is that Jesus is referred to in both as "son," and this within a setting that in each case is tantamount to a sketch in miniature of a particular segment of the history of salvation.

The parable of the Wicked Husbandmen (21:33–46) covers the history of salvation from OT times to the emergence of the church. The "house-holder" (vs. 33) stands for God, the "vineyard" (vs. 33) for Israel as the nation God chose for himself,[83] the "tenants" (vs. 33) for contemporary Israel and its forebears represented by the members of the Sanhedrin (cf. 21:23), the respective "slaves" sent by the householder (vss. 34–36) for the prophets, and the "other tenants" (vs. 41) for the church (cf. vs. 43).[84] The "heir" whom the householder sends "last" (vss. 37–38) and is designated variously as "his son" (vs. 37), "my son" (vs. 37), and "the son" (vs. 38) is obviously Jesus Messiah.

According to the story of the parable, the heir of the vineyard is the final emissary his father dispatches to the tenants to collect from them his due. The tenants, however, "cast him out of the vineyard" and "kill" him (vs. 39). For this reason, the householder punishes these tenants and lets the vineyard out to "other tenants who will give him the fruits in their seasons" (vs. 41).

The terms that point to Jesus in this parable are common coin in the first Gospel for expressing the fact that he is the Son of God. In considera-tion of this and of the other details of the story, it becomes evident that the use to which Matthew puts this parable is not only to rehearse salvation-history that is past (cf. 21:33–36), but also to adumbrate for the reader the events he portrays in 27:31b–54: Jesus will die outside the city of Jerusalem as the Son of God, and his death will result in punishment for Israel on the one hand (cf., e.g., 27:25, 51a) and, on the other hand, in the emergence of that new "nation" called the "church," the eschatological community of God (cf., e.g., 27:54; 21:43; 16:18).

If the parable of the Wicked Husbandmen reaches its culmination

---

83. Cf. Trilling, *Israel*, 63. On the other hand, O. H. Steck (*Israel und das gewalt-same Geschick der Propheten* [WMANT 23; Neukirchen: Neukirchener Verlag, 1967], 297) holds that the "vineyard" refers to the "Kingdom of God." Isa 5:7, however, gives the nod to Trilling.

84. Cf. also J. Jeremias, *The Parables of Jesus*, trans. S. H. Hooke (New Testament Library; revised; London: SCM, 1963), 70.

with the times of Jesus and the emergence of the church, the parable
of the Great Supper (22:1–10) begins with Jesus and depicts the history
of salvation that runs from him to the age of Matthew himself, which is
characterized by the influx of Gentiles into the church.[85] The "king"
(vs. 2) refers to God, the "wedding celebration" (vss. 2–4, 8–9) to the
messianic banquet, that is to say, to the drawing near of the Kingdom of
Heaven in the person of the Messiah,[86] the "ones invited" (vss. 3, 8) to
Israel, the "slaves" (vss. 3, 4, 6, 8, 10) to disciples and Christian missionaries,[87] the disregard of the invitation (vss. 4–5) to the rejection of the
"Gospel of the Kingdom," the mistreatment of the slaves (vs. 6) to
Israelite.persecution, the destruction of the city by soldiers (vs. 7) to
the fall of Jerusalem, and the inbringing of both "bad and good" (vs. 10)
to the inpouring of the Gentiles into the church. The one on whose
behalf the king gives the wedding celebration is termed "his son" (vs. 2),
which of course is a thinly veiled metaphor for Jesus Messiah, the Son
of God.

Of interest to us is the contrasting yet complementary thrust of this
parable in comparison with that of the Wicked Husbandmen. The latter
focuses on the death of the heir, Jesus Messiah Son of God, and the
resultant punishment of Israel and emergence of the church as the
eschatological community of God. This parable, which also portrays
Jesus as Messiah Son of God, likewise deals with the salvation-historical
tragedy of Israel (22:3–7), but clearly does so in preparation (cf. 22:8),
finally, of describing the entrance of the Gentiles into the church

---

85. A. Weiser (*Die Knechtsgleichnisse der synoptischen Evangelien* [StANT XXIX;
München: Kösel, 1971], 66, 69) speaks for a number of commentators (e.g., Jeremias
[cf. *Parables*, 68]) when he claims that the salvation-historical outline of the parable
of the Great Supper begins already with OT times in that it depicts in 22:3 the
sending to Israel of the OT prophets. The difficulty with this position is that it does
not do justice to the opening verse of the parable. According to 22:2b, the "son" is
already on the scene. Since, as we state in the body of this chapter, this "son" is
plainly Jesus Messiah, the "wedding celebration" marks the eschatological age of the
Kingdom he has inaugurated, and the parable's point of departure cannot be OT
times but, again, the times of Jesus (cf. also F. Hahn, "Das Gleichnis von der Einladung zum Festmahl," *Verborum Veritas*, ed. O. Böcher and K. Haacker [Fest-
schrift G. Stählin; Wupertal: R. Brockhaus, 1970], 79).
86. Cf. also W. Trilling, "Zur Ueberlieferungsgeschichte des Gleichnisses vom Hochzeitsmahl Mt 22, 1–14," *BZ* 4 (1960): 260–61; J. Schmid, *Das Evangelium nach
Matthäus* (RNT 1; Regensburg: F. Pustet, 1959), 307–308.
87. There is considerable disagreement as to how "his slaves" in 22:3 and the "other
slaves" in 22:4 are to be interpreted. For three contrasting positions, cf. Jeremias,
*Parables*, 67 (also Weiser, *Knechtsgleichnisse*, 66, 69); Hahn, "Festmahl," 79–80;
and A. Vögtle, "Die Einladung zum grossen Gastmahl und zum königlichen Hochzeitsmahl. Ein Paradigma für den Wandel des geschichtlichen Verständnishorizonts,"
*Das Evangelium und die Evangelien* (Kommentare und Beiträge zum Alten und
Nuen Testament; Düsseldorf: Patmos, 1971), 205–206.

(22:9–10). Hence, if the Wicked Husbandmen prefigures for the reader the events Matthew records in 27:31b–54, the Great Supper prefigures for the reader, at least before going on to paraenetic concerns (cf. 22:11–14), the so-called great commission (cf. 28:18–20). Here Jesus, the resurrected Son of God, no longer speaks of a mission to Israel but instead commands his followers to make disciples of all nations. Following the narration of these two parables the reader has a good idea as to what to expect as he approaches the stories surrounding the death and resurrection of Jesus Messiah, the Son of God.

### Jesus in Gethsemane (26:36–46)

The story of Jesus in Gethsemane (26:36–46) places us within the passion narrative. Of significance for our inquiry are vss. 39 and 42. In both of these, Jesus, addressing God as "my Father," appeals in prayer that, if it be God's will, he be spared the cup of suffering. In Jesus' Thanksgiving to the Father (11:25–27), we encountered two other passages in which Jesus addresses God directly, and here, too, the appellation is "Father" (11:25b, 26). Moreover, in the latter pericope Jesus likewise makes explicit reference to himself as "the Son" (cf. 11:27). Analogously, therefore, in this text Matthew is picturing Jesus in his prayer to God in his capacity as the Son of God. And what this pericope emphasizes concerning the relationship that Jesus Son of God has with God his Father is the total obedience the Son renders the Father.

### The Words of the High Priest at Jesus' Trial (26:62–66)

In the Garden of Gethsemane, Jesus Messiah, the Son of God, is betrayed, arrested, and then taken away to be tried. Of particular importance for us is the circumstance that, during the trial, Matthew has the High Priest ask Jesus whether he is the "Son of God." Jesus' response to the High Priest is in two parts: he first replies with the seemingly noncommittal *sy eipas* ("you have said"), and then proceeds with a statement in which he designates himself as the Son of Man (26:64).

The expression *sy eipas* has been shown to be "affirmative in content" and "circumlocutory in formulation."[88] It appears that at least three considerations prompted Matthew to change Mark's *egō eimi* (14:62). To begin with, Matthew desires that the reply of Jesus be affirmative in con-

---

88. Cf. D. R. Catchpole, "The Answer of Jesus to Caiaphas (Matt. XXVI. 64)," *NTS* 17 (1970/71): 226.

tent because the High Priest has in fact spoken the truth: Jesus is indeed the Son of God. On the other hand, Matthew intends that the reply be circumlocutory in formulation because, although the High Priest has spoken the truth, he has not done so with perception born of revelation, but in order to charge Jesus with blasphemy (26:65). Consequently, Jesus does not unambiguously confirm the truth of the words of the High Priest, which is Matthew's way of underlining the continued ignorance of the High Priest as to the real fact of Jesus' divine sonship. In the third place, the affirmative content and the circumlocutory formulation of *sy eipas* serve Matthew above all in his utter concern that official Judaism should condemn Jesus to death, that is, reject him totally, on the basis of nothing short of that title that conveys the deepest mystery of his person, which is at the same time the most exalted confession of Matthew's church (cf. 26:62–65; 27:39–43).

We shall discuss in principle the relationship in the first Gospel between the predications Son of God and Son of Man in the next chapter. Suffice it to say that, from Matthew's standpoint, the passages 26:63–64 should not be so interpreted that the title Son of Man is made to supersede that of Son of God. These passages are antithetically parallel to 16:16–17. There Peter addresses Jesus in exactly the same vein as the High Priest does here, but whereas Jesus greets Peter's words with a benediction, he responds to the High Priest with a declaration concerning the Son of Man. The language in 26:64 is the type that Matthew regularly employs in his description of the parousia, at which time Jesus Son of Man will function as Judge (cf. 24:30; 25:31). Therefore the point of Jesus' reply to the High Priest is that because he, with the consent of the Sanhedrin, has stated with evil intention the truth of Jesus' divine sonship, at the parousia he, the Son of Man, will hold them accountable.[89]

### Jesus on the Cross (27:38–54)

Jesus, then, is condemned to death by the Sanhedrin precisely as the Son of God. Significant for our purposes in Matthew's narration of Jesus on the cross is the heavily redacted section 27:38–54 (cf. Mark 15:27–39).

That Matthew attaches importance in this section to the title Son of God is evident from the three explicit references to it (vss. 40, 43, 54),

89. Cf., e.g., A. H. M'Neile, *The Gospel according to St. Matthew* (London: Macmillan, 1915), 402; Schniewind, *Matthäus*, 265–66; Lohmeyer, *Matthäus*, 369; Schmid, *Matthäus*, 365; K. Berger, "Die königlichen Messiastraditionen des Neuen Testaments," *NTS* 20 (1973): 19–20.

the first two of which are editorial in character. Indeed, one can even draw up an outline of this text on the basis of this title. (A) Vs. 38 sets the scene for vss. 39–44. (1) In vss. 39–40, Jesus is blasphemed, as the Son of God. (2) In vss. 41–43, Jesus is mocked, as the King of Israel and the Son of God. (3) In vs. 44, the force of *to d' auto* is that "in the same way" as Jesus is blasphemed by the crowds and mocked by the leaders, namely, as the Son of God, so he is ridiculed by the robbers. (B) Vs. 45 sets the scene for vss. 46–54. (1) At the center of vss. 47–50 is the so-called cry of dereliction, which is the final prelude to the death of Jesus. Stylistically, Matthew has changed Mark's *ho theos mou* to the grammatically preferable *thee mou* ("my God"), and, in line with a passage such as Ps 89:26 (LXX 88:27; cf. also Tob 13:4; 3 Mac 5:7; Sir 23:4),[90] it may well be that he proposes to construe "my God" as synonymous with "my Father," a thoroughly Matthaean idiom. Should this be the case, then the cry "my God" may be regarded as testimony on the part of Jesus himself that he is the Son of God (cf. *sy eipas*, 26:64). (2) Vss. 51–53 describe the supernatural portents that God causes to occur (cf. the repeated use of the passive voice) upon the death of Jesus. Matthew's editing of vs. 54 (cf. Mark 15:39) clearly shows that these portents are to be understood as God's own attestation of Jesus' divine sonship: the soldier's confession of Jesus as the Son of God is in direct response to the "quake" and the "things which were happening." (3) In vs. 54, the Roman soldiers are, properly, the recipients of an epiphany (cf. the stark language of vss. 51–54), with the result that, as we just stated, they confess Jesus to be the Son of God.

If this outline reflects the development of 27:38–54, it proves not only that Matthew attaches importance in this section to the title Son of God but that, indeed, the entire section revolves around it and that Matthew is furthermore operating with it according to a definite pattern: three times Jesus is rejected as the Son of God (vss. 38–44), and three times he is attested to as the Son of God (vss. 45–54). But this raises a question: Why is Matthew so concerned to stress the fact that Jesus hangs upon the cross and dies particularly as the Son of God?

To answer this, we must ascertain which aspects of divine sonship in 27:38–54 Matthew intends to accentuate most. In this respect, the Matthaean interpolation of vs. 43 into Mark's text is significant, for in it divine sonship is associated with trust. But this is not the whole of it. In vs. 40, the clause *ei huios ei tou theou* ("if you are the Son of God")

90. Cf. also such related passages as Isa 9:6; 63:16; 64:8; Jer 3:19; Mal 2:10.

is, as is well known, a direct quotation of the words Satan addresses to Jesus at the Temptation (4:3, 6). This explains why Jesus does not come down from the cross as the crowds and the Jewish leaders demand (vss. 40, 42): they are tempting him, but he chooses to do the will of God (cf. *dei* in 16:21). But in that Jesus is pictured as resisting temptation, Matthew informs us that obedience, the companion of trust, is also to be emphasized in our text. To recognize this, however, is to comprehend Matthew's understanding of the cry of derelection: if, as we have suggested, "my God" is a synonym for "my Father," then Jesus declares that even though God should deliver him up to death, he makes no forfeiture of his sonship but remains obedient to the Father's will and continues to rely upon him completely.

Where this line of argument finally comes to rest is in Matthew's doctrine of the forgiveness of sins. The primary passages are 1:21, 20:28, and 26:28, at which places Matthew writes, respectively, that Jesus will save his people from their sins, give his life as a ransom for many (cf. Mark 10:45),[91] and shed his blood of the covenant for the forgiveness of sins.[92] Since in Matthew's eyes the cross is the place where Jesus finally does shed his blood (cf. 27:22–26), it is here, through atonement, that he effects the forgiveness of sins. To Matthew, however, only one who relies totally upon God and renders to him perfect obedience can atone for sin, and this person, in turn, can be none other than Jesus Son of God, ideal Israelite (cf. Exod 4:22–23).

Matthew, therefore, stresses that Jesus hangs upon the cross and dies in his status as the Son of God because it is only the death of God's perfectly obedient and trusting Son that accomplishes the forgiveness of sins. The supernatural portents, in turn, constitute the immediate response of God to the death of Jesus (27:51–53). In view of the charge leveled against Jesus in 26:61 and the blasphemy of the crowds in 27:40, the tearing of the curtain of the temple described in vs. 51 can only be interpreted from Matthew's standpoint in terms of the destruction of the temple:[93] by virtue of the atonement accomplished by the Son of God, the sacrificial system of Israel has been brought to an end. Then, the

---

91. At 20:28, Matthew employs the title Son of Man. For a preliminary explanation of this, cf. n. 63.

92. At 26:28, Matthew appropriates Mark 14:24 but, significantly, adds the phrase *eis aphesin hamartiōn.*

93. Cf., e.g., N. A. Dahl, "Die Passionsgeschichte bei Matthäus," *NTS* 2 (1955/56): 28; Lohmeyer, *Matthäus,* 395–96; Bonnard, *Matthieu,* 407; Hummel, *Kirche und Iudentum,* 83–85.

raising of the saints (vss. 51b–53) and the confession of the Roman soldiers (vs. 54), both of which, according to Matthew, are the result of divine action, prefigure for him his own church of Jewish and Gentile Christians, who are sons of God because the Son of God has died for their sins and been raised (cf. *tēn egersin autou,* vs. 53).

*The Ending of Matthew: The Great Commission (28:16–20)*

The reference to the resurrection of Jesus in 27:53 points ahead to ch. 28. At 28:18b, Matthew shows how he interprets the resurrection: it signifies for him the exaltation of Jesus Son of God to absolute and universal authority, or dominion.

Elsewhere we have endeavored to demonstrate that 28:16–20 is throughout the composition of Matthew and that the christology inform-ing it is that of the Son of God.[94] Thus, this text evinces remarkable affin-ity with other parts of the first Gospel in which the title Son of God is prominent. The setting, for example, is "the mountain" (vs. 16), which, we learned, in itself points to Jesus as the Son of God. The eleven disciples are pictured as coming *eis tēn Galilaian* ("into Galilee," vs. 16), where they will begin the post-Easter ministry of the church to the nations, and this parallels the earlier departure of Jesus Son of God *eis tēn Galilaian* (4:12) to begin his pre-Easter ministry to Israel. The combination of "doubt" and "worship" (vs. 17) occurs only one other place in the NT, in Matthew's pericope of the Walking on the Water (cf. 14:31–33), in which the disciples, we recall, confess Jesus to be the Son of God. The clause *edothē moi pasa exousia* ("all authority has been given to me," vs. 18) is directly related, as we saw, to that of *panta moi paredothē* ("all things have been given over to me") in 11:27, a passage in which Jesus is designated as "the Son." The theme of baptism in the name of the Father, Son, and Holy Spirit (vs. 19) alludes to the baptism of Jesus, at which time the Father calls Jesus "my Son" and empowers him with the Spirit (3:16–17). The promise *egō meth' hymōn eimi* ("I am with you," vs. 20) is simply a post-Easter reiteration of the same truth we encountered in the word of the prophet at the birth of Jesus, namely, in Jesus *meth' hēmōn ho theos* ("God [is] with us," 1:23). Last, Matthew does, after all, employ the term "Son" in an absolute manner (vs. 19) in this peri-cope, which refers pointedly to his Son-of-God christology.

We stated that divine sonship in 28:16–20 connotes for Matthew dominion, which is at the opposite end of the spectrum from the

94. Cf. Kingsbury, "Composition and Christology," 573–84.

obedience unto death stressed in the passion narrative. On the authority of Jesus Son of God, the "post-Easter" disciples engage in their ministry aimed at making disciples of all nations even as the "pre-Easter" disciples on the authority of Jesus engaged in their ministry aimed at making disciples of all Israel (cf. vss. 19–20 to 10:1, 5b–7). On the authority of Jesus Son of God, the disciples baptize and teach. In baptism, one becomes a disciple of Jesus and a son of God and is empowered by the Spirit for ministry: the disciple continues the work of the earthly Son of God (cf. vs. 19 to 3:16–17). Through instruction, the disciple learns what it is to know and do God's will: it is keeping all that Jesus commanded while on earth (cf. vs. 20 to 7:21, 24–27). And under the authority of Jesus Son of God, the doubt, or "little faith" (cf. vs. 17 to 14:31) of the disciple gives way to the assurance of faith that the church will never be without the dynamic, saving presence of Jesus Son of God (cf. vs. 20b to 1:23; 14:22–33; 18:20).

In the light of all this, to what use does Matthew put 28:16–20? As regards Jesus, Matthew utilizes this text to establish the closest possible identification of person between the pre-Easter and post-Easter Son of God. Matthew emphasizes that, whether "then" or "now," God has entrusted to his Son divine authority: "then" to confront Israel with his Rule in teaching, preaching, and healing, "now" to exercise this Rule in heaven and on earth.

As regards the disciples, Matthew utilizes 28:16–20 for all of the following purposes: to outline their ministry to the nations as the ambassadors of Jesus Son of God; to impress upon them that in this world they will live out their Christian existence between the poles of "doubt" and "worship"; and to assure them that they can always be certain of the saving presence of Jesus, in whom "God is with them." Hence, also with reference to the disciples Matthew establishes identification between the "pre-Easter" followers of Jesus and his "post-Easter" followers.

### C.  SUMMARY

We are now in a position to summarize our discussion of the predication Son of God in Matthew's Gospel. Matthew fashions the first main part of his Gospel (1:1–4:16), which treats of the person of Jesus Messiah (1:1), to set forth the confessional truth that, while Jesus Messiah is to be sure the Son of David and the Son of Abraham, he is preeminently the Son of God.

The way in which Matthew basically conceives of Jesus Messiah as the Son of God comes to the fore in the so-called Emmanuel passage (1:23), which is also a formula quotation that stems from the hand of Matthew: in the person of Jesus Messiah, the Son of God (cf. 1:18, 20), God has drawn near to dwell with his people, thus inaugurating the eschatological age of salvation (cf. 1:21). Through his use in the first part of his Gospel of such related idioms as "his people" (1:21), "my people" (2:6), "my Son" (2:15; 3:17), and "Son of God" (4:3, 6), Matthew expands upon the concept Son of God. The result is that this first part of his Gospel already yields the following, relatively comprehensive, description of the person of Jesus Messiah as the Son of God: Jesus Messiah, in the line of David (1:21), is the Son of God (2:15; 3:17), that is to say, he has his origin in God (1:20) and is the one chosen to shepherd the eschatological people of God (2:6) for, empowered by God for messianic ministry (3:16–17), he proves himself in confrontation with Satan to be perfectly obedient to the will of God (4:3–4, 5–7, 8–10) and, as such a one, he saves his (God's) people from their sins (1:21). If we look beyond the first main part of the Gospel, we discover that there are three other passages that, in conjunction with 1:23, reflect to a remarkable degree Matthew's understanding of Jesus as the Son of God, viz., 14:27 (*egō eimi* ["I am"]), 18:20, and 28:20.

In his development of the concept Son of God, Matthew defines it broadly enough so that messianic expectation associated, for example, with Abraham and David can be ascribed to Jesus precisely as the Son of God. Thus, the promise in Genesis that through Abraham the nations will find blessing (cf. 12:3; 18:18; 22:18; 26:4; also Matt 8:11) comes to fulfillment, finally, in Jesus Son of God (cf., e.g., 2:1–12, 15; 28:18–20). Similarly, passages of Scripture said in the OT to be addressed to David and his successors likewise reach their fulfillment in Jesus as the Son of God (cf., e.g., 1:23 to Isa 7:13–14; 2:6 and 15 to 2 Sam 5:1–2; 3:17 and 17:5 to Ps 2:7; 4:15–16 to Isa 9:1–2, 7).

But these observations should not, in fact, occasion surprise, because the very roots in the OT of Matthew's Son of God christology are Davidic in nature (cf. 2 Sam 7:13–14; Pss 2:7–8; 89:26–27; 1 Chr 17:12–13; 22:10). At the same time, Matthew's particular view of the divine sonship of Jesus Messiah is of course without parallel in the OT. According to Matthew, Jesus is not son of God after the manner of ancient kings in the line of David, who were "begotten" by God at the time of their coronation. Instead, Jesus is Son of God in that he is conceived by the Holy Spirit in a virgin, whose husband scrupulously refrains from having relations with her until the birth of her son, so that Jesus, born of a woman, in reality has his origin in God (1:18, 20, 23, 25). Then, too, whereas ancient sons of God from the house of David died and were gathered to their fathers, Jesus Son of God from the house of David is raised from the dead by God the Father to reign with all authority in heaven and earth (28:18–20). Still, like ancient sons of God from the house of David, Jesus Son of God is indeed a royal figure chosen by God to rule. But whereas they ruled over Israel or a portion of Israel at best and merely laid claim, though in the name of Jahweh, to dominion over the nations (cf. Ps 2:7–8), Jesus Son of God is the reigning figure, as we shall see in Chapter IV, in the Kingdom of God, which establishes itself in the face of both Israel and the nations. Accordingly, if the roots of Matthew's Son-of-God christology can be traced back to "Davidic" portions of the OT, the concept as defined by him is far more elevated than anything found there and surpasses in both depth and breadth the two titles he also affirms, Son of Abraham and Son of David, as we shall show in the next chapter.

Therefore, Matthew introduces Jesus Messiah to the reader foremost as the Son of God, and in the second and third main parts of his Gospel he elaborates further upon this central concept. In the second main part of the Gospel (4:17–16:20), Matthew portrays the public ministry of Jesus Messiah, the Son of God, to Israel. In Galilee, Jesus presents himself to the crowds in proclaiming to them the Gospel of the Kingdom, the message of the gracious nearness of the Reign of God (4:17, 23). Furthermore, he calls his first disciples (4:18–22), who through him become sons of God (5:9, 45), and, followed by them, undertakes his messianic ministry of teaching, preaching, and healing (4:23–25; 9:35; 11:1). Seeing the crowds, he ascends the mountain, a setting that in itself alludes to his divine sonship, and teaches his disciples and all Israel with authority (5:1–7:29). Descending from the mountain, he goes about Galilee, and heals and performs mighty acts with authority (8:1–9:34). Then, out of compassion for the crowds, he empowers and dispatches his disciples to discharge through the cities of Israel a ministry of preaching and healing patterned after his own (9:35–10:42). And what, at the deepest level, is transpiring in the messianic ministry of Jesus? He, the Son of God, who enjoys a unique relationship with the Father and has been chosen by him to be his exclusive representative among men, employs the divine authority with which the Father has entrusted him to confront men in his words and deeds with the eschatological Kingdom and so to reveal the Father to whomever he will, especially to those whom he makes his disciples (11:25–27). Personally, Jesus Messiah, the Son, acknowledges his election by the Father by living in complete fellowship with him, relying upon him totally and being perfectly obedient to his will (11:25–27).

But Israel, continues Matthew, does not perceive Jesus to be its Messiah, the Son of God, and utterly rejects him (chs. 11–12). As a result, Jesus turns on the people and addresses them regarding the Kingdom, not openly, but in parables, in speech they cannot comprehend (13:1–15, 24–35). On the other hand, he turns toward his disciples, and because they do comprehend, he imparts to them the mysteries of the Kingdom (13:10–11, 16–17, 18–23, 36–52). More particularly, through a christophany he discloses to them on one occasion the truth of his divine sonship (14:22–33), and, on another, leads them to confess it (16:13–20). In other respects, this truth, which involves insight into the deepest mystery of his person and can be known only by revelation of God, becomes, in turn, the most exalted confession of his church (16:16–18).

Because Israel rejects him, the direction the ministry of Jesus Messiah, the Son of God, takes is toward death (16:21). Matthew devotes the third main part of his Gospel to the development of this theme (16:21–28:20). In another christophany, that of the Transfiguration, Jesus Messiah is again revealed to be the Son of God, this time to a select group of his disciples (17:1–8). Here on the mountain these disciples furthermore receive the command to give ear to him, and what Jesus subsequently tells them has to do with his approaching death (17:5, 12). Later, in the temple, in confrontation with the members of the Sanhedrin (21:23), Jesus again speaks of his impending death as the Son of God, but he does so in parables (21:33–41; 22:1–10). Finally, in the Garden of Gethsemane, Jesus calls upon his Father to remove the cup of suffering from him, but even as he prays he expresses his willingness to submit obediently to whatever his Father has ordained (26:36–46).

With this, Matthew has brought his gospel-story of Jesus Messiah, the Son of God, to the point where it moves rapidly toward its culmination, which it achieves in the narratives that describe his trial, his death on the cross, and his resurrection. Jesus, condemned to death by the Sanhedrin for not disclaiming for himself divine sonship (26:63–66), and ridiculed as the Son of God by the people (27:39–40), dies upon the cross, singularly trusting in God and, again, rendering to him absolute obedience (27:38–54). Still, in his death Jesus brings to pass all of the following: he accomplishes for humankind the forgiveness of sins (1:21; 26:28), brings the sacrificial cult of Israel to an end (27:51a), and lays the foundation for the emergence of the church (cf. 27:54), that community of the end-time that comprises disciples of both Jewish and Gentile background. Then, after Jesus' death and burial, God raises Jesus Messiah, his Son, to life (28:6–7), and exalts him to absolute and universal authority in heaven and on earth (28:18–20). By virtue of the death and resurrection of Jesus Messiah, the Son of God, and on his authority, disciples of Jesus henceforth become sons of God through baptism, and are themselves empowered by the Spirit for an eschatological ministry that aims at making disciples of all nations (28:18–20). And discharging this ministry, the disciples of Jesus are assured of the dynamic and saving presence of the exalted Son of God, through whom God continues to the end of the age to dwell among his people (28:20).

The content of the title Son of God alone is sufficient to mark it as the central christological category of Matthew's Gospel. But there is yet further indication that it occupies a preeminent position in the theology of Matthew. Matthew uses it in such a way that it is the one christological predication that extends to every phase of the "life" of Jesus: conception, birth, and infancy; baptism and temptation; public ministry; death; and resurrection and exaltation. For another thing, it is the natural complement of a thoroughly Matthaean idiom, "my Father," which Matthew attributes to Jesus some sixteen times in his Gospel, fifteen of which give semblance of being redactional in origin.[95] And in other respects the force of this title is such that it (a) expresses for Matthew the deepest mystery of the person of Jesus Messiah, (b) represents the most exalted confession of his Christian community, and (c) can be uttered by people only by "revelation of God" if such utterance is not to be accounted as blasphemy. The importance of the latter observation is that it marks Son of God as a "confessional" title, one that is inaccessible to the unbelieving "public."

---

95. Cf. 7:21; 10:32–33; 11:27 (// Luke 10:22); 12:50; 15:13; 16:17; 18:10, 19, 35; 20:23; 25:34; 26:29, 39, 42, 53. At 18:14 and 25:41, the idiom "my Father" is textually uncertain. In one passage for sure (25:34; cf. also 7:21; 20:23), the words "my Father" are predicated to Jesus, not as the Son of God, but as the Son of Man. Note that 25:34 (cf. also 7:21; 20:23) pictures Jesus as Judge at his parousia. At the point of the parousia, however, Matthew, as we shall see in the next chapter, envisages a coalescence of the categories of Son of God and Son of Man under the sign of the latter. But short of the parousia, the expression "my Father" refers to Jesus as the Son of God.

In the next chapter we shall show how a comparison of the predication Son of God with other christological predications in the first Gospel only serves to confirm that the most fundamental christological category in Matthew's Gospel is that of Son of God.

Chapter III

# The Christology of Matthew: Other Titles

Our objective in this chapter is to argue the thesis that "Son of God" is the central christological title of Matthew's Gospel by discussing the meaning and function of titles other than Son of God and the relationship Matthew establishes between the latter and these others. For the sake of convenience, we have divided the terms we shall consider into two categories, those that are of minor and those that are of major importance. The criteria on the basis of which any given term is placed in the one or the other category are the significance Matthew attaches to it and the extent to which he employs it. At the same time, these categories are in no sense intended to be absolute; they result merely from a desire on our part to group the numerous terms according to a principle that is at once recognizable and practicable. In line with this principle, then, we shall deal with the two groups of terms in the following order: (a) minor christological terms: "Jesus," "Son of Abraham," "the Coming One," "Shepherd," "prophet," "rabbi-teacher," "Servant," and "Emmanuel"; (b) major christological terms: "Messiah–King," "Son of David," "Kyrios," and "Son of Man."

## A.  MINOR CHRISTOLOGICAL TERMS

### Jesus

From the standpoint of frequency alone, the christological term "Jesus" (*Iēsous*) occurs in the first Gospel more than any other (150 times). In essence, it means "savior" ("Jahweh is salvation"), and in 1:21 in may be said to approach the status of a christological title: "You

shall call his name 'Jesus,' for he shall *save* his people from their sins."
Still, if we look closely at 1:21, we see that Matthew is interested in this
term, not so much as a predication of majesty per se, but as a definition
of the mission of the Messiah. While one may of course argue in view
of 1:21 that "Jesus" retained for the members of Matthew's church the
fundamental significance of "savior," the general use to which Matthew
puts it shows that he construes it in the main as a personal name.

That the latter is indeed the case is evident from Matthew's genealogy (1:16) and from the two passages in which he tells of the naming
of the Messiah (1:21, 25). In the course of the Gospel, "Jesus" designates
its bearer as, among other things, the one born in "Bethlehem" (2:1,
5–6) but raised in "Nazareth" (cf. 2:23; 21:11; 26:71) who is the "son
of the carpenter," whose mother's name is "Mary" (13:55), and who has
both "sisters" and "brothers," the names of the latter being "James,"
"Joseph," "Simon," and "Judas" (13:55–56). As an adult, the one called
Jesus is depicted as moving from Nazareth to "Capernaum" (4:13),
which can be described as "his own city" (9:1), where he apparently
has a "house" (cf. 9:10, 28; 13:1, 36; 17:25). In Jerusalem to the south,
he can be recognized, as can also his disciples, as one who comes "from
Galilee" (cf. 26:69, 73; also 21:11). On the whole, therefore, the character of "Jesus" as a personal name in the first Gospel is unmistakable.

### Son of Abraham

The term "Son of Abraham" (*huios tou Abraam*) appears but one time
in Matthew's Gospel, in the "superscription" to the first main part
(1:1–4:16). Most immediately, this term designates Jesus Messiah as
the one in whom the entire history of Israel, which had its beginning in
Abraham, reaches its culmination (1:17).[1] Because Matthew portrays
Jesus as recapitulating in his person a significant portion of this history
(4:1–11), this title seems to allude to him as the ideal Israelite.[2]

The figure of Abraham also has relevance for the Gentiles. As the book
of Genesis puts it, through Abraham and his descendants God will extend
his blessing to all the nations of the earth (cf. Gen 12:3; 18:18; 22:18;
26:4). In 8:11, Matthew sounds this very theme in words of Jesus: "But

---

1. Cf. A. Vögtle, "Das Schicksal des Messiaskindes," *Bibel und Leben* 6 (1965):
272–73; C. Burger, *Jesus als Davidssohn* (FRLANT 98; Göttingen: Vandenhoeck &
Ruprecht, 1970), 99, 102.
2. Cf. E. Krentz, "The Extent of Matthew's Prologue," *JBL* 83 (1964): 411, 414.

I say to you, many from east and west will come and recline at table with Abraham, Isaac, and Jacob in the Kingdom of Heaven."

It is important to observe that in the pericope in which Matthew describes Jesus Messiah as recapitulating a significant portion of the history of Israel, Jesus is designated as "the Son of God" (4:1–11; cf. also 2:15). Similarly, the direct command to proclaim the Gospel of the Kingdom to the Gentiles and so to make them disciples is also found in a pericope in which, as we saw, Jesus stands before the reader as the Son of God (28:16–20). From these two observations we learn that in the first Gospel the title Son of God supersedes the title Son of Abraham. The function of the latter is, finally, to broaden and enrich selected facets of Matthew's Son-of-God christology.

### The Coming One

Matthew employs the term "the Coming One" (*ho erchomenos*) four times. In three instances, it is plainly messianic in coloration. At 3:11, for example, Jesus is said to be the Coming One in the sense that he, the Mightier One, can be expected to appear publicly in Israel as soon as John has completed his ministry of baptism for repentance. Then, in the subsequent pericope on his Baptism (3:13–17), Jesus is pictured as empowered by the Spirit and declared by the voice from heaven to be God's beloved Son (3:16–17). Consequently, by juxtaposing 3:11–12 to the pericope on the Baptism of Jesus, Matthew makes it eminently clear that the Coming One is Jesus Son of God.

At 11:3 and 21:9, the term the Coming One is likewise messianic in character. In the first passage it has direct reference to the title "Messiah" (cf. 11:2) and in the second to the title "Son of David" (cf. 21:9). At 23:39, on the other hand, it is not messianic in nuance but is suggestive of Jesus as the Son of Man who will come for judgment.[3]

The most striking thing about the term the Coming One in the first Gospel is that it consistently points beyond itself to some other, more definitive, christological title: Messiah, Son of David, Son of God, or Son of Man. This indicates, in turn, that to Matthew's way of thinking this term does not stand on its own but, technically, serves as a surrogate for, again, some other christological title. Hence, "the Coming One" in the first Gospel is of the nature, not of a primary, but of a secondary, or

---

3. Cf. G. Strecker, *Der Weg der Gerechtigkeit* (FRLANT 82; Göttingen: Vandenhoeck & Ruprecht, 1962), 113–15; W. Trilling, *Das Wahre Israel* (StANT X; 3d ed; München: Kösel, 1964), 87–88.

auxiliary, christological title. Theologically, the pattern does obtain that Jesus, who once "came" (Messiah, Son of David, Son of God), will "come" again (Son of Man), even if Matthew does not seem concerned to stress it.

## Shepherd

Whereas Matthew brings the term "Shepherd" (*poimēn*) only three times and the verb "to herd" (*poimainō*) but once, the word "sheep" (*probaton*) occurs in his Gospel no fewer than eleven times. In OT thought, God himself is the Shepherd of his people, but Ezekiel applies this title also to the Davidic Messiah whom God will send (cf. 34:23–24; 37:24).[4] In Judaism, both Moses and David are said to be true shepherds.[5]

Except for those passages in the first Gospel in which the word "sheep" retains its literal meaning (cf., e.g., 12:11–12), the terms "Shepherd," "to herd," and "sheep" tend to be messianic in tone and to convey the notion of eschatological rulership in relation to a "flock." Thus, Matthew depicts "Israel" as a flock; and in the sense that it has no shepherd, or ruler, it is considered to be "lost" (cf. 9:36; 10:6; 15:24). By the same token, the "disciples," too, can be pictured as a flock. Their leader, or ruler, is Jesus, who dispatches them, for instance, on a mission "in the midst of wolves" (10:16); according to Scripture, however, he will be "struck down," and they for their part will be scattered (26:31). Finally, in the apocalyptic context of the Last Judgment, those who will be declared to be "the righteous" are also held up as a flock; their king, or ruler, is of course Jesus Son of Man (25:31–34).

Jesus in Matthew's Gospel is never once directly named by the term "Shepherd." This circumstance, together with the fact that Matthew lends great prominence to the verb "to herd" ("to shepherd") in 2:6 and is liberal in his use of the word "sheep," demonstrates that while he desires to draw upon the messianic and eschatological imagery surrounding the term "Shepherd," he is not disposed to elevate this title to the status of a major christological predication.

In what capacity does Matthew think of Jesus as the Shepherd? In answer to this, his use of the verb *poimainō* in 2:6 is revealing, for the ruler who "will shepherd 'my people' Israel" is, we remember, "my Son" (2:15). Furthermore, when Jesus in words of Scripture describes himself

4. Cf. J. Jeremias, *TDNT*, VI, 488.
5. Cf. ibid., 489.

as the Shepherd who is about to be struck down (26:31), the reference is to his death, as the following remark concerning the resurrection proves (cf. 26:32). But Jesus dies in Matthew's Gospel above all as the Son of God (cf. 27:40, 43, 54). In other respects, the kingly figure who at the Great Assize will divide the nations into two groups after the manner of a shepherd is, we know, Jesus Son of Man (25:31–33). On the basis of these passages, therefore, it is obvious that for Matthew the title Shepherd is, like that of the Coming One, of the nature of an auxiliary christological title: it points beyond itself to Jesus as the Son of God or the Son of Man.

### Prophet

Whenever Matthew applies the term "prophet" (*prophētēs*) to such OT figures as, for example, Isaiah or Jeremiah, or to a circle of Christians within his own church (cf. 10:41; 23:34), he gives it a thoroughly positive ring. But in those passages in which he applies it to Jesus, he does not even raise it to the rank of what may properly be construed as a christological title.[6]

The truth of this can be seen already in the way in which Matthew operates with the word "prophet" in relation to John the Baptist. The Jewish "crowd" may well think of John as a prophet (14:5; 21:26), but Jesus, on the other hand, declares to them that John is "more than a prophet" (11:7, 9). He is, in reality, Elijah redivivus, the forerunner of the Messiah (11:10, 14; 17:10–13).

With reference to Jesus, too, the term "prophet" comprises no more than the core of the "confession" that some "men" (16:13b–14) or the "crowds" (21:11, 46) are disposed to make. For Matthew, however, such a confession has only negative value: by contrast, the leaders of the people cannot even look upon Jesus favorably enough to recognize in him a prophet. At the same time, the lack of personal commitment which the term "prophet" connotes for Matthew as applied to Jesus is well documented in the pericope on Peter's Confession (16:13–20): whereas those to whom Matthew never ascribes the attitude of faith ("men" [or the "crowds"]) are said to regard Jesus as "one of the prophets" (16:14),

---

6. A. Sand (*Das Gesetz und die Propheten* [Biblische Untersuchungen 11; Regensburg: F. Pustet, 1974], 141) wrongly claims for Matthew the argument that "precisely this Jesus of Nazareth and no other is the eschatological prophet." Sand errs in that he attributes to the word "prophet" in 16:14, 21:11, and 21:46 an inflated significance and to the Israelite "crowds" a crucial role in the development of Matthew's christology.

the disciples assert with Peter that he is the Christ, the Son of God (16:16; cf. 14:33). Because the relationship in this pericope between the confession of Peter and that of "men" is one of antithesis, this "confession of men" simply pales into insignificance. Once this is clear, we can begin to appreciate the scorn with which Matthew imbues the comment of Jesus to the Jews of Nazareth, who take offense at him (13:57): his former neighbors, like his worst enemies but unlike even the crowds, will not afford him so much as the honor due a prophet.

At this juncture, we should also like to speak a word on the matter of new-Moses typology as reflected in the first Gospel. G. Bornkamm,[7] E. P. Blair,[8] F. Hahn,[9] and J. L. McKenzie,[10] to cite but these, assert that the theme of Jesus as the "new Moses" stands out most prominently in Matthew's treatment of his subject matter.

In general, new-Moses typology has been claimed for many parts of Matthew's Gospel, but there are certain passages in which it is thought to be especially conspicuous. Thus it is said, in this instance correctly, that in ch. 2 the infant Jesus is miraculously saved through flight from the murderous designs of Herod even as the infant Moses was miraculously saved from the murderous designs of Pharaoh (and, as an adult, fled to Midian to escape death) (Exod 1–4).[11] The baptism of Jesus in the Jordan river is held to be typical of the crossing of the Red Sea by Moses and the children of Israel (Exod 14). Jesus' fasting forty days and forty nights prior to his confrontation with Satan (4:2) allegedly recalls the fasting of Moses forty days and forty nights prior to momentous events confronting him (cf., e.g., Exod 34:28; Deut 9:9, 18).[12] Jesus' ascending the mountain to teach the law to his disciples and the crowds (5:1) is believed to allude to the ascent of Moses into Mt. Sinai to receive the law and give it to the people of Israel (Exod 24).[13] The ten

---

7. "End-Expectation and Church in Matthew," *Tradition and Interpretation in Matthew*, trans. P. Scott (Philadelphia: Westminster, 1963), 35.

8. *Jesus in the Gospel of Matthew* (Nashville: Abingdon, 1960), 133.

9. *The Titles of Jesus in Christology*, trans. H. Knight and C. Ogg (London: Lutterworth, 1969), 385–86.

10. "The Gospel according to Matthew," *JBC* (Englewood Cliffs: Prentice-Hall, 1968), II, 62, 64.

11. Cf. A. Vögtle, *Messias und Gottessohn* (Theologische Perspektiven; Düsseldorf: Patmos, 1971), 72, 82.

12. Cf. A. Schlatter, *Der Evangelist Matthäus* (5th ed.; Stuttgart: Calwer, 1959), 100; Blair, *Matthew*, 134; Hahn, *Christology*, 386; J. Dupont, Les tentations de Jésus au désert (StudNeot 4; Tournai: Desclée, 1968), 28–29.

13. Cf. G. Bornkamm, "End-Expectation," 35; W. D. Davies, *The Setting of the Sermon on the Mount* (Cambridge: Cambridge University, 1964), 61, 85; Hahn, *Christology*, 385–86; McKenzie, "Matthew," 69.

miracles Jesus performs in chs. 8–9 are considered to be reminiscent of the ten miraculous plagues Moses effected in Egypt (Exod 7–12).[14] The circumstances surrounding the transfiguration of Jesus, namely, that it takes place on a mountain, that his face is described as shining like the sun, and that a voice from a bright cloud commands the three disciples to hear him (17:1–5), ostensibly refer, respectively, to the shining of the face of Moses as he descended from Mt. Sinai with the tables of the law (Exod 34:29–35) and to the command Moses gave to Israel to give heed to the prophet like himself whom God would raise up for them (Deut 18:15).[15] And, it seems, like Moses on Mt. Sinai, who was the recipient of the law that was henceforth binding on Israel, so the resurrected Jesus on a mountain in Galilee enjoins his disciples with a view to the future to "keep all that I have commanded you" (28:16–20).[16]

It lies beyond the purview of this discussion to attempt the difficult task of ascertaining the exegetical soundness of each of these reputed allusions. What strikes us as extraordinary, however, is the fact that these allusions have all been drawn from portions of the Gospel in which Matthew is at pains to develop his Son-of-God christology. Consider the following: "the child" who through flight miraculously escapes death at the hands of Herod is identified as "my Son" (2:15); at his baptism in the Jordan, Jesus is openly declared to be "my Son" (3:17); following his fast of forty days and forty nights, Jesus is tempted by Satan as "the Son of God" (4:3, 6); Jesus, ascending the mountain to teach his disciples and the crowds, occupies a setting that in itself alludes to him as the Son of God; the ten mighty acts Jesus performs in chs. 8–9 are the works of the Messiah who "heals" with divine authority (cf. 4:23; 9:35) and whom Matthew has introduced in 1:1–4:16 as being preeminently the Son of God; on the mountain where Jesus is transfigured, he is once again declared to be "my Son" (17:5); and on the mountain in Galilee on which the resurrected Jesus enjoins his disciples to keep what he has

14. Cf. E. Klostermann, *Das Matthäusevangelium* (HNT 4; 2d ed.; Tübingen: J. C. B. Mohr, 1927), 72; Blair, *Matthew*, 134–35; Hahn, *Christology*, 385; W. Grundmann, *Das Evangelium nach Matthäus* (HKNT I; Berlin: Evangelische Verlagsanstalt, 1968), 245–46.

15. Cf. McKenzie, "Matthew," 93. Cf. also Davies' discussion of these points (*Setting*, 51–52, 61).

16. Cf. K. Stendahl, "Matthew," *PCB* (London: Nelson, 1962), 798; McKenzie, "Matthew," 114; also B. J. Hubbard (*The Matthean Redaction of a Primitive Apostolic Commissioning: An Exegesis of Matthew 28:16–20* [SBL Dissertation Series 19; Missoula: Scholars' Press, 1974], 91–94), who, without wanting to exaggerate the implications, nevertheless maintains that there is a "material linking" of Jesus to Moses in 28:16–20.

commanded them, the christological term by which Jesus refers to himself is that of "the Son" (28:19).

To concentrate further on the passages 5:1 and 28:16–20, the very way in which Matthew works editorially with the term "Moses" helps to illuminate his understanding of the person of Jesus in these two places. On the one hand, Matthew does not appear to be adverse to following the tradition according to which pronouncements of the law can be described as the pronouncements of "Moses," for he has done so in words of Jesus once directly (8:4 // Mark 1:44) and once obliquely (cf. 23:2). On the other hand, three times he abandons this custom, and his procedure in each instance is most revealing. In debate with the "Pharisees and scribes" over the law and the tradition of the elders, Matthew does not, like Mark, have Jesus introduce his quotation of the law with the words "For *Moses* said . . ." (Mark 10:7), but with the words "For *God* said . . ." (15:4). Again, in debate with the "Pharisees" on divorce Matthew redacts Mark's pericope in order to emphasize more strongly than the latter the supersession of the will of Moses by the will of God (cf. 19:4b, 7–8 with Mark 10:3b–6). Third, in debate with the "Sadducees" over the question of the resurrection, Matthew emends Mark's version of the words of Jesus (". . . have you not read *in the book of Moses* . . . how *God* said to him . . .": Mark 12:26) to read: ". . . have you not read what was said to you by *God* . . ." (22:31), thus eliminating a reference to Moses and making the reference to God stand out more starkly. In addition, J. M. Gibbs has also shown that the expression "my yoke" in 11:30 cannot be understood as relating Jesus to Moses.[17]

Obviously, the point of the various editorial changes is that Matthew, in treating of the law, is intent upon following the thrust of a passage such as Exod 20:1 (the one who "spoke" atop Mt. Sinai was "God") at the expense of other pentateuchal passages which stress the mediating role of Moses. But why should this be? Because the Jesus who ascends the mountain in the first Gospel and declares the will of God which is henceforth binding on his disciples is the Son of God and not, strictly speaking, a new Moses. To refer to Jesus as a "new Moses" is to import into Matthaean christology a category Matthew himself repeatedly refuses to invoke.

Accordingly, however many of the aforementioned allusions to Moses one may finally decide are legitmiate, Matthew's position is clear: it is

17. J. M. Gibbs, "The Son of God as the Torah Incarnate in Matthew," *SE IV* (Berlin: Akademie, 1968), 44.

not with a new Moses that the reader has to do in these portions of the first Gospel, but with the Son of God.

### Rabbi–Teacher

In 23:8, Matthew seems to indicate that he regards the terms "rabbi" (*hrabbi*) and "teacher" (*didaskalos*) as synonymous (cf. John 1:38). Moreover, on the basis of 23:7–8 it also appears that "rabbi" by the time of Matthew had become a common title of respect by which Jewish scribes in general were addressed.

Twice in the first Gospel Jesus himself is addressed as "rabbi," both times by Judas Iscariot (26:25, 49). Of significance is the fact that the one verse falls within a pericope (26:20–25) in which each of the true disciples of Jesus is depicted as addressing him as "Lord" (cf. 26:22). We shall discover below that the latter title is "confessional" in nature, the connotation being that the person who utters it is seen as approaching Jesus in faith acknowledging his exalted status and divine authority. Hence, what we have in 26:20–25 is a pericope in which Matthew has pointedly contrasted the term "rabbi" with the term "Lord," disclosing thereby how he would have us understand the former: in that Judas, a disciple of Jesus, addresses him as "rabbi," he pays him the honor and respect that a pupil owes his teacher or a learner his master; by the same token, in that Judas does not address Jesus as "Lord," he is characterized as one who is devoid of that perception of the person of Jesus which is born of faith. The conclusion, therefore, is compelling: Matthew does not view "rabbi" as a christological title per se but simply as a term of human respect.

The situation with the term "teacher" is not appreciably different. Thus, never once does Matthew record that the disciples use it to address Jesus. On the contrary, those who do use it to address Jesus or to refer to him in discussion with his disciples are such as the following: a scribe (8:19), the Pharisees (9:11), some of the scribes and Pharisees (12:38), Jewish tax officials (17:24), the rich man who asks what he must do to inherit eternal life (19:16), the disciples of the Pharisees and the Herodians (22:15–16), the Sadducees (22:23–24), and a lawyer from among the Pharisees (22:36). To be sure, in one case Jesus does instruct his disciples to designate him as "the teacher," but the point is that they are to do this in dealing with the man to whom Jesus dispatches them to secure a place for celebrating the passover (26:17–19). Consequently, in all these examples "teacher" proves itself to be no more than a term of human respect.

Except perhaps for the two-part aphorism in 10:24–25, there is only one passage in the first Gospel in which the term teacher even approximates the status of christological predication: 23:8. The thing to note, however, is that 23:8a–b goes with 23:10 to form an inclusion. The result is that the two words *didaskalos* and *kathēgētēs*, both of which mean "teacher," stand in effect in apposition to the title "Messiah" (23:10b), which occupies a position of stress. Hence, what Matthew is about in 23:8a–b, 10 is to set forth the fundamental truth that it is none other than the Messiah who is the one teacher of the disciples.

In Matthew's view, therefore, the Messiah is the teacher par excellence. At the same time, we learned in the last chapter that Matthew casts the Messiah in a particular light, viz., he is the Son of God. Accordingly, it is Jesus Messiah, the Son of God, who wanders about Galilee teaching (4:23; 9:35; 11:1), who ascends the mountain and instructs his disciples and the crowds with divine authority (5:1–2; 7:28–29), who invites those who labor and are heavy-laden to "learn from me" (11:25–30), who wields in teaching and in healing in the temple of God the authority of God (21:23–27), and who, after his resurrection, appears to his disciples on a mountain in Galilee enjoining them to teach the nations to observe all that "I have commanded you" (28:16–20). But once we recognize this, it becomes evident why Matthew does not permit the terms "rabbi" and "teacher" to achieve the status of christological titles: the one who teaches with divine authority is in reality Jesus Messiah, the Son of God; but because Judas and the leaders of the people and their cohorts do not perceive the mystery of Jesus' person, they address him as "rabbi" or "teacher" and so attribute to him merely the respect due a Jewish scribe.

*Servant*

As a christological title, the term "Servant" (*pais*) is also found but once in the first Gospel (12:18), in a free adaptation of the song of Isa 42 which appears to combine elements from the Septuagint, the Masoretic Text, and the Targum.[18] To what end does Matthew make use of this term?

---

18. Cf. K. Stendahl, *The School of St. Matthew* (reprinted; Philadelphia: Fortress, 1968), 109–15; R. H. Gundry, *The Use of the Old Testament in St. Matthew's Gospel* (NovTSup XVIII; Leiden: E. J. Brill, 1967), 111–16; W. Rothfuchs, *Die Erfüllungszitate des Matthäus-Evangeliums* (BEvT 8: Stuttgart: W. Kohlhammer, 1969), 72–77.

Matthew's adaptation in 12:18–21 of the text of Isaiah is tantamount to a summary of the ministry of Jesus Messiah, here called "Servant" (12:18a). But if this observation seems to suggest that Matthew attaches great importance in his Gospel to the title Servant, it must be balanced by the recognition that he develops no "Servant christology" as such. On the contrary, everything that is said of the Servant in the words of Isaiah in 12:18–21 Matthew otherwise says in much more detail of Jesus as the Son of God. Hence, within the overall pattern of his christology, it looks as though Matthew employs the term "Servant" in the same manner as "Son of Abraham" or "Emmanuel," viz., to assert that in Jesus Messiah, who is preeminently the Son of God, OT prophecy concerning the Servant of Isaiah (ch. 42) comes to fulfillment.

That Matthew does indeed subsume the title of Servant under the broader category of Son of God can be seen from a comparison of the statements he relates in 12:15–21 to the Servant to those he makes elsewhere about Jesus as the Son of God. The notation in 12:14 that the Pharisees take counsel to destroy Jesus is a veiled reference already to the cross, upon which Jesus dies in the main as the Son of God (cf. 27:40, 43, 54). The withdrawal of Jesus from his enemies mentioned in 12:15a is attributed by Matthew, though not by Mark (cf. 3:7a), to Jesus' (unmediated) knowledge of his opponents' evil intentions, a feature that accords well with Matthew's portrait of Jesus Messiah as the Son of God who is endowed with the *exousia* ("authority") of God (cf., e.g., 26:53; also 11:27; 21:23–27; 28:18; 16:8; 22:18; 26:10). The Matthaean emphasis in 12:15b that Jesus, followed by many people as he withdraws, heals them "all" (cf. Mark 3:10: "many") calls to mind other scenes in the first Gospel in which mass healings are ascribed to Jesus as Messiah Son of God (cf. 15:29–31; 4:23–25; 9:35; also 8:16–17; 11:5). This contrasts, incidentally, with the Matthaean tendency to portray Jesus as the Son of David as, for example, healing particular individuals (cf., e.g., 9:27; 12:22–23; 15:22; 20:30). The unobtrusiveness of Jesus depicted in 12:16, which is the thematic link that binds the Isaianic quotation (cf. 12:19) to its context,[19] is a trait that is typical of the Matthaean Jesus almost across the board. It is especially reminiscent, however, of 16:20, where Jesus, confessed by Peter to be the Messiah Son of God (16:16), "warns" (*epetimēsen*) his disciples not to tell anyone that he is this Messiah.

To turn from the context to the OT quotation itself, we discover in

19. Cf. Strecker, *Weg*, 69; Rothfuchs, *Erfüllungszitate*, 74, 77.

12:18a–b, the very verse in which the title "Servant" occurs, that Matthew places the accent, not on this word per se, but on "God" (cf. the three-fold use of *"mou"* [= "God"]);[20] this further mitigates any notion that Matthew is introducing into his Gospel at 12:18–21 a Servant christology as an independent strain. What is more, 12:18b ("my beloved with whom my soul is well pleased" [RSV]) reflects editorial assimilation to 3:17 and 17:5, passages in which Matthew likewise quotes from the song of Isa 42, yet not so as to enhance a Servant christology but to present Jesus in definitive fashion as the Son of God. In other respects, the declaration of 12:18c ("I will put my Spirit upon him") alludes to the empowerment with the Spirit of Jesus Son of God at his baptism (cf. 3:16), and 12:18d ("and he shall proclaim [God's saving and judging] justice[21] to the Gentiles") finds its concrete articulation in the Gospel in 28:20, where Matthew focuses on the resurrected Son of God as he enjoins his disciples to teach "all nations" to "observe all that I have commanded you." Finally, the description of the Servant's ministry to Israel in 12:20 and to the nations in 12:21 calls to mind, on the one hand, the appeal of the Son of God to the weary and heavy-ladened (cf. 11:28) and his compassion for the harassed and driven (9:36) and, on the other hand, the commission that he, the exalted Son of God, gives to his followers, namely, to go and make disciples of all the Gentiles (cf. 28:19; also 24:14; 26:13).

In the light of these parallels, we conclude, therefore, that Matthew's purpose with the Servant-passage 12:18–21 is manifestly not to establish an independent christological strain in his Gospel, but to stress the fact that, again, in Jesus Messiah, the Son of God, OT prophecy concerning the Servant has reached its fulfillment (cf. 12:17). In the last analysis, the role this Servant-passage plays in the Gospel is to enrich Matthew's more comprehensive picture of Jesus as the Son of God.

## Emmanuel

"Emmanuel" (*Emmanouēl*) occurs exclusively in the pericope on the Origin of Jesus (1:23). But by itself, this datum is deceiving: the importance of "Emmanuel" in the first Gospel is immense. Although the text reads that it is the "name" that the son born to the virgin will bear (cf. 1:23), we know from the story that "Jesus" and not "Emmanuel" is the name the son finally receives (cf. 1:21, 25).

20. Cf. also Rothfuchs, *Erfüllungszitate*, 123.
21. Cf. V. Herntrich, *TDNT, III* 932–33; Grundmann, *Matthäus,* 326.

This ostensible anomaly, however, only serves to call attention to the nature of the term Emmanuel: it is a name not in an appellative sense but in the sense that it sets forth the significance of a person,[22] viz., Jesus Messiah: he is "God with us." Functioning in this way, the term Emmanuel, as we noted before, admirably reflects Matthew's understanding of Jesus Messiah as the Son of God: in the person of Jesus Messiah, the Son of God, God has drawn near to dwell with his people, thus inaugurating the eschatological age of salvation.

Focusing as it does on Jesus Messiah as the Son of God, the entire first Gospel may be regarded as an attempt on the part of Matthew to draw out the implications of what it means to say in 1:23 that in him God dwells with his people. By means of his topical outline, Matthew describes the person of Jesus Messiah, the Son of God, and explains what God has effected in his public ministry and death and resurrection. By means of his outline of the history of salvation, Matthew shows that Jesus Messiah, the Son of God, has ultimate meaning for people of every age, Israelite and Gentile alike. Hence, the abiding presence of God with his people in the person of Jesus Messiah, his Son, who lived, died, was raised, and has ultimate meaning for all people, is the foundational motif of Matthew's Gospel, and has determined both its structure and its content. The nub of this thought is, again, explicitly stated in this "Emmanuel passage" of 1:23, and then reiterated in various ways in such related passages as 14:27 (*egō eimi*), 18:20, and 28:20.

### B.  MAJOR CHRISTOLOGICAL TERMS

*Messiah–King*

The term "Messiah" (*christos*), or "Christ," belongs with the major christological titles of Matthew's Gospel. Of the sixteen or seventeen times it occurs (it is textually uncertain at 16:21), it appears to be redactional in nature eleven or twelve times.[23]

Matthew employs the term Messiah on more than one level. At 1:1, it has the status of a personal name ("Jesus Messiah"), which is also the case in 1:18 and 16:21, provided that "Jesus Messiah" is the correct reading.[24] Even as a personal name, however, "Jesus Messiah" conveys

22. Cf. also Hahn, *Christology*, 262.
23. Cf. 1:1, 16, 17, 18; 2:4; 11:2; 16:20, 21; 23:10; 26:68; 27:17, 22.
24. On 1:18, cf. Vögtle (*Gottessohn*, 17), who follows H. Pirlot and R. Pesch in opting for the single word "Messiah" (*christou*) as the correct reading. On 16:21, note that most ancient Greek manuscripts read simply "Jesus."

in the first Gospel the basic truth that Jesus is the Messiah (cf. 1:1, 18 to 1:16; 16:21 to 16:20).

As a christological title, Matthew understands the term Messiah as follows: the Messiah, the Coming One foretold by the prophets and awaited by Israel (11:2–6), is Jesus (1:16; 16:20; 24:5), that royal figure in the line of David (1:1, 16, 17) who brings the history of Israel (Abraham) to its culmination (1:1, 17) and who, wielding the authority of God, means salvation or damnation for people (1:21, 3:11). Throughout his Gospel, Matthew is concerned to qualify the title of Messiah further, in two directions: in terms of "King of the Jews (Israel)" on the one hand and "Son of God" on the other.

In those places in the Gospel where "Messiah" is related epexegetically to "King of the Jews," it possesses, from the standpoint of the characters of the story, political overtones. Herod, for example, because he fears the loss of his throne, plots to kill the Messiah, the King of the Jews (2:2, 4, 13, 16). For their part, Pilate and the Roman cohort accede to the charge that "Jesus . . . the King of the Jews . . . who is called the Messiah"[25] is a political throne-pretender (27:11, 17, 22, 29, 37). And in that the leaders of the people mock the crucified Messiah as the "King of Israel," Matthew pictures them as taking up where the Romans have left off, the thought being that this Jesus whom the Romans have placed on the cross as the Jewish king (cf. 27:37) does not even have at his command sufficient power to get himself down and so establish this messianic "claim" for which he is being executed (cf. 26:63, 68 and 27:41–42).

The preceding are examples of what we may designate as the "public" concept of Jesus as the Messiah: such figures in the gospel-story as Herod and Pilate attempt to deal with Jesus the Messiah as though he were claiming for himself politically the throne of Israel. In stark contrast to this is what we may designate as Matthew's "confessional" description of Jesus as the Messiah. To project this, Matthew relates, both directly and indirectly, the word "Messiah" to the term "Son of God."

Thus, at 16:16 and 26:63, which contain the confession of Peter and the question of the High Priest, Matthew places "the Son of God" in

25. W. Bauer, W. F. Arndt, and F. W. Gingrich (*A Greek-English Lexicon of the New Testament* [Chicago: University of Chicago, 1957], 895) translate the expression *Iēsous ho legomenos christos* as "Jesus the so-called Messiah." Although this translation may seem appropriate in the mouth of Pilate at 27:17, 22, it does not fit 1:16, where the Greek manifestly does not connote that it is questionable to call Jesus the Messiah. To do justice to this expression in all three passages, therefore, it is best to translate it each time as "Jesus who is called the Christ (Messiah)."

direct apposition to "the Messiah."[26] Obliquely, Matthew relates the two terms to each other in the pericopes on the Origin of Jesus (1:18–25) and on the Question about David's Son (22:41–46). In the first pericope, Matthew shows that the origin of "[Jesus] Messiah" (1:18) is such that, while he is the Son of David according to adoption (1:20–21, 25), he is the Son of God from conception (1:18, 20, 23, 25a). In the second pericope, which we shall treat in greater detail below, he shows in words of Jesus that although "the Messiah" is indeed the Son of David, he is of yet higher station, namely, the Son of God (22:42, 45). On the basis of these four passages, therefore, it is plain that Matthew intends that the term Messiah be interpreted, at its most profound level, in the light of the title Son of God. And since the "public" (e.g., Herod, Pilate, the Roman soldiers, and the leaders of the people) have an erroneous concept of Jesus as the Messiah, only those who are his disciples, by revelation of God (cf. 16:16–17), perceive the "confessional" truth that Jesus the Messiah is the Son of God.

Two additional conclusions follow from these observations. If an investigation of Matthew's use of the term Messiah reveals that it properly issues in the title Son of God, then this corroborates (a) interpreting, as we did, the activity of Jesus Messiah in the chapters following 4:17 as the activity of Jesus Son of God, and (b) understanding, as we argued above, the term Messiah as a surrogate for the title Son of God especially in such passages as 11:2–3 and 23:10. The present analysis of the term Messiah serves to confirm the view stated in the last chapter that in Matthew's Gospel Jesus fulfills the role of Messiah in the main as the Son of God.

The term "King" (*basileus*), where it functions as a christological predication in the first Gospel, is likewise employed by Matthew in both a positive and negative fashion. Negatively, it characterizes Jesus in the eyes of his opponents as, again, a political figure, and forms the basis of the now familiar expression "King of the Jews (Israel)" (cf., e.g., 2:2; 27:11, 29, 37, 42).

Positively, Matthew makes use of this title to counter such political misunderstanding of the person of Jesus by associating it with his suffering. When Jesus, for example, enters Jerusalem as the Son of David (21:1–11), Matthew inserts into his Marcan text (cf. 11:1–10) a formula

---

26. Cf. also Hummel, *Die Auseinandersetzung zwischen Kirche und Judentum im Matthäusevangelium* (BEvT 33; München: Chr. Kaiser, 1963), 113; Hahn, *Christology*, 285; A. Vögtle, "Zum Problem der Herkunft von 'Mt 16, 17–19,'" *Orientierung an Jesus*, ed. P. Hoffmann (Festschrift J. Schmid; Freiburg: Herder, 1973), 385.

quotation describing Jesus Son of David as the "humble King" (21:5). This reference prepares for ch. 27, which tells of the suffering that Jesus endures as King at the hands of Pilate (vss. 11–31) and on the cross (vss. 38, 42). In the pericope 27:27–31, Matthew provides a detailed portrait of the true nature of Jesus' kingship: as he stands draped in a scarlet robe with a crown of thorns on his head and a reed for a scepter in his right hand, the soldiers abuse him and, kneeling in mock obeisance before him, hail him as "King of the Jews." At the same time, after Jesus has been placed on the cross, the title "King" is mentioned in the succeeding narrative only once (27:42), giving way to the title Son of God. Consequently, if "King" marks Jesus as a political throne-pretender in the perspective of his enemies, in the perspective of Matthew it marks him as the one in the line of David (cf. 1:6; 21:9) who establishes his rule, not by bringing his people to heel, but by suffering on their behalf in order to atone, as the Son of God, for their sins.

In the story of the Last Judgment (25:31–46), Matthew twice (vss. 34, 40) designates the Son of Man as *basileus*. Perhaps this word "king," used absolutely in these passages, can be regarded as a christological predication. But this is unlikely.[27] Instead, it functions in this pericope in an auxiliary capacity, viz., to emphasize the circumstance that the apocalyptic Son of Man is a figure of majesty who will exercise judgment over all nations at the end of time in the same way as a king presides over his court.

### Son of David

Some commentators, such as G. Strecker,[28] R. Hummel,[29] and A. Suhl,[30] hold that the foremost title in the first Gospel for the earthly Jesus is "Son of David" (*huios tou Dauid*). In the succeeding paragraphs, we hope to demonstrate that this cannot be the case. Still, that "Son of David" is of great importance to Matthew is indisputable, for of the eleven times it is found in the Gospel, Matthew uses it editorially seven times.[31] What role, therefore, does this title play in the first Gospel?

27. Hummel (*Kirche und Judentum*, 114) believes that the term "king" in 25:34 serves as a "bridge" to connect the messianic title of "King" with the apocalyptic concept of the "Son of Man": "the King of Israel comes again as the Judge–King of the world."
28. Cf. *Weg*, 118–20.
29. Cf. *Kirche und Judentum*, 116–22.
30. Cf. "Der Davidssohn im Matthäus-Evangelium," ZNW 59 (1968): 68–69, 81.
31. Cf. 1:1, 20; 9:27; 12:23; 15:22; 21:9, 15.

Matthew's initial description of Jesus as the Son of David is that he is the royal Messiah from the house of David promised and sent specifically to Israel (1:1–17, 20–21; 15:22–24; 21:5, 9; 22:42). Hence, the title Son of David in the first Gospel complements the title Son of Abraham: even as the latter points to Jesus as the one in whom the nations are to find blessing, so this title points to Jesus as the one in whom Israel is to find blessing. Nevertheless, both of these titles, we should add, are limited in application and subsumed by Matthew under the broader messianic category of Son of God.

Matthew's presentation of Jesus as the Son of David is not only positive in character but apologetic as well. To begin with, Jesus is of course Son of David from infancy: his birth is in fulfillment of prophecy made to the house of David (1:23; 2:6), and Joseph son of David gives him his name, adopting him into his line (1:21, 25). In addition, the fact that the name of David stands out prominently in Matthew's genealogical schematization of the history of Israel (1:1, 6a–b, 17), which culminates in the birth of Jesus, serves to associate Jesus in a pronounced way with David.

One of the most striking features of the activity of Jesus as the Son of David in the first Gospel is its narrow scope: aside from his entrance into Jerusalem, at which time he is hailed by the crowds and assumes the posture of the humble King (21:5, 9), the public activity of Jesus Son of David is set forth by Matthew within the confines of a double restriction: it extends exclusively to healing,[32] and, except for the "blind and lame" in the temple (21:14–15), only to particular individuals (cf. 9:27; 12:22; 15:22; 20:30) and not to the masses per se (cf., e.g., 4:23–25; 8:16; 9:35; 11:5; 12:15; 14:14; 15:29–31). What is more, the status of the persons whom Jesus Son of David heals is that of the "no-accounts" of contemporary Jewish society ("blind," "dumb," "lame," "daughter" of a Gentile woman). In other respects, conspicuously absent from the positive side of Matthew's description of Jesus as the Son of David is any hint whatever that Jesus somehow satisfies the political expectations of the people and their leaders. That concept of the Son of David, suggests Matthew, is false.

Accordingly, Jesus as the Son of David, says Matthew, is one who heals selected "no-accounts" in Israel and shows himself in Jerusalem to be the humble King. But, continues Matthew, Israel not only does not receive Jesus as the Son of David, it does not even recognize him to be

32. Cf. also Burger, *Davidssohn*, 79, 90.

such.[33] In this regard Israel, contends Matthew, is without excuse. For one thing, the "blind," a "dumb" man, the "children," and even a Gentile "woman" are able to "see" and "confess" what Israel does not (cf. 9:27; 12:22; 15:22; 21:15 with 13:13; 15:14; 23:16–17, 19, 24, 26). For another thing, there is no lack of publicity in the land of Galilee to the effect that Jesus is the Son of David (cf. 9:31). Indeed, at risk to his life (12:14–16) Jesus dares to carry out in public that ministry of healing by which he reveals himself to be the Son of David (12:22–24), and upon his entry into Jerusalem the crowds eagerly greet him with this title (21:9). At the last, even in the temple itself the shouting children, again, proclaim him to be the Son of David (21:15).

But to repeat, Israel does not so much as recognize Jesus to be the Son of David. The leaders of the people witness his ministry of healing, but this only provokes them to anger (21:15) or motivates them to charge him with being an emissary of Satan (9:32–34; 12:22–24). The crowds, it is true, at least pose the question as to whether he is the Son of David, but the manner in which they frame it is negative (cf. *mēti*; 12:23). And when Jesus enters Jerusalem and the crowds do hail him as the Son of David, they reveal that this title means no more to them than that he is the "prophet . . . from Nazareth" (21:9–11).

So much for Matthew's sketch of Jesus as the Davidic Messiah. Before we attempt to draw the balance, we must first compare the title Son of David with that of Son of God.

Is "Son of David" the principal christological predication that Matthew attributes to the "earthly" Jesus? On the contrary, the evidence is decidedly in favor of the title Son of God. First of all, there are two key pericopes in the Gospel in which Matthew ranks "Son of God" above "Son of David." The one pericope, on the Origin of Jesus (1:18–25), we have already discussed. Suffice it to say that the adoption of Jesus by Joseph, which makes him Son of David, cannot compare to his conception by the Holy Spirit, which makes him Son of God.

The second pericope, on the Question about David's Son (22:41–46), illustrates the same difference in degree. Matthew edits the text so that Mark's question, "How can the scribes say that the Christ is the Son of David?" (12:35) becomes absolute in character: "Whose son is he?" (vs. 42). In this way, the opening question is made to harmonize with the closing question: ". . . how is he his [David's] son?" (vs. 45). Now

33. Cf. Suhl, "Davidssohn," 69–73, 78–81.

the counterpart of *kyrios* (cf. vss. 43–45) is not "son" but "slave";[34] Matthew, however, shows with his editing of the text that it is the sonship of Jesus which is the issue at point. In this connection, we note that Matthew has Jesus accept at face value the reply of the Pharisees that the Messiah is the Son of David (vs. 42) yet prove, on the basis of Ps 110, that the Messiah must be understood to be of still higher station (vss. 43–45). In terms of sonship, the station that surpasses Davidic sonship is divine sonship. Accordingly, it becomes clear that what Matthew intends for Jesus to assert in this pericope is that the Messiah is, to be sure, the Son of David but, what is more, he is the Son of God.[35]

In addition to these pericopes, there is yet further evidence that weighs heavily against the thesis that Son of David is Matthew's primary christological title for the earthly Jesus. In the first place, following Jesus' dialogue with the Pharisees on the Question about David's Son (22:41–46), the title Son of David does not appear again in the Gospel. The upshot is that Matthew develops his entire passion narrative apart from any mention of this title. This is strange procedure if Son of David were in fact Matthew's chief title for the earthly Jesus.

In the second place, it is of decisive significance that the disciples, while they openly confess Jesus to be the Son of God (14:33; 16:16; cf. also 27:54), never once in the Gospel confess him to be the Son of David. Not only this, but they do not so much as even address him by this title. On the contrary, at one place in the Gospel Matthew even goes out of his way to avoid giving the impression that the disciples address Jesus as the Son of David. In Mark's account of Jesus' entry into Jerusalem, it appears as though the disciples are depicted as joining with the people in their joyful acclamation of Jesus (cf. 11:9). But Matthew in his account of this scene explicitly states that it is exclusively the "crowds" who point to Jesus as the Son of David (21:9). Now since the disciples function in the Gospel as the representatives of Matthew's church,[36] their silence throughout the Gospel as regards "Son of David" can only mean that Matthew's church has "outgrown" this title: these believers serve and worship Jesus no longer as the Son of David but as the Son of God.

---

34. Cf. W. Grundmann, "Sohn Gottes," *ZNW* 47 (1956): 126.
35. Cf. also W. Wrede, "Jesus als Davidssohn," *Vorträge und Studien* (Tübingen: J. C. B. Mohr, 1907), 174; J. M. Gibbs, "Purpose and Pattern in Matthew's Use of the Title 'Son of David,'" *NTS* 10 (1963/64): 461, 463–64; Suhl, "Davidssohn," 61; D. M. Hay, *Glory at the Right Hand* (SBLMS 18; Nashville: Abingdon, 1973), 116–17.
36. Cf. J. D. Kingsbury, *The Parables of Jesus in Matthew 13* (London and Richmond, Va.: S.P.C.K. and John Knox, 1969), 41–42.

In the light of the preceding discussion, to what use does Matthew put the title Son of David? He employs it for theological and apologetic purposes. Theologically, Matthew takes great care, particularly in 1:1–2:6, 15:24, and 21:1–9, to portray Jesus as Israel's royal Messiah in whom OT prophecy concerning David is fulfilled. At the same time, Matthew does not honor popular notions of the Davidic Messiah according to which he is to be a political and military figure, but instead shows him to be a humble King and attributes to him the activity of healing. Yet even such healing activity is sharply restricted in scope. The result is that Jesus comes to the fore as the Son of David in the first Gospel in a very particular way and in certain passages only. This, in turn, enables Matthew to picture the public ministry of Jesus Messiah to Israel in the greatest measure as that of the Son of God, a christological category that Matthew defines broadly and under which he can subsume that of Son of David.

Apologetically, Matthew utilizes the title Son of David in order to underline the guilt that devolves upon Israel for not receiving its Messiah. To this end Matthew calls attention to the "no-accounts" of Jewish society—the blind, a blind and dumb man, the children, and a Gentile woman—in reproach of Israel: these perceive and confess what Israel does not (13:13; 15:14), and the faith with which they approach Jesus Son of David (cf. 9:28–29; 15:28) serves both as an example and a warning also for the Israel of Matthew's day.

### Kyrios

In some quarters redaction-critics have virtually made a dogma of the view that *kyrios* ("Lord") is a principal, or indeed the primary, christological title of Matthew's Gospel. Lucan research and the continued influence of W. Bousset's *Kyrios Christos*[37] without doubt helped create the atmosphere in which this dogma could flourish, but, most directly, it was G. Bornkamm who solidly established it.

In his essay "End-Expectation and Church in Matthew," Bornkamm picks up on the suggestion of W. Foerster and points out that whereas strangers, enemies, and Judas Iscariot always greet Jesus in the first Gospel with *"didaskale"* ("teacher") or *"hrabbi"* ("rabbi") but never with *"kyrie,"* the disciples and those who search Jesus out in the belief he can heal and save never approach him with *"didaskale"* or *"hrabbi"* but al-

---

37. Second ed.; Göttingen: Vandenhoeck & Ruprecht, 1921.

ways with *"kyrie."*[38] From Matthew's use of the term *kyrios,* Bornkamm concludes that "the title and address of Jesus as *kyrios* in Matthew have throughout the character of a divine Name of Majesty."[39]

The effect of Bornkamm's essay was to put an end for all practical purposes to the dispute, as far as Matthew's Gospel is concerned, over whether *kyrios* is a christological title or merely an expression of human respect. The passage 10:24, "A disciple is not above his teacher, nor a slave above his master [*kyrion*]," has henceforth generally been seen as enunciating the principle that the disciples and others in Matthew's Gospel who approach Jesus uttering the word *kyrie* are acknowledging thereby that he is a figure not merely of human but of lordly, or divine, dignity.[40]

In assessing the overall importance of the title *kyrios* for Matthew, Bornkamm himself regards it along with Son of David, Son of God, and Son of Man as one of the four chief titles with which Matthew operates.[41] By contrast, other Matthaean specialists, while appropriating Bornkamm's insights, have nevertheless attributed to the term *kyrios* a considerably higher status in relation to the other christological titles of the Gospel. G. Strecker, for example, contends that *kyrios* ranks with "Son of David" as one of the two most significant titles in the first Gospel,[42] and W. D. Davies advances the same claim on behalf of *kyrios* and "Son of Man."[43] For their part, W. Trilling[44] and H. Frankemölle[45] are prepared to award *kyrios* absolute preeminence in Matthew's hierarchy of christological concepts.

On what evidence, other than that already mentioned, is this trend toward an escalation of the importance of the title *kyrios* in Matthew's Gospel based? While numerous passages are of course cited in support of the case, the *locus classicus* to which appeal is made is the ending of the Gospel (28:18–20; but cf. also 7:21–22; 21:3; 22:43–45; 24:42).[46] Now

38. Cf. Bornkamm, "End-Expectation," 41.
39. Ibid., 42–43.
40. Ibid., 42.
41. Ibid., 33.
42. Cf. Strecker, *Weg,* 118–20, 123–26.
43. Cf. Davies, *Setting,* 96–99, 360.
44. Cf. *Israel,* 21–51.
45. Cf. *Jahwebund und Kirche Christi* (NTAbh 10; Münster: Aschendorff, 1974), 80, 89, 144, 377, 398.
46. The study of Trilling (cf. *Israel,* 21–51) is an excellent example of the key role that 28:18–20 plays in any attempt to claim for Matthew a christology with major orientation toward Jesus as the *kyrios;* cf. also Strecker, *Weg,* 211–14; Hahn, *Christology,* 109; Davies, *Setting,* 97, 360; A. Vögtle, "Das christologische und ekklesiolo-

concerning 28:18–20, H. E. Tödt in 1959 already warned that one must exercise the "greatest caution . . . against all the attempts to interpret Matt. 28:18 as a statement about the *Kyrios* or even the Son of Man,"[47] and we have attempted elsewhere to prove the truth of this caveat by demonstrating that the christology informing Matt 28:16–20 is not at all that of *kyrios* or Son of Man but that of Son of God.[48] If this is correct, then obviously this passage can no longer be used to support the claim for the preeminence in the first Gospel of *kyrios* as a christological title.

But this, in turn, leads us to ask the further question (notwithstanding the passages 7:21–22; 21:3; 22:44; and 24:42 [see below]) as to whether Strecker, Davies, Trilling, Frankemölle, and even Bornkamm have not misjudged the importance Matthew attaches to the word *kyrios*? To be sure, this is not to say that we care to argue that *kyrios* is, after all, simply a term of human respect. On this point there is no going behind Bornkamm's position that *kyrios* in Matthew's Gospel is indeed a christological title. But what exactly is the status of this title in the first Gospel? This is the question that has yet to be satisfactorily resolved. In answer to this question, we should like to advance the argument that Matthew employs *kyrios* as an auxiliary christological title in order to attribute to Jesus divine authority in his capacity as the Messiah, Son of David, Son of God, or Son of Man.

Matthew uses the word *kyrios* on at least three levels. At 27:63, for example, he does so in a purely conventional fashion so that the leaders of the people address Pilate with the equivalent of the English "sir."[49] From a strictly theological standpoint, *kyrios* denotes "God" numerous times in the first Gospel (cf., e.g., 4:7, 10; 5:33; 9:38; 11:25; 21:9, 42; 22:37; 23:39; 27:10; 28:2). And of course it can also have a christological coloration.

---

gische Anliegen von Mt. 28, 18–20," *SE II* (TU 87; Berlin: Akademie, 1964), 277–83; G. Bornkmamm, "Der Auferstandene und der Irdische. Mt 28, 16–20," *Zeit und Geschichte,* ed. E. Dinkler (Festschrift R. Bultmann; Tübingen: J. C. B. Mohr, 1964), 173; Frankemölle, *Jahwebund,* 79–80, 96, 143. Some commentators, in treating 28:18–20, make no distinction whatever between Jesus as the exalted Son of Man and as the exalted *Kyrios* (cf. E. Lohmeyer, "Mir ist gegeben alle Gewalt! Eine Enogooo von Mt. 28, 16 20," *In Memoriam Ernst Lohmeyer,* ed W Schmauch [Stuttgart: Evangelisches Verlagswerk, 1951], 28, 33–35, 42, 47; O. Michel, "Der Abschluss des Matthäusevangeliums," *EvT* 10 [1950/51], 22; G. Barth, "Matthew's Understanding of the Law," *Tradition and Interpretation in Matthew,* trans. P. Scott [Philadelphia: Westminster, 1963], 133–36; Vögtle, "Mt. 28, 18–20," 290–93).
47. Cf. H. E. Tödt, *The Son of Man in the Synoptic Tradition,* trans. D. M. Barton (New Testament Library; London: SCM, 1965), 290.
48. J. D. Kingsbury, "The Composition and Christology of Matt 28:16–20," *JBL* 93 (1974): 573–84.
49. Cf. Bauer–Arndt–Gingrich, *Lexicon,* 460.

We have made no reference thus far, out of methodological considerations, to the parables of Jesus.[50] For if it is possible for us to determine Matthew's understanding of *kyrios* apart from the parables, it should follow that his use of the term there will fundamentally comply with this understanding. Nevertheless, in one respect the parables are of primary importance in the study of *kyrios*, namely, in setting forth the general nature of the word. Because in that *kyrios* designates in the parables the "master" as opposed to the "slave,"[51] the owner" as opposed to the "workmen,"[52] or the "father" as opposed to the "son,"[53] its essentially relational character stands out as well as its propensity for attributing both authority and the more exalted station to the one to whom it points.[54]

As it applies to Jesus, Matthew employs *kyrios* overwhelmingly in the vocative case,[55] another factor which points to its relational character. Moreover, it also proves to be a "confessional" term in the sense that, apart from the accursed in the scene of the Last Judgment (cf., e.g., 7:21–23; 25:37), it crosses the lips exclusively, as we noted, of the disciples[56] or of those who come to Jesus in the belief that he can heal or save.[57] But if, as applied to Jesus, *kyrios* in the first Gospel is both "relational" and "confessional," then we can state provisionally that the purpose for which Matthew employs it is to attribute authority and an exalted status to Jesus. And since in Matthew's view the authority Jesus wields and the exalted station that is his are derived from God himself (cf. 11:27; 21:23–27; 28:18), we see that Matthew employs *kyrios* in order to attribute an exalted station to Jesus and an authority that is specifically divine. Perhaps the passage that best illustrates Matthew's intention with *kyrios* is 12:8 (cf. Mark 2:28): "For the Son of Man is lord of the Sabbath."

We mentioned above that those who take the position that Matthew presents Jesus in a principal way as the *kyrios* base their case, aside from

50. As J. A. T. Robinson has had occasion to observe ("The 'Parable' of the Sheep and the Goats," *Twelve New Testament Studies* [SBT 34; London: SCM, 1962], 76), the narrative of the Last Judgment (Matt 25:31–46) is not, properly speaking, a parable but a "combination of parabolic, apocalyptic, and ethical teaching. . . ." In this study, therefore, we shall not categorize this unit as a parable.

51. Cf., e.g., 13:27–29; 18:23–35; 24:45–51; 25:1–13, 14–30.

52. Cf., e.g., 20:1–16.

53. Cf., e.g., 21:28–31.

54. Cf. W Foerster, *TDNT*, III, 1086.

55. Cf. 7:21–22; 8:2, 6, 8, 21, 25; 9:28; 14:28, 30; 15:22, 25, 27; 16:22; 17:4, 15; 18:21; 20:30–31, 33; 25:37, 44; 26:22.

56. Cf. 8:21, 25; 14:28, 30; 16:22; 17:4; 18:21; 26:22. Cf. also 25:44.

57. Cf. 8:2, 6, 8; 9:28; 15:22, 25, 27; 17:15; 20:30–31, 33.

28:18–20, also on such passages as 7:21–22 and 24:42. The passage 24:42 is an exhortation and reminds the members of Matthew's church that at the Latter Day "your Lord comes (*erchetai*)." And 7:21–22 depicts the workers of lawlessness in the church as appealing to Jesus, the eschatological Judge, as "Lord."

A close look at these passages, however, shows that in reality Jesus stands behind the term *kyrios* as the Son of Man. To begin with, if 24:42 warns Christians that "your Lord comes," one should not overlook the circumstance that, on the one hand, this verse is parallel to 24:44, which states that "the Son of Man comes (*erchetai*)," and, on the other, is preceded by 24:37 and 39, which likewise tell of "the coming (*parousia*) of the Son of Man." Then, too, if the workers of lawlessness in 7:21–22 address Jesus, the eschatological Judge, as "Lord," so do "all the nations" in 25:31–46, except that here Jesus is further identified as the "Son of Man" (25:31).

The question, then, is one of primacy: which term takes precedence over the other? The answer is that Son of Man takes precedence over *kyrios*, for three reasons. First, the passages in which Matthew reveals that the figure he associates most closely with the parousia and the Last Judgment is not Jesus *kyrios* per se but Jesus Son of Man predominate in the Gospel by a wide margin.[58] Second, Matthew twice attributes a "kingdom" to Jesus as the Son of Man (13:41; 16:28) but not at all to Jesus as the *kyrios*. Last, at 12:8 Matthew gives direct indication as to how he would have us resolve the question of the primacy of the two terms: whereas "Son of Man" is the subject of the sentence, "*kyrios*" is the predicate nominative and thus functions to make a statement about the Son of Man.

Consequently, there can be no doubt that in 7:21–22 and 24:42 Matthew intends that the term *kyrios* should refer beyond itself to Jesus as the Son of Man. Jesus Son of Man is called *kyrios* because, as the eschatological Judge, he exercises dominion with authority derived from God himself.

The relationship that Matthew establishes between the term *kyrios* and such titles as "Messiah," "Son of David," and "Son of God" is basically the same as that which prevails between *kyrios* and Son of Man. The following is an attempt to show this.

In four pericopes, the story of the Triumphal Entry (21:1–9) and three miracles of healing (9:27–31; 15:21–28; 20:29–34), Matthew relates

58. Cf. 10:23; 13:41; 16:27–28; 19:28; 24:27, 30, 37, 39, 44; 25:31; 26:64.

the word *kyrios* to "Son of David." As for the story of the Triumphal Entry, Matthew follows Mark in making *kyrios* absolute (21:3 // Mark 11:3). The result is that the force of the term in this passage is a matter of considerable debate. Some commentators, for example, contend that *kyrios* in 21:3 does not at all refer to Jesus but to the man who owns the donkey and the colt that Jesus borrows.[59] Other commentators, however, aver that *kyrios* certainly does refer to Jesus but that it is conventional in meaning so that Jesus is described as the "master" of the animals upon which he will ride as he enters Jerusalem (cf. 21:5, 7).[60] On the other end of the spectrum, there are those who stoutly maintain that *kyrios* in 21:3 is thoroughly christological in tenor and anticipates before Easter the majestic office Jesus will assume at his exaltation.[61]

In our view, to determine Matthew's understanding of the word *kyrios* in 21:3, we dare not isolate it from either the immediate context of the pericope or the wider context of the Gospel. Thus, to claim that *kyrios* does not refer to Jesus but to the owner of the animals is to raise a most secondary figure to a level of prominence in the story which conflicts with Matthew's objective, viz., to highlight the person of Jesus. By the same token, to see in the meaning of *kyrios* no more than conventional usage is to revert to a position that especially Bornkamm has shown to be untenable. On the other hand, to point to Matthew's use of *kyrios* in 21:3 as proving that it has for him the status of a principal, as opposed to an auxiliary, christological title is to ignore both the position and the function *kyrios* has in this pericope.

Even a cursory glance at the text reveals that *kyrios* is not the chief christological term. For whereas Matthew has appropriated *kyrios* from Mark (cf. 11:3), the two terms "King" (*basileus*, vs. 5) and "Son of David" (vs. 9) owe their presence in the text to Matthaean redaction. But of the latter two terms, "Son of David" has the position of greater stress. The relationship, therefore, that Matthew establishes among the three christological terms in this pericope may be sketched as follows. The importance of the term *kyrios* to Matthew is that it underlines the lordly authority with which Jesus the King commands for himself the animals upon which he will ride into Jerusalem (cf. the use of the im-

59. Cf., e.g., M.–J. Lagrange, *Évangile selon Saint Matthieu* (7th ed.; Paris: J. Gabalda, 1948), 397; Klostermann, *Matthäus*, 166; J. Schmid, *Das Evangelium nach Matthäus* (RNT 1; Regensburg: F. Pustet, 1959), 299.

60. Cf., e.g., P. Bonnard, *L' évangile selon Saint Matthieu* (CNT 1; Neuchâtel: Delachaux & Niestlé, 1963), 303; W. Foerster, *TDNT*, III, 1093.

61. Cf., e.g., Bornkamm, "End-Expectation," 42–43; Hahn, *Christology*, 82; P. Gaechter, *Das Matthäusevangelium* (Innsbruck: Tyrolia, 1963), 656.

peratives and of *euthys* ["immediately"] in vss. 1–3). But in what particular way is the person of Jesus the King to be understood? As the crowds are made to shout in vs. 9, he is the Son of David. In the last analysis, therefore, the use to which Matthew puts the term *kyrios* in 21:1–9 is to attribute a high station and dominical authority to Jesus, King and Son of David.

We stated that Matthew also relates the term *kyrios* to "Son of David" in three stories of healing (9:27–31; 15:21–28; 20:29–34). Although in four instances in these stories direct appeal is made to Jesus not only as *kyrios* but also as Son of David (cf. 9:27; 15:22; 20:30–31), Matthew may have preferred to cast only *kyrios* in the vocative and to render Son of David each time in the nominative.[62] While the nominative case can of course function as the vocative,[63] could it be that Matthew intended that even his style in these instances should be a sign that the term *kyrie* is meant to refer beyond itself to Son of David as the primary title?[64] However the latter may be, the first of these three stories sets the example for all in clearly indicating that the title Son of David is to take precedence over the title *kyrios* ( cf. 9:27 with 9:28).

The texts read that Jesus, as the Son of David (cf. 9:27; 15:22; 20:30–31), heals, respectively, two blind men, the daughter of a Canaanite woman, and an additional two blind men, all of whom call upon him with *kyrie* (cf. 9:28; 15:22, 25, 27; 20:30–31, 33). In two of these accounts, explicit reference is made to the "faith" with which the suppliants approach Jesus (cf. 9:29; 15:28), and in the third account such faith is strongly implied by virtue of the persistence the men display in their desire, despite the crowd's rebuke, to reach Jesus (20:31). In the first story, the faith of the men in question is defined as belief that "I [Jesus Son of David (9:27)] am able to do this" (9:28). Accordingly, if we

62. Text-critically, all of the readings which render "Son of David" in the nominative case are disputed (cf. 9:27; 15:22; 20:30–31). The Nestle text (*Novum Testamentum Graece* [25th ed.; Stuttgart: Württembergische Bibelanstalt, 1963]; cf. also K. Aland, *Synopsis Quattuor Evangeliorum* [5th ed.; Stuttgart: Württembergische Bibelanstalt, 1968]), apparently following especially the codex Vaticanus and considerations of an internal nature as to the harder reading, opts each time for the nominative case in place of the vocative. S. C. E. Legg (*Evangelium secundum Matthaeum* [Oxford: Clarendon, 1940]) prefers the nominative case three times and the vocative once (9:27). By contrast, the text published by the American Bible Society (*The Greek New Testament*, ed. K. Aland, M. Black, B. Metzger, and A. Wikgren [New York, 1966]) reverses the ratio, retaining the nominative case only at 15:22.
63. Cf. R. W. Funk, *A Beginning-Intermediate Grammar of Hellenistic Greek* (Sources for Biblical Study 2; Missoula: Society of Biblical Literature, 1973), II, 710; J. H. Moulton, *A Grammar of New Testament Greek* (Edinburgh: T. & T. Clark, 1908), I, 71.
64. Cf. also Burger, *Davidssohn*, 73–74.

consider the several features of the three stories, what they reveal is that the word *kyrie* in the mouth of these needy persons, who are portrayed as approaching Jesus as the Son of David in faith for healing, is, once again, intended by Matthew to attribute to Jesus Son of David a high station and dominical authority, in these cases to heal.

In the pericope on the Question about David's Son (22:41–46), Matthew relates *kyrios* to "Messiah." Here Matthew twice writes in words of Jesus that "David calls him [the Messiah] Lord" (vss. 43, 45). To ascertain the meaning of these words, it is helpful to take note of the scope of the text. From previous discussion we will recall that what Matthew intends for Jesus to assert in this pericope is that the Messiah is, to be sure, the Son of David but, what is more, he is the Son of God.[65]

Should this be correct, what role is Matthew ascribing in this text to the term *kyrios?* Taking the twofold statement "David calls him [the Messiah] Lord" (vss. 43, 45) as indicating how Matthew proposes that the words of the psalmist should be understood ("The Lord [God] said to my lord [the Messiah], 'Sit at my right hand,'" etc.), we see that Matthew employs *kyrios,* not after the fashion of an independent christological category as such, but in order to attribute to Jesus as the Messiah a more exalted station (i.e., divine sonship; cf. 1:18, 20, 23) than the "Pharisees" have a mind to accord the Messiah in their understanding of his person (Davidic sonship). And since, in Matthew's eyes, central to the divine sonship of Jesus the Messiah (cf. 1:18, 23) is the divine authority God has entrusted to him (cf. vs. 44; also 1:18 and 23 to 11:27; 21:23–27; 28:18–20), we conclude that in this pericope on the Question about David's Son the term *kyrios* stands in essentially the same relationship to the term Messiah as we discovered is the case with it and Son of Man: Jesus the Messiah is not merely of human but of divine station, the one who wields divine authority.

In 22:41–46, then, Jesus the Messiah stands behind the term *kyrios* as the divine Son who wields divine authority. In two other pericopes, the stories of the Walking on the Water (14:22–33) and of the Transfiguration (17:1–9), Matthew associates the term *kyrios* more immediately with Jesus as the Son of God. In the first story, Peter calls upon Jesus as *kyrios,* first, that he might receive the command to walk on the water (14:28–29), and second, after he has done so but has become afraid and begins to sink, that Jesus might save him (14:30). Once Jesus has rescued Peter and the two climb into the boat, Matthew records that the

65. See above, n. 35.

disciples in the boat worship Jesus and confess him to be the Son of God (14:33). In both the command Peter requests of Jesus and the cry for rescue, the vocative *kyrie* functions to attribute majesty and divine authority to Jesus, this time identified as the Son of God.

Nor is the situation appreciably different in the story of the Transfiguration (17:1–9). Matthew again has Peter address Jesus as *kyrios* (17:4), and the "voice from the cloud" names him "my beloved Son" and exhorts the disciples to "hear him" (17:5). Since one of the points Matthew is concerned to make in this story is that Peter's desire to remain on the mountain (17:4) is superseded by Jesus' act of taking the disciples down from there and instructing them as to his death and resurrection (17:9), Peter, in addressing Jesus with *kyrie* in 17:4, is implicitly acknowledging that Jesus' words are with divine authority. As the voice from the cloud puts it, he is God's beloved Son, one invested with divine authority.

It remains for us to discuss briefly several passages in Matthew's Gospel not yet treated in which Jesus is approached by a disciple or someone else with *kyrie* but in which there is either no direct reference in the same unit to another christological title (cf. 8:2, 6, 8, 21, 25; 16:22;[66] 17:15; 18:21) or there appears to be no immediate connection between *kyrios* and the other christological title (cf. 26:22). Do these passages break the pattern we have thus far established, namely, that the purpose of the term *kyrios* as Matthew utilizes it is to point beyond itself to some other, more definitive, christological term?

We think not, for as regards the initial set of passages, the Jesus we encounter in them is the one whom Matthew has presented in the first main part of his Gospel (1:1–4:16) as the Messiah who is preeminently the Son of God. Hence, we see that as Matthew portrays Jesus in his Gospel as discharging his public ministry to Israel, those disciples and others who approach him uttering the word *kyrie* are doing so in acknowledgment of the divine authority with which the Messiah, the Son of God, heals (8:1–4, 5–13; 17:14–18), saves (8:23–27), and teaches (8:21–22; 16:21–23; 18:21–22). This element of divine authority stands

---

66. If there seems to be a problem in relating *kyrios* in 16:22 to "Christ" in 16:21, it has to do with the nature of 16:21: this verse is both a passion prediction and the "superscription" to the third main part of the Gospel (16:21–28:20), so that its formal character tends to set it apart from its immediate context. Vss. 22–23 build upon it, but, strictly speaking, they have a setting all their own, as can be seen from vs. 22a. In the final analysis, therefore, Matthew's use of *kyrie* in 16:22 corresponds exactly to his use of it in the other passages we have listed in the body of the chapter where no other christological title appears.

out markedly in particular verses of these pericopes (cf., e.g., 8:2, 8, 22, 27; 16:21; 17:16; 18:21).

In 26:22, the word *kyrios* seems to have little or no association with Son of Man, the other christological title present in the pericope (26:20–25). But this ostensible anomaly can be readily explained. In 26:24, Jesus solemnly speaks of himself as the Son of Man who is to be betrayed in the same vein as he speaks of himself in the passion predictions (cf. 17:22–23; 20:17–19). Here Jesus is interacting primarily with Judas, with one who does not "believe" in him, as Judas' use of "rabbi" in his reply to Jesus discloses (26:25). But in 26:22, where *kyrios* appears, Jesus is interacting with the true disciples, who know him as the Messiah who must go the way God has determined (cf. 16:21). In formal terms, therefore, Matthew's use of *kyrios* in 26:22 is no different from his use of it in those passages just discussed, where *kyrios* at first glance seems not to refer to another christological title but, upon closer examination, can be shown to point to Jesus in general as the Messiah and, more exactly, as the Son of God.

It has been said that, for Luke, Jesus is first of all the *kyrios* who, exalted by God to dominion, presides over the community of believers in the "time of the church" through the agency of the Spirit.[67] So understood, the term *kyrios* designates a highly profiled christological category that can stand quite apart from any other such category. One of the principal reasons the title *kyrios* is said to have increasingly gained the ascendancy over other primitive titles was the need of the early church for epiklesis, for interaction especially in the cult with the Risen One.[68]

However appropriate this schema may be to Luke, the burden of this analysis is that it does not apply in the greatest measure to Matthew, so that students of the first Gospel should be on their guard against adopting it uncritically. Matthew's application of the term *kyrios* is considerably less sophisticated than this. To be sure, he does place it in the service of epiklesis, indeed almost totally so, as his extensive use of it in the vocative case shows. But in the overall manner in which he employs *kyrios*, Matthew gives no evidence that he regards it as an independent christological title on a par with the other titles most central to his Gospel.

Matthew, then, utilizes the term *kyrios* in such a way that Jesus stands behind it in his capacity as the "Messiah," "Son of David," "Son of God,"

---

67. Cf., e.g., H. Conzelmann, *The Theology of St Luke*, trans. G. Buswell (New York: Harper, 1960), 176–79, 184; Tödt, *Son of Man*, 290–92.

68. Cf. Bousset, *Kyrios Christos*, 80–81, 84–91; Tödt, *Son of Man*, 288–90.

or "Son of Man." Found only in the mouths of disciples and "believers" (apart from those who will be condemned at the Latter Day), *kyrios* characterizes the person who utters it as acknowledging that Jesus is the one of exalted station who wields divine authority, even if it be for judgment. Accordingly, we find the term *kyrios* functioning in the first Gospel to depict (a) Jesus the Messiah as a more authoritative figure than the Pharisees conceive the Davidic Messiah to be (22:42–45), or (b) Jesus Son of David as possessing the authority to command or to heal, or (c) Jesus Son of God as possessing the authority to teach, to heal, and to save, or (d) Jesus Son of Man as possessing the authority to regulate the Sabbath or to judge. Although Matthew can use *kyrios* in a purely conventional sense (27:63), there is no doubt that when he applies it to Jesus it assumes christological overtones. At the same time, because it basically refers beyond itself to some other more definitive title, it is most properly to be regarded in the first Gospel, not as one of the chief titles with which Matthew develops his christology (or indeed the primary one), but, again, as of the nature of an auxiliary christological title.

### Son of Man

The term "Son of Man" (*huios tou anthrōpou*) has long been recognized as one of the principal christological titles of Matthew's Gospel. Recently, however, this established opinion has been challenged, a matter we shall discuss shortly. Nevertheless, in Matthew as in Mark, Luke, and John, Jesus alone is portrayed as employing it, to refer to himself. But as unmistakable a fact as this may be, there are still several questions regarding Son of Man to which students of the first Gospel have not yet given adequate answer. What is the precise use to which Matthew puts it? Why does he not bring it in his Gospel prior to 8:20? What is the relationship between it and "Son of God"? In an attempt to answer these questions, we shall endeavor to establish the thesis that, for Matthew, "Son of Man" is indeed a christological title of the first order which is furthermore "public" in nature and is meant to complement the title Son of God, which is, as we know, "confessional" in nature.

It is common knowledge that "Son of Man" relates to three distinct phases of Jesus' activity: to his public ministry; to his suffering, death, and resurrection; and to his parousia. In addition, there is one passage in which Matthew seems to think of Jesus Son of Man as discharging a ministry also between Easter and the parousia (cf. 13:37–38).

Editorially, Matthew increases considerably the number of Son-of-Man references made available to him from the tradition, according to the following distribution. Whereas it is questionable whether he adds any Son-of-Man reference of the first type (but cf. 13:37; 16:13//Mark 8:31), it appears that he may well have added two references of the second type (17:12; 26:2) and six of the third (10:23; 13:41; 16:28; 19:28; 24:30; 25:31). These statistics give clear indication that Matthew's primary interest in the term Son of Man has to do with its association with the parousia.

There is no need for us to delineate here Matthew's description of each of the three phases of the activity of Jesus Son of Man.[69] What is important, however, is that we observe that on such matters as possessing authority,[70] giving one's life for others,[71] enduring mockery and abuse,[72] dying,[73] being raised,[74] and being entrusted by God with dominion,[75] Matthew's portrait of Jesus as the Son of Man coincides with his portrait of Jesus as the Son of God. At the same time, whereas the term Son of Man is only marginally significant in the first Gospel as a vehicle for setting forth the so-called "present" activity of Jesus, the title Son of God plays no role whatever as a vehicle for setting forth the activity of Jesus at the parousia.

As we see it, it is rather fruitless to attempt to determine the relationship Matthew establishes between the terms Son of Man and Son of God solely on the basis of the association of ideas surrounding each one (the "content"). Proceeding in this manner, we can draw only one of two conclusions: either that there is much similarity of "content" between the two and that the principle of discrimination is largely contextual or simply not easily discernible; or that the distinction Matthew draws between them is primarily not material in nature but formal. The latter proves to be the case.

The most striking feature about Matthew's use of Son of Man is that it assumes a totally "public," as opposed to "confessional," character. In

69. (a) The "present" activity of Jesus: 8:20; 9:6; 11:19; 12:8, 32; 13:37; 16:13; (b) the suffering and resurrection of Jesus: 12:40; 17:9, 12, 22; 20:18–19, 28; 26:2, 24, 45; (c) the parousia of Jesus: 10: 23; 13:41; 16:27–28; 19:28; 24:27, 30, 37, 39, 44; 25:31; 26:64.

70. Son of Man: 9:6; cf. 12:8. Son of God: 21:23–27; 28:19.

71. Son of Man: 20:28. Son of God: cf. 1:21; 26:28 to 27:38–54.

72. Son of Man: 17:12; 20:18–19. Son of God: 27:38–44.

73. Son of Man: 12:40; 17:23; 20:18–19; 26:2. Son of God: 21:38–39; 27:45–54.

74. Son of Man: 17:9, 23; 20:19. Son of God: cf. 28:5–7 to 28:16–20 (cf. 18:20).

75. Son of Man: 13:41; 16:27–28; 19:28; 24:30; 25:31; 26:64. Son of God: 28:16–20.

addition, except for the "righteous" in the scene of the Last Judgment, it marks the people in view of whom it is used as being unbelievers or opponents of Jesus. Two leading passages for illustrating what we are designating as the "public" character of this title are 16:13–15 and 13:37–38a. At 16:13, Matthew has redacted Mark so that Jesus' question to the disciples is: "Who do *men* say that the *Son of Man* is?" By contrast, Jesus asks Peter at 16:15: "Who do *you* say that *I* am?" The thing to note is that Son of Man is made to correlate, not with the disciples, but with "men." At 13:37–38a, Matthew writes in words of Jesus: "He who sows the good seed is the *Son of Man*; and the field is the *world*." In that Jesus stipulates the "world" as the place where the Son of Man is active, this passage attests directly to the "public" character of the title Son of Man.

A leading passage for illustrating the fact that Son of Man marks the people in view of whom it is used as unbelievers or opponents of Jesus is 26:20–25. At vs. 21, Jesus tells the disciples: "One of you will betray *me*." Each disciple replies: "Is it I, *Lord*?" (vs. 22). To Judas, however, Jesus says: "The *Son of Man* goes as it is written of him, but woe to that man by whom the *Son of Man* is betrayed" (vs. 24). Judas replies: "Is it I, *Rabbi*?" (vs. 25). The point of interest in this dialogue is the correlation between "me" and "Lord" in the case of the true followers of Jesus (28:16) and "Son of Man" and "rabbi" in the case of Judas.

One series of passages in which both the "public" and the "unbelieving" connotations of the title Son of Man stand out in sharp relief is 8:19–22. In the first scene, Matthew writes that a "scribe" approaches Jesus, addresses him as "Teacher" and says that he will follow him (vs. 19). Jesus, however, counters: ". . . the *Son of Man* has not where to lay his head" (vs. 20). In the antithetical second scene, Matthew writes that "another of the disciples" addresses Jesus as "Lord" and asks permission to bury his father (vs. 21). Jesus answers: "Follow *me* . . ." (vs. 22). So again, we have what is now a familiar correlation: in the one instance, "scribe" and "teacher" and "Son of Man"; in another instance, "another of the disciples" and "Lord" and "me."

These latter Son-of-Man passages belong to the larger group having to do with the "present" activity of Jesus. A survey of this group of passages according to the formal principle we have now defined reveals that in them the term Son of Man consistently bears the two connotations just identified. Consider the following examples. Some *scribes*, seeing Jesus forgive the sins of a paralytic, charge him in the presence of the *crowds* with blasphemy (9:2–3, 8); in this context Jesus declares: "The *Son of*

*Man* has authority on earth to forgive sins" (9:6). In the audience of the
*crowds* (11:7), understood apologetically as "this generation" (11:16),
Jesus cries out: ". . . the *Son of Man* came eating and drinking, and they
say, 'Behold, a glutton and a drunkard, a friend of tax collectors and
sinners!'" (11:19). The *Pharisees* claim that plucking grain on the Sabbath is a violation of the law (12:2); in response, Jesus asserts that "the
*Son of Man* is lord of the Sabbath" (12:8). And with the *crowds* as spec-
tators, the *Pharisees* contend that Jesus casts out demons by Beelzebul
(12:23–24); in reaction to this, Jesus informs his adversaries that "whoever speaks a word against the *Son of Man* will be forgiven, but whoever
speaks against the Holy Spirit will not be forgiven . . ." (12:32).

When we turn to the Son-of-Man sayings associated with the suffering
of Jesus or his parousia, we notice at once that Matthew casts three of
them in the same mold as the sayings we have just reviewed. Thus, the
*scribes and Pharisees* demand of Jesus a sign (12:38); he acquits their
demand with the reply that "as Jonah was three days and three nights in
the belly of the sea-monster, so will the *Son of Man* be three days and
three nights in the heart of the earth" (12:40). In the presence of the
*mother of the sons of Zebedee*, who requests for her offspring the seats
of greatest honor in Jesus' coming Kingdom (20:20–21), Jesus tells his
disciples that "the *Son of Man* came not to be served but to serve . . ."
(20:28). And at his trial, the *High Priest* and the *Sanhedrin* seek to condemn Jesus to death (26:59, 62); Jesus' words to them are that "hereafter
you will see the *Son of Man* seated at the right hand of Power, and coming on the clouds of heaven" (26:64).

The second of these three passages is spoken by Jesus principally to
the disciples, not to outsiders (cf. 20:24–25a). The rest of the "suffering"
and "apocalyptic" Son-of-Man sayings in the first Gospel are addressed
by Jesus exclusively to the disciples. But despite this change in audience,
the title Son of Man continues to be "public" in character and to mark
the persons in view of whom it is used (again, apart from the "righteous"
at the Last Judgment) as being opponents of Jesus who do not believe
in him.

The passion predictions demonstrate this well, for they describe in ever
greater detail the nature of the suffering that "men" (17:22; also "Judas,"
cf. 26:2, 24, 45) and the leaders of the people (20:18) and "Gentiles"
(20:19) will inflict upon specifically the Son of Man (17:12, 22–23; 20:
18–19; 26:2, 24–25, 45). In this connection, to return a final time to the
pericope that treats of the request for seats of honor on behalf of the sons

of Zebedee (20:20–28), we cannot fail to observe that here Jesus' words concerning the death of the Son of Man set forth the significance this death will have for especially the world: it is said to be a "ransom *for many*" (20:28). Reference to the resurrection, too, is of a piece with the passion predictions (17:22–23; 20:18–19; cf. also 17:9), for Matthew records that the Jews and the bribed soldiers spread the word that the body of Jesus Son of Man has been stolen (cf. 12:40 and 28:11–15). And as for the parousia, it constitutes of course the dramatic appearance of Jesus Son of Man at the end of the age in the "public" view of all the nations (25:31–46). As Judge, the Son of Man will confront the "cursed" and the "righteous" alike, consigning the former to eternal punishment but the latter to eternal life (25:46).

Perhaps a word about Matthew's picture of the end-time judgment of the church as such is in order. It is noteworthy that only twice (16:27; 24:44), once in a parable, does Matthew imply that the "coming of the Son of Man" will have to do also with the judgment of the church. As Matthew portrays it, the Son of Man is the one who will judge the nations (13:38, 41–43; 24:30; 25:31–46) and Israel, or "this generation" (cf. 24:32–39; 26:59, 64; cf. 19:28), but in contexts where the judgment of the church comes in for discussion, Matthew employs either no title whatever (cf. 13:47–50), or the idiom "my heavenly Father" (cf. 18:35), or, what is most frequent, he brings the term *kyrios* into play (cf. 7:21–22; 20:8, 15–16; 24:42, 45–51; 25:1–11, 14–30). Even if, as we believe, the term *kyrios* in these contexts is an allusion to the Son of Man, it strikes us that so accustomed is Matthew to associate the term Son of Man with those beyond the church that he avoids it with remarkable consistency when speaking of the judgment that the church, too, must undergo.

However the latter may be, our conclusion is that "Son of Man" in the first Gospel is the term with which Jesus encounters the world, first Israel and then the Gentiles, and particularly his opponents and unbelievers. Once we recognize this, it becomes obvious why it does not occur in Matthew's Gospel before 8:20: prior to this exchange with a scribe the occasion has not yet arisen for Jesus to engage in discussion with any of his opponents other than Satan. Hence, Matthew had no cause to use the term Son of Man.

Thus far we have scarcely broached the central question of this analysis: how does "Son of Man" in Matthew's Gospel relate to "Son of God"? In preparation for giving answer to this question, we must now consider the argument advanced recently by G. Vermes[76] and R. Leive-stad[77] to the effect that the historical Jesus is indeed to be understood as having employed the term "son of man" (*bar nasha; huios tou anthrō-pou*) but simply as a circumlocution for the personal pronoun ("I," "me") and not in any titular sense. The reason this argument is of concern to us is that Leivestad maintains that the Synoptists, too, use the term *ho huios tou anthrōpou* in the same manner as he contends the historical Jesus used *bar nasha.*[78]

It cannot be our purpose to ascertain what *bar nasha* may have meant to the historical Jesus. But as for Matthew, we believe that he does indeed construe the term *ho huios tou anthrōpou* as a christological title and not merely as a circumlocution for the personal pronoun. In order to set forth Matthew's position on this matter, we shall discuss particular Son-of-Man passages in the first Gospel which appear to be redactional rather than traditional in character.

The redactional Son-of-Man passages in the first Gospel number approximately ten. Of these ten, six are apocalyptic in nature (10:23; 13:41; 16:28; 19:28; 24:30; 25:31) and a seventh is related to them because it treats of the activity of Jesus Son of Man in the time following Easter and leading up to the parousia (13:37; cf. 13:41). A review of these passages shows first of all that they resist the easy substitution of the personal pronoun for the term *ho huios tou anthrōpou.* This is especially true, for example, of 13:37, 19:28, 24:30, and 25:31, where to make the substitution is to destroy the otherwise uniform imagery of the units in which these passages are embedded. But such resistance to easy substitution is an initial sign already that Matthew considers *ho huios tou anthrōpou* in the apocalyptic passages of the Gospel as more than the mere equivalent of a personal pronoun, viz., as a title.

Perhaps the outstanding feature of the redactional apocalyptic passages as far as we are concerned is that the figure called Son of Man takes on sharp profile in them: his coming and his activity are in fulfillment of OT prophecy (16:27; 24:30–31; 26:64);[79] he speaks (cf. 25:31,

76. *Jesus the Jew* (New York: Macmillan, 1974), 177–86.
77. "Exit the Apocalyptic Son of Man," *NTS* 18 (1971/72): 244–45, 254–55.
78. Ibid., 244–45, 255–60, 263–66.
79. According to J. J. Collins ("The Son of Man and the Saints of the Most High in the Book of Daniel," *JBL* 93 [1974]: 64), the Matthaean passages 13:41, 16:27, and 24:31 stand in a tradition that runs via the Similitudes of Enoch back to Daniel (cf. 7:13) and finds its focus in a heavenly being of angelic type (the archangel Michael in Daniel) called "son of man" who stands at the head of a host of angels. If Collins is correct in this, it would seem that Jewish tradition does prepare the way for the titular use of "son of man."

34–36, 40–43, 45); he performs definite functions (cf. 13:41; 16:27; 24:31; 25:32–46); he is ascribed a Kingdom (13:41; 16:28); and he refers to God as "my Father" (25:34; cf. 16:27) and to the righteous as "my brothers" (25:40). In short, what these observations reveal is that in these redactional passages *ho huios tou anthrōpou* is not a colorless or unemphasized term but assumes all the marks of a christological title that Matthew desires to apply to Jesus in his capacity as the one who will come again to judge the world and to rule.

Support for this conclusion comes from another quarter: Matthew subordinates three, and possibly four, other christological titles to *ho huois tou anthrōpou*. Exactly because Matthew's apocalyptic imagery is remarkably consistent and finds its center in the term Son of Man, one does not do justice to the intention of Matthew if one argues that in the first Gospel it is simply "Jesus" who will come again. Not simply Jesus, but Jesus as precisely *"ho huios tou anthrōpou"* is the figure in the first Gospel who will come again. Thus, the one in 7:22, 25:37, and 25:44 (cf. also 24:42) whom the judged at the Latter Day will address as *"kyrios"* is specifically the Son of Man, as is "the Coming One" in 23:39, whom the inhabitants of Jerusalem will at the last call "blessed." Similarly, it is, again, none other than the Son of Man who, "as the Shepherd," will, according to 25:32, separate the nations at the end of the age into two groups and gather the righteous as his flock. And in 25:34, 40, if, contrary to our opinion, *basileus* ("king") is held to be a christological title, then this title, too, is made subordinate to "Son of Man" in the scene of the Last Judgment. Now when we recall that it is only major titles such as "Messiah," "Son of David," and "Son of God" to which Matthew in his Gospel subordinates other titles, the fact that he proceeds in this manner also in the case of *ho huios tou anthrōpou* suggests that in his eyes the latter is on a par with these other major titles.

In the event that Matthew does in fact regard *ho huios tou anthrōpou* in a titular sense in the apocalyptic passages in which he has placed it, it is logical to assume that he would furthermore regard it as a title in the other passages of the Gospel in which it occurs. On this view, therefore, it would appear that Matthew applies this title Son of Man to Jesus along the following lines. As to its nature, "Son of Man" is the "public" title by which Jesus refers to himself as he interacts in Israel with the crowds and the leaders of the people (also Judas) or tells his disciples of what his enemies will do to him or what his death will mean for the world. From their standpoint, however, the people of Israel think of Jesus Son of Man simply as a man (cf. 9:8; 16:13): they hold him to be at best "John the Baptist" or "Elijah" or "Jeremiah" or "one of the prophets" (16:14). For their part, the leaders of Israel are hostile to this one who refers to himself as the Son of Man and enlist the support of Judas, of the crowds, and of the Gentiles to see to it that he is put to death (17:22–23; 20:18–19; 26:23–25). What is more, when God raises Jesus Son of Man from the dead, the leaders of Israel spread false rumors about his empty tomb (cf. 12:40 to 28:11–15). In the aftermath of Easter, Jesus Son of Man stands before the inhabited world as a king before his kingdom (13:37–38a). Indeed, he raises up in the world sons of the Kingdom (13:38), which means in Matthew's perspective that, among other things (cf. 25:37–40), people are made disciples of Jesus and take their place in the community that confesses him to be the Son of God (14:33; 16:15–17; 28:18–20). Finally, at the end of the age Jesus Son of Man can be expected to come suddenly with his angels on the clouds of heaven in power and great glory, so that he who was rejected by both Israelite and Gentile will at the last be seen by both Israel and the nations to be the Judge of all.

Should this be Matthew's portrait of Jesus as the Son of Man, in what way does he relate the title Son of Man to the title Son of God? We have already noted the similarity in "content" between the two. Formally, the difference between the two is, again, that whereas the title Son of Man is a "public" term, the title Son of God is a "confessional" term. Still, this is not the whole of it, for Matthew seems to indicate that although at one point the title Son of God coalesces with that of Son of Man, it otherwise "outranks" it.

The story of Peter's Confession (16:13–20) informs us in what way the title Son of God is superior to the title Son of Man. On the one hand, "men," to whom Jesus presents himself as the "Son of Man," hold him to be no more than John the Baptist or one of the great prophets come back to life (vss. 13–14). "Peter," on the other hand, as a disciple of Jesus to whom God reveals the deepest mystery of his person, holds him to be the "Son of the living God" (vss. 15–17). Consequently, Matthew shows in this story that the title Son of God supersedes the title Son of Man in the same way as enlightenment by divine revelation supersedes purely human powers of insight.

The point at which the titles Son of God and Son of Man coalesce in the first Gospel is the parousia and the appearance of Jesus Son of Man for judgment. Following the resurrection, it is said of Jesus Son of God that he possesses all authority in heaven and on earth and that, until the close of the age, he presides over and resides in his church (28:18, 20).[80] But if the church knows and confesses Jesus as the Son of God, from the perspective of humankind in general it can be said that he rules over the world as the Son of Man (13:37–38, 41). Then, at the end of time Jesus Son of Man will appear in heavenly splendor as King before all humankind in order to carry out the judgment that will issue in salvation or damnation for all. At the point of the parousia and the Last Judgment, therefore, the secret of the person of Jesus will be disclosed to every eye, and what the church has hitherto known by revelation of God the world, too, is given to perceive. In christological categories, what the latter signifies is that the titles Son of God and Son of Man have coalesced.

Is there further proof that Matthew is indeed thinking along these lines? At 16:27 and 25:34, we find the expression "his (my) Father" and in 25:40 the expression "my brothers." In the first Gospel, "Father-talk" and "brother-talk" are indicative of Jesus as the Son of God. In these passages, however, the two expressions are predicated to Jesus Son of Man as the King who comes for judgment. What they demonstrate, therefore, is that in these three passages the titles Son of God and Son of Man have, again, coalesced, under the sign of the latter.

We can now attempt a systematic presentation of our findings. To begin with, we have endeavored to establish that the title Son of Man in the first Gospel is above all "public" in character: it serves to describe Jesus in terms of his relationship to the world, Israel first and then the Gentiles, and especially as he interacts with the crowds and his opponents. Accordingly, Jesus, in his encounters in the course of his ministry with the people and the leaders of Israel, openly refers to himself as the Son of Man, and in his passion predictions he foretells what his enemies, in fulfillment of Scripture, will do to him who has so designated himself to them. Following Easter, Jesus Son of Man stands before the world as a king before his kingdom, and at the end of time he will confront all nations, Israel and the Gentiles, as their Judge, bestowing eternal life upon the righteous and consigning the accursed to eternal punishment.

The counterpart to the title Son of Man in the first Gospel is the title Son of God. For Matthew, this has an exclusively "confessional" character; that is to say, it conveys what for Matthew's church is the deepest mystery concerning the person of Jesus: his origin is in God and therefore it is in him that God dwells with his people. Unless it is in

80. Cf. Kingsbury, "Matt 28:16–20," 579–84.

blasphemy and thus ignorance of its true meaning, the only humans who can utter this title are the disciples of Jesus and the confessing Roman soldiers, by revelation of God. As the Son of God, Jesus presides over and resides in his church until the end of the age, at which time he will confront both church and world as, again, the Son of Man.

Consequently, "Son of Man" and "Son of God" prove themselves to be christological titles of paramount importance in the first Gospel. Because the one assumes a "public" and the other a "confessional" character, they complement each other. Moreover, their centrality to Matthew's christology is also evident from the fact that they describe Jesus, the one from the standpoint of the world and the other from the standpoint of the church, in ways in which Matthew's community thought of Jesus in its own day. At the same time, both titles relate to the person and ministry of the earthly Jesus, so that they underline the continuity and identification of person as regards Jesus, a matter for which Matthew displays no little concern. Nevertheless, even as knowledge by divine revelation supersedes purely human knowledge in Matthaean categories, so the title Son of God is superior to that of Son of Man throughout this age. But, in terms of what they signify, Matthew permits the titles to coalesce at that point in his concept of salvation-history, namely, the parousia, at which he can portray the eyes of the nations as perceiving with respect to Jesus what until then only the eyes of faith had ever been given by God to comprehend. At the parousia, then, it is precisely Jesus Son of Man whom both church and world will behold in all the majesty and splendor of God, but this side of the parousia the worship and work of the church are due Jesus Son of God.

### C.  SUMMARY

A casual reading of the first Gospel may give the impression that Matthew has inherited from the tradition a bewildering array of christological terms all of which seem to lie on virtually the same plane.[81] At first glance, it may appear to make little difference whether Jesus is designated as, for example, Messiah, Son of David, King, Son of God, or even Kyrios. Unfortunately, most commentaries on Matthew do little to disabuse the reader of this impression.

---

81. H. Frankemölle (*Jahwebund*, 169–70, 262, 377, 385, 398), for example, takes the position that the notion of "fulfillment" is the principle governing Matthew's christology so that Jesus, the exalted Lord who is identical with the earthly Jesus, is simply the "fulfiller" across the board of the whole range of OT predications that are applied to him.

Careful scrutiny of the christology of Matthew, however, shows that in reality he works with christological terms with plan and design. The key to an understanding of the whole is above all the first main part of the topical outline of the Gospel (1:1–4:16). This part, devoted to the person of Jesus, informs the reader that Matthew would present him preeminently as the Son of God. What this means in a nutshell Matthew explains in the formula quotation at 1:23: in the person of Jesus, his Son, God has drawn near to dwell with his people, thus inaugurating the eschatalogical age of salvation (cf. also 18:20; 28:20).

In the course of his Gospel, Matthew elaborates on this central thought. As for the person of Jesus Son of God, he is a royal figure in the line of David who nevertheless has his origin in God and is chosen by God to shepherd the eschatalogical people of God; to this end, God empowers him with his Spirit for messianic ministry and he, in turn, shows himself to be perfectly obedient to God (1:1–4:16). As for the ministry of Jesus Son of God, he proclaims to Israel the Gospel of the Kingdom, calls disciples to follow him, teaches and heals with divine authority and so reveals God to those whom he will, imparts the mystery of his person to his disciples and thus leads them to confess him, atones for sin and brings to an end the Jewish cult through death on the cross, is raised from the dead by God and entrusted with all authority in heaven and on earth, and will to the end of the age reside in the presence of his followers as they go forth to make disciples of all nations (4:17–28:20).

Once the reader is clear as to the Gospel's basic presentation of Jesus, he gains further insight into Matthew's christology from his concept of the history of salvation. An analysis of this concept reveals that the fundamental motif of the abiding presence of God with his people in the person of the earthly and exalted Son of God (1:23; 14:27, 33; 18:20; 28:20) serves to divide the history of salvation into two epochs: the "time of Israel (OT)" (= the time of prophecy) and the "time of Jesus" (= the time of fulfillment), which extends from birth to parousia but does not burst onto the scene of history until John the Baptist begins his ministry to Israel (3:1–2). The age in which Matthew lives, the so-called time of the church, is a subcategory of the overarching time of Jesus. In this age, Jesus is worshiped (cf., e.g., 14:33; 28:9, 17), confessed (14:33; 16:16–17; 27:54), and "followed" (cf., e.g., 4:18–22; 9:9; 10:38; 16:24; 19:27–29) as the Son of God by the church. At the same time, the church sees Jesus as standing before the world as the Son of Man: he who once openly designated himself in Israel as the Son of Man (cf., e.g., 16:13), and whom Israelite and Gentile crucified (cf., e.g., 17:22–23; 20:17–19), presently raises up sons of the Kingdom in the world (13:37–38) and will return at the consummation to judge the world (cf., e.g., 25:31–46). In the age of Matthew, therefore, the church knows Jesus most immediately by the "confessional" title Son of God and the "public" title Son of Man, but short of the parousia the former surpasses the latter (cf. 16: 13–20).

The remaining christological terms Matthew employs relate in some fashion to the title Son of God, though with qualification in particular cases. Terms that relate less directly or only partially to the title Son of God are "Jesus," "prophet," "rabbi–teacher," "*kyrios*," "the Coming One," and "Shepherd." Thus, the term "Jesus," meaning in essence "savior," defines in 1:21 the mission of Emmanuel, the Son of God (1:23), and in this verse it may be said to approach the status of a christological title; otherwise it functions in the Gospel as a personal name. For their part, the terms "prophet," "rabbi," and "teacher" do not even approach the rank of a true christological title in the first Gospel. "Prophet," applied to Jesus, connotes no personal commitment to him and is merely indicative of the way in which the unbelieving "crowds" or "men" think of him (16:14; 21:11, 46). And "rabbi" and "teacher," forms of address used, respectively, by Judas and the leaders of Israel and their cohorts, attribute to Jesus purely human respect.

By contrast, the terms "*kyrios*," "the Coming One," and "Shepherd" do attain in the first Gospel the status of auxiliary christological titles. "*Kyrios*," for instance, occurs (save for the "accursed" at the Last Judgment) on the lips of persons who address Jesus in faith, and therefore also has the character of a "confessional" title. While Matthew uses this term most often to attribute divine authority and an exalted station to Jesus as the Messiah, the Son of God (cf., e.g., 8:2, 6, 8, 21, 25; 14:28, 30), he also uses it to make the same attributions to Jesus as the Son of David (cf., e.g., 20:30–31) and the Son of Man (cf., e.g., 25:37, 44). In similar fashion, "the Coming One" points to Jesus as, respectively, the Messiah, Son of David, Son of God, or Son of Man, and "Shepherd" refers to him in his capacity as the Son of God or Son of Man.

These designations aside, Matthew utilizes a select number of christological terms to underline the salvation-historical significance of the Jesus whom his church confesses to be the Son of God. In the attempt to comprehend these titles, the hermeneutical implications of the circumstance that Matthew's church does, in point of fact, know Jesus most immediately as the Son of God become apparent. For if the latter is indeed the case, then the purpose of these christological terms necessarily becomes that of enhancing some aspect of Matthew's Son-of-God christology. Moreover, Matthew himself proves the truth of this observation, for he himself relates these terms to Son of God in such a way that through definition (e.g., "Emmanuel," cf. 1:23; "Messiah," cf. 16:16; 26:63), assimilation (e.g., "Servant," cf. 12:18 to 3:17 and 17:5; "King," cf. 27:11, 29, 37, 42 to 27:40, 43, 54), comparison (e.g., "Son of David," cf. 1:18–25; 22:41–46), or supersession (e.g., "Son of Abraham," cf. 1:1 and 8:11 with 28:16–20) they become subsumed under the title Son of God, the one christological category that in the first Gospel is both broader and "superior" to any other.

In line with this, we can observe how the following christological terms fall into place in the first Gospel. The term "Emmanuel," for example, describes Jesus Son of God as, again, the one in whose person God dwells with his people and inaugurates the eschatological age of salvation (cf. 1:23). The term "Messiah," although it, too, has become a personal name by the time of Matthew (cf. 1:1, 18; 16:21), nevertheless serves to describe Jesus Son of God as the Coming One foretold by the prophets and awaited by Israel whose appearance as the culmination of Israelite and Davidic history means salvation and damnation for people (cf., e.g., 1:1–17, 21; 3:11; 11:2–6). The term "Son of David" describes Jesus Son of God as the royal figure from the house of David who in the course of his earthly ministry healed certain "no-accounts" of Jewish society who approached him in faith, was not recognized by the crowds and their leaders, and who at the end entered Jerusalem, revealing himself to be the humble King (cf., e.g., 1:1, 6, 17, 18–25; 2:6 and 15; 9:27; 12:22–24; 21:1–11, 14). The term "King (of the Jews [Israel])" describes Jesus Son of God as the royal figure who was not, as his Jewish and Roman opponents made him out to be, a political throne-pretender, but the one who humbled himself to suffer and die on behalf of his people (cf., e.g., 2:2–3; 21:5; 27:11, 29, 37, 42). The term "Son of Abraham" describes Jesus Son of God as the ideal Israelite, the one in whom the history of Israel, begun in Abraham, reached its culmination and in whom the nations will find blessing (cf., e.g., 1:1; 8:11; 28:18–20). And the term "Servant" describes Jesus Son of God as the one who bore the burdens of his people in that he healed them, who was unobtrusive in public, and who likewise is the hope of the Gentiles (cf. 12:15–21).

In the preceding sketch of christological terms, there is a matter of importance which is largely implicit but which should be made explicit. From the vantage point of Matthew's church, some of these terms can be seen to be "current" in this community in that they apply to the exalted Jesus, and some to be associated primarily with the past in that they apply especially to the earthly Jesus. The terms "Jesus" and "Messiah," for example, live on in this community as proper nouns that combine to name the exalted Son of God. *"Kyrios"* is the term with which this community appeals in worship and prayer to the exalted Son of God and, at the parousia, will address the triumphal Son of Man. "Son of God," of course, is the term par excellence for the exalted One who presides over this community; it embraces the mystery of his person which comes to expression in the translation of the term "Emmanuel," is known by revelation of God only to the believer, and is at the heart of the community's Gospel of the Kingdom. And "Son of Man" is the term by which this community knows the exalted One to stand before the world as a king before his kingdom and to return at the Latter Day as the Judge of all the nations.

In contrast to these terms, such others as "Son of Abraham," "Son of David," "King (of the Jews [Israel])," "Servant," "Shepherd" (for the most part), "the Coming One" (for the most part), "prophet," "rabbi," and "teacher" can all be recognized to apply to the earthly Jesus. Their major purpose is to describe the exalted Son of God whom the community confesses in post-Easter times in terms of his background and appearance in Israel during the days of his public ministry. So understood, they have a value that is above all didactic and paraenetic in nature.

Matthew in his Gospel, then, poses for his church the central question as to who Jesus Messiah is. The reply is that *he is characteristically the Son of God,* a title that properly comprehends his person at every phase of his "life" from conception, birth, and infancy through exaltation to absolute dominion. Thus, he is eminently more than the prophet or teacher the Jewish public thought him to be. *Indeed, in him OT prophecy associated with the name "Emmanuel" and with Abraham, David, and the Servant of Isaiah has come to fulfillment.* "Then" during his ministry he wielded divine authority, and he likewise wields it "now," for which reason he is addressed as *kyrios.* Moreover, *at the parousia,* when the whole world will be enabled to see what the church presently knows by faith, this same Jesus, the one crucified by Israelite and Gentile but raised by God from the dead, *will be unveiled before all as the Son of Man, the Judge of all.*

Should this delineation of the christology of the first Gospel reflect the mind of Matthew, one task remains: to determine how Matthew relates Jesus the Son of God to the Kingdom of God, which he proclaims.

## Chapter IV

# Matthew's View of the Son of God and the Kingdom of Heaven

The single most comprehensive concept in the first Gospel is without doubt that of the Kingdom of Heaven.[1] It touches on every major facet of the Gospel, whether it be theological, christological, or ecclesiological in nature. If Son of God is the foremost christological category with which Matthew operates, we can be certain that he relates it in some basic way to his concept of the Kingdom. The purpose of this final chapter is to place the christology of Matthew within the context of his wider thought, and we propose to do this by probing his concept of the Kingdom of Heaven and the relationship he establishes between it and Jesus Messiah, the Son of God. At the same time, since the counterpart of the "confessional" title Son of God is the "public" title Son of Man, we must also take note of the role that Matthew ascribes in his concept of the Kingdom to Jesus as the Son of Man.

### A. THE GOSPEL OF THE KINGDOM

An investigation of the expression "the Gospel of the Kingdom" (*to euaggelion tēs basileias,* 4:23; 9:35; 24:14; cf. also 26:13) provides insight into the relationship that Matthew establishes between Jesus

---

1. Works which may be consulted with profit in any treatment of Matthew's concept of the Kingdom of Heaven are: G. Dalman, *Die Worte Jesu* (2d ed.; Leipzig: J. C. Hinrichs, 1930), 75–119; H. Windisch, "Die Sprüche vom Eingehen in das Reich Gottes," *ZNW* 27 (1928): 163–92; G. Strecker, *Der Weg der Gerechtigkeit* (FRLANT 82; Göttingen: Vandenhoeck & Ruprecht, 1962), 166–72; W. Trilling, *Das wahre Israel* (StANT X; 3d ed.; München: Kösel, 1964), 143–51; A. Kretzer, *Die Herrschaft der Himmel und die Söhne des Reiches* (SBM 10; Stuttgart: Katholisches Bibelwerk, 1971).

128

Messiah, the Son of God, and the Kingdom of Heaven. Still, the initial importance of this expression is that it constitutes Matthew's capsule-summary of his document.

In 4:23 and 9:35, passages in which he sums up the messianic activity of Jesus, Matthew speaks of him as "proclaiming the Gospel of the Kingdom." These words, in turn, recall 4:17, where Matthew presents a succinct summation of Jesus' gospel: "From that time on Jesus began to proclaim and say: 'Repent, for the Kingdom of Heaven is at hand.'" By the same token, these words are also suggestive of 10:7, where Matthew pictures Jesus, as an extension of his own activity, as commissioning his disciples, too, to go to Israel with the same announcement as he: "And as you go, proclaim and say: 'The Kingdom of Heaven is at hand.'" Now 4:17, a literarily well-rounded verse that can stand apart from its immediate context, functions in other respects, we will remember, as the "superscription" of the second main part of Matthew's Gospel (4:17–16:20). This part has to do with the public ministry of Jesus Messiah, the Son of God, to Israel. The point we wish to make, therefore, is that "the Gospel of the Kingdom," considered in the light of 4:17 and 10:7, serves as Matthew's summary-expression of the message with which Jesus and his disciples confront Israel in the course of his earthly ministry.

In the third main part of the Gospel (16:21–28:20), in Jesus' so-called Eschatological Discourse, the expression "the [this] Gospel of the Kingdom" appears again (24:14), and in 26:13 it occurs yet a fourth time, in abbreviated form ("this Gospel"). As regards Matthew's use of this expression in these verses, several matters call for comment.

The first matter is perhaps not germane to the larger argument we are pursuing, but is worthy of attention so that further reference in this chapter to the expression "the Gospel of the Kingdom" will not occasion confusion. Historically speaking, this expression in 24:14 and 26:13 no longer denominates the message of the earthly Jesus as such, but that with which the post-Easter disciples of Jesus (i.e., the church) confront "the whole world." What this means, however, is that Matthew does what historical research forbids the present-day exegete to do: he makes no distinction at all between the pre-Easter proclamation of Jesus and the post-Easter proclamation of the church, but utilizes the same expression to designate both. Why is this the case? Because Matthew's overwhelming concern in the application of this expression is to stress the element of continuity that he believes exists between the preaching of the earthly Jesus and that of his church. And that this is indeed Matthew's concern is apparent from the circumstance that the exalted Son of God, in his commission to the eleven to make disciples of all the nations, is pictured as enjoining his followers to teach the nations to observe all that none other than the earthly Son of God has commanded them (28:20).

Accordingly, in Matthew's vocabulary the expression "the Gospel of the Kingdom" refers without distinction both to the message of the earthly Jesus and to that of his post-Easter church. Of significance is the fact that in neither 24:14 nor 26:13 does Matthew supply a definition of it in the context.[2] On the contrary, he simply assumes that the reader will know what it means. On what grounds is he able to do this? On the grounds that the reader has access to the substance of this expression in the document Matthew has written for his community. Hence, it becomes clear that although Matthew would not identify the expression "the [this] Gospel of the Kingdom" with a literary document (genre) per se,[3] nevertheless he does employ the contents of his document to explicate it.[4]

But to say this is to raise an additional question: How much of his document does Matthew regard as explication of the expression "the Gospel of the Kingdom"? W. Marxsen[5] claims that it is merely the great discourses of Jesus and E. Schweizer[6] that it is the "teaching" of Jesus. Matthew, on the other hand, seems to indicate otherwise. In 26:13, his text associates with the proclamation of "this Gospel" throughout the world mention of the woman's act of pouring ointment on the head of Jesus. In other words, in 26:13 we have evidence that in Matthew's community the term "gospel" embraces not merely traditions of logia of

2. J. Schniewind (*Das Evangelium nach Matthäus* [NTD 2; Göttingen: Vandenhoeck & Ruprecht, 1936], 258) and, following him, Strecker (*Weg*, 129) and P. Stuhlmacher (*Das paulinische Evangelium* [FRLANT 95; Göttingen: Vandenhoeck & Ruprecht, 1968], 242) argue that "this Gospel" in 26:13 refers to the passion of Jesus. Strictly speaking, however, this connection is not made in the text. Although mention of the woman's act of pouring ointment on the head of Jesus is associated with the proclamation of "this Gospel" throughout the world, the latter expression is as "absolute" and undefined here in 26:13 as is "the [this] Gospel of the Kingdom" in 4:23, 9:35, and 24:14 (cf. also 13:19).
3. Cf. also Stuhlmacher, *Evangelium*, 242.
4. Cf. also Schniewind, *Matthäus*, 241; F. Hahn, *Mission in the New Testament* (SBT 47; London: SCM, 1965), 121–22; W. Grundmann, *Das Evangelium nach Matthäus* (HKNT I; Berlin: Evangelische Verlagsanstalt, 1968), 504.
5. Cf. *Mark the Evangelist,* trans. R. Harrisville (Nashville: Abingdon, 1969), 124, 138–41.
6. Cf. "Observance of the Law and Charismatic Activity in Matthew," *NTS* 16 (1969/70): 217.

Jesus but traditions of narratives about him as well.[7] In the light of this, we have good reason to believe that in the mind of Matthew the expression "the [this] Gospel of the Kingdom" can properly be explicated only in terms of the subject matter of his entire document.[8]

In support of the preceding is the pericope on the Interpretation of the Parable of the Sower (13:18–23). Matthew has Jesus address this pericope to the disciples (cf. vs. 18 to vs. 10), the representatives of his church, in contrast to "them" (cf. vss. 10, 13, 24), the Israelite crowds,[9] and the conditions described are indicative of the age of Matthew.[10] Following the lead of Mark (cf. 4:13–20), Matthew five times brings the absolute term "the Word" (vss. 20–23), but at its first occurrence he edits it to read "the Word of the Kingdom" (vs. 19), a turn of phrase that represents at once an assimilation to, and a qualification of, the term "the Word."

What has prompted this editorial change? Matthew makes it because in his view "the Word of the Kingdom" is quite plainly a variant expression of "the Gospel of the Kingdom," which in this passage designates for him the proclamation of the church. Thus, in Matthew's time it is the hearing of precisely this proclamation which, if not understood, Satan will subvert (13:19), and which, if superficial, leaves the Christian vulnerable to apostasy when experiencing tribulation and persecution (13:21), and which, if held to be of secondary importance, will not result in works of love in the face of worldly cares and the seduction of wealth (13:22). And where would Matthew have us look to discover his understanding of this proclamation, or "Word of the Kingdom," which he nowhere defines? Obviously, to the document he has written, for it is, again, coterminous with the Word, or Gospel, of the Kingdom.

The Gospel of the Kingdom, then, is Matthew's own capsule-summary of his work. Consequently, it is all the more noteworthy that exactly this expression should reveal the manner in which he relates Jesus Messiah, the Son of God, to the Kingdom of Heaven. To get at this relationship, we will need to examine the constituent terms of this expression, "gospel" and "kingdom."

---

7. Cf. also Strecker, *Weg*, 129; Stuhlmacher, *Evangelium*, 241–42.
8. Cf. also Schniewind, *Matthäus*, 241; R. Walker, *Die Heilsgeschichte im ersten Evangelium* (FRLANT 91; Göttingen: Vandenhoeck & Ruprecht, 1967), 81 n. 24.
9. Cf. J. D. Kingsbury, *The Parables of Jesus in Matthew 13* (London and Richmond, Va.: S.P.C.K. and John Knox, 1969), 47.
10. Cf. ibid., 52–63.

*The Term "Gospel"*

The stem of the Greek term for "gospel" is *euaggel-*, and it appears that the conceptual roots of the words used in the NT which derive from this stem (e.g., *euaggelion* ["gospel"] and *euaggelizomai* ["to proclaim," "to announce news"]) lie in the OT and in Aramaic-speaking Judaism.[11] Theologically, of great importance in the development of the concept of gospel is the prophecy of Deutero- and Trito-Isaiah.[12] This gave rise in Judaism to the intense hope that the tidings the "glad-messenger" (*mᵉbaśśēr;* LXX: *euaggelizomenos*) would one day bring to the people of God would be those of "peace" and "salvation" and that "God has become king" in Zion (Isa 52:7; cf. 61:1–3).

Whether or not the earthly Jesus ever employed terms denoting either "gospel" or "to announce news" in connection with the proclamation of his message of the Kingdom is perhaps impossible to know.[13] What we do know, however, is that Matthew was heir to the documents Q and Mark. The document Q, it seems, emanated from a Jewish-Christian community that arose in the first years following the resurrection and maintained itself in a Palestinian milieu.[14] In this community, the verb "to announce news" (*euaggelizomai;* cf. 11:5 // Luke 7:22) most likely referred to a preaching of the coming in the immediate future, not just of the eschatological Kingdom,[15] but, as Norman Perrin argues, more particularly of Jesus as the Son of Man.[16]

---

11. Cf. Stuhlmacher, *Evangelium*, 122, 152–53, 177–78, 204–206.

12. Cf. G. Friedrich, *TDNT*, II, 708–709; Stuhlmacher, *Evangelium*, 117–22.

13. J. Wellhausen (*Einleitung in die drei ersten Evangelien* [Berlin: Georg Reimer, 1905], 109) believes that this is "improbable." Dalman (*Worte,* 84) likewise doubts that Jesus made use of either a noun meaning "gospel" or a verb meaning "to announce news." Friedrich (*TDNT*, II, 727–29) is more cautious and leaves the question open on both counts, although he seems to be more confident in deriving such a verb from Jesus. By contrast, W. G. Kümmel ("Die Eschatologie der Evangelien," *Heilsgeschehen und Geschichte* [Marburg: N. G. Elwert, 1965], 53–54) is convinced, on the basis of Matt 11:5, that Jesus did utilize the verb, and is even "relatively certain" that he designated his message as "gospel." Marxsen (*Mark*, 124–25, 146–47) does not speculate as to Jesus' utilization of the verb, but holds that Mark was the one who first introduced the noun into the synoptic tradition. Stuhlmacher (*Evangelium*, 243–44, 287) states simply that Jesus' possible use of terms corresponding to "gospel" or "to announce news" is something that can no longer be determined with any certainty.

14. Cf., e.g., H. E. Tödt, *The Son of Man in the Synoptic Tradition* (New Testament Library; London: SCM, 1965), 249, 273–74.

15. Cf. Stuhlmacher, *Evangelium*, 222–23, 243. Cf. also W. D. Davies, *The Setting of the Sermon on the Mount* (Cambridge: Clarendon, 1964), 385–86.

16. Norman Perrin pointed this out to me in a private conversation; he discusses the matter in his forthcoming book, soon to be published by Fortress Press under the title *Jesus and the Language of the Kingdom: Symbol and Metaphor in New Testament Interpretation.*

But Matthew also appropriated the document written by the Evangelist Mark. Here the term "gospel" (*euaggelion*) is indissolubly joined to the person of Jesus as the Messiah[17] with emphasis not only on the parousia but especially on his death and resurrection. Indeed, "gospel" in this writing is a definite and absolute term ("the gospel"; cf. 1:15; 8:35; 10:29; 13:10; 14:9), and denotes the proclamation of God's decisive act on behalf of humankind in Jesus Christ, above all in his death and resurrection (cf., e.g., 1:1, 14–15).

In Matthew's Gospel, the Q tradition, in which is found the verb *euaggelizomai* ("to announce [the immediate coming of Jesus Son of Man]"), and the Marcan tradition, which focuses on the noun *to euaggelion* ("the gospel [Jesus Christ]"), converge. Since Matthew employs the verb *euaggelizomai* only once (in the Q logion 11:5) but works redactionally with the noun *euaggelion* (cf. 4:23; 9:35; 24:14; 26:13), it is plain that the expression "the Gospel of the Kingdom" (*to euaggelion tēs basileias*) is what is especially reflective of his thinking. In substance, even though Matthew refrains from using *euaggelion* in an absolute manner and modifies it with a genitive ("of the Kingdom," 4:23; 9:35) or a demonstrative ("this," 26:13) or both (24:14), the expression "the [this] Gospel of the Kingdom" is nevertheless thoroughly christological in coloration. We see this not only from a passage such as 26:13, but also from the topical outline Matthew has fashioned for his document and from his concept of the history of salvation. With his topical outline, Matthew treats of the person, of the public proclamation, and of the death and resurrection of Jesus Messiah. And with his concept of the history of salvation he sets forth the significance of Jesus Messiah for Israel and for the nations. At the same time, Matthew's further definition of the person of Jesus Messiah is that he is preeminently the Son of God. Accordingly, from Matthew's perspective the term "gospel" in the expression "the Gospel of the Kingdom" is to be defined as the news about the Kingdom, which saves or condemns, that is revealed in and through Jesus Messiah, the Son of God, and is announced first to Israel and then to the nations.

## The Term "Kingdom"

How is the term "kingdom" to be understood? Linguistically, the absolute expression "the Kingdom" is merely an abbreviation of the fuller

17. Cf. Marxsen, *Mark*, 126–38.

expression "the Kingdom of Heaven."[18] Moreover, while statistics show that Matthew prefers the latter, there is no discernible difference in meaning between it and the similar expression "the Kingdom of God."[19] Since the genitive "(of) Heaven" (*tōn ouranōn*) is subjective in nuance and a metonym for "God,"[20] the purpose of the expression "the Kingdom of Heaven" is to assert the truth that "God rules (reigns)." Hence, "the Rule of God" or "the Reign of God" is a proper paraphrase of it.

Although "the Kingdom of Heaven" (Hebrew: *malkuth shamayim*) does not occur as a fixed phrase in the OT, conceptually its roots are embedded there.[21] The idea that "God rules," that he is "King," is one of Israel's elemental affirmations (cf., e.g., Exod 15:18; Deut 33:5; Pss 47:2; 93:1; 96:10; 103:19; 145:10). According to the OT, the Rule of God is "eternal" (Exod 15:18; Ps 145:13) and encompasses all creation (Pss 95:3–5; 103:19). As such, it is directed also toward humankind, toward Israel (Isa 33:22; 43:15; Jer 8:19) and toward the nations (2 Kgs 19:15; Pss 22:28; 96:10). The result is that it is not looked upon as being impersonal, static, or local in nature but as being personal, dynamic, and universal (Pss 18:1–48; 103:19; Zech 14:9). In addition, because God the King is righteous, salvation and punishment for Israel (Isa 25:6–9; 33:22) and for the nations (Ps 96:10; Isa 26:21; Jer 25:30–31; Zech 2:11) are held to accompany his Rule. And even though God exercises dominion in the present (Pss 47:2; 93:1; 96:10), "that [eschatological] day" can be seen as coming when he will openly and decisively visit his people as King and manifest his sovereignty to all (Isa 24:21–23; 33:22; 52:7; Jer 30:8–9; Mic 4:6–7; Zech 14:9).

Judaism, of course, appropriated the faith of Israel as regards the

---

18. Cf. also Trilling, *Israel*, 144.

19. Cf. also Str-B, I, 172; Dalman, *Worte*, 76; Strecker, *Weg*, 17, 166; Trilling, *Israel*, 143. By contrast, Kretzer (*Herrschaft der Himmel*, 21–31) avers that a material, and not merely a formal, distinction can be detected in the first Gospel between the terms "Kingdom of God" and "Kingdom of Heaven." But as we have argued in our review of his book (cf. J. D. Kingsbury, *Bib* 55 [1974]: 118), if the term Kingdom of Heaven denotes that God's Reign manifests itself as a reality that governs all that is, that comes from heaven to earth, and that effects the salvation of humankind, as Kretzer maintains, cannot the same also be said of the term "Kingdom of God"? Is not, therefore, the alleged material distinction between these terms more apparent than real?

20. Cf. Str-B, I, 172; Dalman, *Worte*, 75.

21. On the OT background of this term, cf. N. Perrin, *The Kingdom of God in the Teaching of Jesus* (New Testament Library; London: SCM, 1963), 160–64; idem, *Rediscovering the Teaching of Jesus* (New York: Harper & Row, 1967), 55–57; R. Schnackenburg, *God's Rule and Kingdom*, trans. J. Murray (New York: Herder and Herder, 1963), 11–40; G. E. Ladd, *The Presence of the Future* (Grand Rapids: Wm. B. Eerdmans, 1974), 45–75.

kingship of God. Still, it likewise developed its own characteristic thoughts on the matter. For one thing, it was in Judaism that the idiom *malkuth shamayim* achieved prominence, as an abstraction for the divine name.[22] In other respects, the approach Judaism took to the concept of the Kingdom of Heaven, or the Rule of God, gradually assumed the contours of what we might designate as salvation-history. Thus, it was said that humankind in the wicked days of Noah threw off the Rule of God.[23] Indeed, from that time until the coming of Abraham the sovereignty of God was restricted to heaven alone.[24] With Abraham, however, God again became King over the earth.[25] Still, not until Israel, at the Red Sea and at Sinai, confessed the name of the true God and placed itself under the law, thereby taking upon itself the "yoke of the Kingdom of Heaven," did God's Rule once more become firmly established on earth.[26] In line with this the Jew, who daily recites the *shema* (cf. Deut. 6:4–9), is continually reenacting his acceptance of the yoke of the Kingdom of Heaven.[27] In the present age, because Israel alone has the law through which God reveals himself and reigns in the hearts of those who do his will, the Rule of God is fully acknowledged only in Israel.[28] But at the consummation of this age God will suddenly cause his Rule to "appear," that is to say, he will set Israel free from foreign domination and establish his dominion in splendor over the world in the sight of all the nations.[29]

Within Judaism, one can distinguish the movement known as apocalyptic,[30] regardless of how limited or how broad its influence is conceived to have been. In apocalyptic circles, there was a strong sense of the radical transcendance of God.[31] God appeared, among other things, to be remote from the present age and from his people.[32] Because the voice

---

22. Cf. Str-B, I, 172; K. G. Kuhn, *TDNT*, I, 571.
23. Cf. Str-B, I, 172.
24. Cf. Str-B, I, 172; Dalman, *Worte*, 79.
25. Cf. Dalman, *Worte*, 79.
26. Cf. Str-B, I, 172; Dalman, *Worte*, 80.
27. Cf. Str-B, I, 173; Dalman, *Worte*, 80.
28. Cf. Str-B, I, 172–73, 178; Dalman, *Worte*, 80.
29. Cf. Str-B, I, 178–79; Dalman, *Worte*, 80–83.
30. On the Jewish apocalyptic understanding of the Kingdom of God, cf. Perrin, *Kingdom of God*, 164–70, 176–77; Schnackenburg, *God's Rule*, 63–75; Ladd, *Presence of Future*, 76–101.
31. Cf. W. A. Beardslee, "New Testament Apocalyptic in Recent Interpretation," *Int* 25 (1971): 424.
32. Cf. R. Bultmann, *Jesus and the Word*, trans. L. P. Smith and E. H. Lantero (New York: Charles Scribner's Sons, 1958), 137–39.

of prophecy had fallen silent in Israel (cf., e.g., 2 Bar 85:3; 1 Mac 4:46; 9:27; 14:41), the secrets of God concerning such matters as the composition of the universe, the heavenly world, or the course and consummation of history were to be ascertained either through an inspired exegesis of biblical texts as in Qumran or through revelations mediated by dreams, visions, or heavenly journeys conducted by angels.[33] Though not without sin, Israel was nonetheless held to be a righteous people that was inscrutably subjected to tribulation at the hands of evil nations which seemed to prosper.[34] Indeed, it was thought that the entire world had come under the control of Satan (Azazel, Mastema, Beliar, Belial), who was wreaking havoc in nature and afflicting the faithful with the diverse evils attendant to the so-called Messianic Woes.[35] But since time had already run its predetermined course, the Kingdom, or Rule, of God, which is intimately linked in 1 Enoch (chs. 37–71) and 4 Ezra (ch. 13), for example, with the transcendent figure of the Son of Man, was regarded as on the verge of bursting into history, bringing salvation to the righteous and punishment to the wicked and putting an end to the suffering of "this age" by inaugurating the paradisaical "age to come."[36]

Against this background, we recognize that if the term "gospel" (*euaggelion*) in the Matthaean expression "the Gospel of the Kingdom" finds its center in the person of Jesus Messiah, the Son of God, the term "kingdom" (*basileias*) finds its center in the person of God. As Matthew records it, Jesus' gospel in a sentence is, again, that "the Kingdom of Heaven is at hand (*ēggiken*)" (4:17). Concerning this gospel, the Greek word *eggizō* denotes a "coming near," an "approaching," that is spatial or temporal in character.[37] Since "the Kingdom of Heaven" can be paraphrased as "the Rule of God," what Matthew depicts Jesus as proclaiming in 4:17 is that the Rule of God has drawn near. But should this be the meaning Matthew associates with the term "kingdom" in the expression "the Gospel of the Kingdom," then Matthew's understanding of the entire expression may be delineated as follows: *"the Gospel of the Kingdom" is the news, which saves or condemns, that is revealed in and*

---

33. Cf. D. S. Russell, *The Method & Message of Jewish Apocalyptic* (The Old Testament Library; Philadelphia: Westminster, 1964), 73–82, 161–73, 180–87; H. Ringgren, "Apokalyptik," *RGG³*, I, 465–66.

34. Cf. Russell, *Apocalyptic,* 300–303; Ladd, *Presence of Future,* 94, 99–101.

35. Cf. Russell, *Apocalyptic,* 254–57, 266–76; Ringgren, "Apokalyptik," *RGG³*, I, 466.

36. Cf. Russell, *Apocalyptic,* 324–31; Ringgren, "Apokalyptik," *RGG³*, I, 466.

37. Cf. W. Bauer, W. F. Arndt, and F. W. Gingrich, *A Greek-English Lexicon of the New Testament* (Chicago: University of Chicago, 1957), 212.

*through Jesus Messiah, the Son of God, and is proclaimed to Israel and the nations alike to the effect that in him the Rule of God has drawn near to humankind.*

This attempt to delineate the content of the Matthaean expression "the Gospel of the Kingdom" gives further indication of the paramount importance in the Gospel of the passage 1:23 (cf. also 18:20; 28:20). In 1:23, Matthew writes in words from Isaiah of both "God" and the "son," namely, that the significance of the person of the son the virgin will bear is that in him God comes to be with his people. This statement, however, is substantially a paraphrase of the implied meaning of the expression the Gospel of the Kingdom. Consequently, we discover that, in essence, the point of the passage 1:23, which is Matthew's thumbnail definition of his Son-of-God christology, and of the expression the Gospel of the Kingdom, which is his foremost description of the document he writes, is the same. This, in turn, reveals how completely Matthew's central theological concept, the Kingdom of Heaven, apart from his doctrine of the parousia of Jesus as the Son of Man, has been penetrated by his central christological concept, Jesus Messiah, the Son of God. At the heart of Matthew's concept of the Kingdom of Heaven, therefore, stands Jesus Messiah, the Son of God, and Matthew's document represents the endeavor on his part to set forth the implications for his church of what it means to confess that in Jesus Messiah, his Son, God has drawn near to be with his people.

## B.  THE CONCEPT OF THE KINGDOM OF HEAVEN

We have argued that Matthew's summary-statement of his document and of the proclamation of Jesus and of his church is that in the person of Jesus Messiah, the Son of God, the Rule of God has drawn near to humankind. This statement, however, is global in nature, and so begs for explication. What we propose to do in this section, therefore, is to discuss the "salvation-historical," the "cosmic," and the "ethical" dimensions of Matthew's concept of the Kingdom of Heaven.[38]

38. One of the strengths of A. Kretzer's study (cf. *Herrschaft der Himmel,* esp. 261–64) is that he has shown that these three dimensions are indeed integral to Matthew's concept of the Kingdom of Heaven. But while recognizing the wisdom of operating with this general schema, we have developed it in a manner that is quite different from what Kretzer has done. The emphasis of his study is theological and ecclesiological in nature, whereas ours is christological.

*The Salvation-Historical Dimension of the Kingdom*

The salvation-historical dimension of Matthew's concept of the Kingdom of Heaven is decidedly temporal in orientation, but not exclusively so. In an effort not to accentuate the temporal element overmuch, W. Trilling contends that Matthew's statements concerning the Kingdom reveal that he works with the "static" category of "above and below" as well as with the "dynamic" category of "now and then."[39]

What is correct about Trilling's contention is that, as we shall discuss shortly, Matthew certainly does see "God in heaven" as in control of the universe and, in the present "time of Jesus," as at work in unparalleled fashion to bring "people on earth" into the gracious sphere of his eschatological Rule and have them respond with lives that reflect the "greater righteousness." Still, it is inappropriate to describe this "vertical order" as "static" and it is misleading to claim that the category of "above and below" is as prominent in Matthew's concept of the Kingdom of Heaven as is that of "now and then."

In Matthew's language, "the Kingdom of Heaven 'has drawn near (*ēggiken*)'" (3:2; 4:17; 10:7). Such "drawing near," we said, has both spatial and temporal connotations.[40] "Spatially," God in the person of his Son resides even now with those who live in the sphere of his eschatological Rule (1:23). In this sphere, disciples of Jesus, for example, seek first God's Kingdom and righteousness (6:33) and pray for his will to be done on earth as it is in heaven (6:10); and in this sphere the promise obtains that whatever is bound or loosed on earth shall be bound or loosed in heaven (16:19; 18:18). "Temporally," the drawing near of God's eschatological Rule means that the present is to be viewed in the light of the future and everything seen as moving toward the consummation of the age. Consequently, while we affirm the intention of Trilling to provide a balanced presentation of Matthew's understanding of the Kingdom, the evidence suggests that the exegete should not avail himself of the adjective "static"; it is best to discuss Trilling's category of "above and below" within the framework of the Matthaean dogma that in the person of the earthly and exalted Son of God, God has come to dwell with his own. In a sentence, then, Matthew's salvation-historical characterization of the Kingdom of Heaven is that of a transcendent, eschatological reality that confronts people already in the present but will be consummated only in the future.

39. Cf. Trilling, *Israel*, 146–51.
40. Cf. Bauer–Arndt–Gingrich, *Lexicon*, 212.

In view of decades of research on the subject, it may seem commonplace to describe the Kingdom of Heaven as being eschatological, but for Matthew this is nevertheless the crucial point. Moreover, to understand the word eschatological from the perspective of Matthew, we must invest it with overtones that are at once theological, christological, and temporal in nature.

The temporal aspect of the word eschatological as applied to the Kingdom of Heaven comes to the fore the first time Matthew speaks of the Kingdom, in his summation of the preaching of John the Baptist (3:2). This preaching is said to take place "in those days" (3:1). In Chapter I, we observed that the phrase "in those days" denotes the time that precedes the parousia and the Final Judgment (cf. 24:3, 19, 22, 29), the so-called last times. In addition to John's proclamation of the Kingdom, however, these "last times" also encompass, respectively, the proclamation of the Kingdom by Jesus (cf. 4:17, 23; 9:35) and by his pre-Easter (cf. 10:7) and post-Easter (cf. 24:14; 26:13) disciples, the latter concluding only with the consummation of the age (cf. 28:18–20). In Matthew's eyes, therefore, the Kingdom of Heaven is eschatological in a temporal sense because the open proclamation of it occurs "in those days," that is to say, in the "time of Jesus," or the "last times."

Still, this strictly temporal aspect of Matthew's understanding of the Kingdom as eschatological is of little consequence if isolated from the theological and christological aspects. The thrust of the proclamation of the Kingdom is, after all, that God has in fact drawn near to humankind in the person of Jesus Messiah, his Son. Accordingly, the truly important thing about the proclamation of the Kingdom is that it is of ultimate significance for Israel and for the nations. That Matthew portrays this proclamation as taking place in fulfillment of OT prophecy (cf., e.g., 11:5) is evidence that he believes God is presently at work in his Son in an unprecedented way to bring his eschatological Rule to people. In the proclamation of the Kingdom, Israel and the nations encounter God's Rule, a Rule that is tending toward its consummation. God's will is that the proclamation of his Kingdom be received with understanding, or faith, and that people enter the sphere of his sovereignty to their salvation; they can, however, reject the word and perish. Yet either way, the Kingdom still proves itself to be an eschatological reality: it is openly proclaimed in the "time of Jesus" (the "last times"), and such proclamation is of ultimate significance as regards the eternal destiny of humankind.

In defining the adjective eschatological as it pertains to the Kingdom of Heaven for Matthew, we have already gone some distance in elucidating the notion that the Kingdom of Heaven is a reality that can only be described in terms of both the present and the future. The verb *ēggiken* ("is at hand," "has drawn near"), which according to Matthew is indicative of the proclamation of John (cf. 3:2), of Jesus (cf. 4:17), and of the disciples (cf. 10:7) concerning the Kingdom, harbors within it just this tension between present and future. On the one hand, this verb connotes that the Kingdom is indeed near, so near that the authority (*exousia*) of God impinges upon the present and decisively qualifies it. By what means does this take place? As the passages 1:23, 11:27, 18:20, 21:23–27, and 28:20 reveal, this takes place, again, in the person of the earthly and exalted Son of God; through him God comes with his Rule and in his community of disciples this Rule is obediently acknowledged. On the other hand, the verb *ēggiken* connotes that the Kingdom has not yet arrived; God has not yet miraculously consummated his Rule in all power and outward splendor. When will this occur? As the apocalyptic Son-of-Man sayings stipulate, this will occur at the end of the age when Jesus Son of Man returns for judgment.

If the verb *ēggiken* at 3:2, 4:17, and 10:7 embodies a tension between the present and the future modes of the Kingdom, in numerous places in the Gospel the stress is more clearly on either the one pole or the other. Thus, Matthew in a wide variety of ways gives expression to his conviction that in the recent past God has been, and is presently, at work in his Son to visit people with his Rule. It is this conviction, for example, that prompts Matthew to utilize the eschatological phrase "in those days" and the schema of prophecy and fulfillment, especially as the latter is applied in the case of the formula quotations. It is likewise this conviction that motivates Matthew to attribute to Jesus divine authority, so that he delivers the Sermon on the Mount as the Son who stands above Moses (cf. chs. 5–7) and also dares to forgive sins (cf. 9:2, 5–6),[41] incurring thereby the charge of blasphemy (cf. 9:3).

Matthew furthermore points to the presence of the Kingdom in Jesus through his appropriation from the tradition of a number of eschatological images. Pertinent are the following: the Matthaean Jesus declares that "something greater" than either Jonah or Solomon is here (12:41–

---

41. On the forgiveness of sins as an eschatological act suggesting the nearness of the Kingdom, cf. Perrin, *Kingdom of God,* 75 n. 6; idem, *Rediscovering,* 90–102; W. Foerster, *TDNT,* VII, 991.

42); he warns that one should not attempt to place a "piece of unshrunk cloth" on an old garment (9:16) or to put "new wine" in old wineskins (9:17); he designates himself in quotation of the OT as the "Shepherd" (26:31) and describes his mission in terms of gathering the flock (cf. 15:24; also 2:6; 9:36; 10:6); he refers to himself also as the "bridegroom" (9:15) and to his time as one of joy and celebration as at a wedding (cf. 9:15; 11:19; 22:1–10); and he anticipates the eschatological banquet (cf. 8:11; 26:29) by granting table fellowship[42] to tax-collectors and sinners (cf. 9:10; 11:19).

In connection with the matter of eschatological imagery, one word for which Matthew shows great affinity is *makarios* ("blessed"). This word, which portrays the present in the light of the future[43] and hence attests to the tension between the two in Matthew's understanding of the Rule of God, nevertheless bears strong witness to the Kingdom as a present reality in that it expresses the unique religious joy that springs from those who share in the salvation God bestows upon all who live in the sphere of his sovereignty.[44] These people are "blessed," for they have not taken offense at Jesus Messiah (cf. 11:6) but have received in faith the revelation imparted by his Father to the effect that he is the Son of God (cf. 16:17). Because of this, they can be said to have eyes that see and ears that hear the many things the prophets and righteous ones desired to see and hear but were not priviliged to do so (13:16–17). In point of fact, these people are like faithful slaves who do the will of their lord (24:45–47), who reflect in their lives the eschatological reversal of values (cf. 5:3–9),[45] and who rejoice in the face of persecution, knowing that their reward lies with God and that, in enduring affliction, they are following in the footsteps of the OT prophets (cf. 5:10–12).

Last, there are yet three passages in the first Gospel which, owing to the intensity with which they depict the Kingdom as a present reality, merit special attention. The one passage we have in mind is 12:28. In substance, it underlines an important truth we have not yet mentioned, namely, that the Rule of God effects the destruction of the rule of Satan. Of equal interest, however, is the circumstance that Matthew does not hesitate in this verse to make the Kingdom the subject of a verb in the aorist tense: "The Kingdom of God has come (*ephthasen*) upon you."

42. On the granting of table fellowship as indicative of the nearness of the Kingdom, cf. Perrin, *Rediscovering*, 102–108.
43. Cf. F. Hauck, *TDNT*, IV, 369.
44. Cf. ibid., 367–68.
45. Cf. ibid., 368–69.

In the whole of the Gospel, this passage represents one of Matthew's most direct overtures to "realized" eschatology.[46]

The second passage is 21:43. Here "the Kingdom of God" functions as the subject of a double predicate. As a logion of the earthly Jesus, the two verbs have been cast in the future tense, but the thing to note is that from Matthew's vantage point in history they refer to an event of the immediate past.[47] At any rate, this logion ascribes to the Kingdom such a degree of reality in the present that it can "be taken away" (*arthēsetai*) by God from Israel and "be given" (*dothēsetai*) to another nation that will produce its fruits.

The third passage is 11:12. As before, the Kingdom is the subject of the sentence, but this time the verb is in the present tense (*biazetai*). Exegetically, 11:12 is a *crux interpretum*, but the following translation captures its meaning: "From the days of John the Baptist until now the Kingdom of Heaven has suffered violence, and violent ones plunder it."[48] Who, specifically, are these "violent ones"? As we suggest in a footnote,[49] from Matthew's perspective they are the devil and all the false Christians, Israelites, and Gentiles who are his "sons" ("the sons of the Evil One"), those who resist the Rule of God and "plunder" it in that through various means they lead "sons of the Kingdom" astray and bring them to fall (cf., e.g., 7:15–23; 12:45d; 13:19–21, 38–39, 49; 23:13; 24:9–11; 25:41–46).

46. Cf. Strecker, *Weg*, 168–69.

47. Cf. Strecker, *Weg*, 169; Trilling, *Israel*, 62.

48. Our understanding of 11:12 is the following (for a clear statement of the exegetical options, cf. R. H. Hiers, *The Kingdom of God in the Synoptic Tradition* [University of Florida Humanities Monograph 33; Gainesville: University of Florida, 1970], 37–41). Parallels from Greek literature, few though they are (cf. Bauer–Arndt–Gingrich, *Lexicon*, 140), suggest that *biastai*, a *hapax legomenon*, must be construed in a bad sense ("violent ones"), and G. Schrenk (*TDNT*, I, 610–11) makes a sound case for taking the related verb *biazetai* both in a bad sense and as passive in voice ("is treated violently," "suffers violence"). As for the verb *harpazousin*, it basically means "seize" or "snatch" (cf. Bauer–Arndt–Gingrich, *Lexicon*, 108), and Matthew employs it in two other passages in the sense of "steal," "rob," or "plunder" (cf. 12:29; 13:19).

The question is, who are the "violent ones" at the hands of whom the Kingdom suffers and is plundered? Now in 13:19, Matthew speaks of the "Evil One," or the devil, as "stealing," or "robbing" (*harpazei*), the Word of the Kingdom from the heart of one who has not heard it with understanding, and in 13:38–39 he speaks of the devil as the Enemy of the Son of Man who raises up in the world "sons of the Evil One." In line with these passages, the violent ones who plunder the Kingdom would be the devil and his "sons," that is to say, all those who live in such a way that they do his bidding. Cases in point are false Christians (cf., e.g., 7:15–23; 24:11), "this generation" (contemporary Israel; cf., e.g., 11:16; 12:41–42, 45; 23:36), especially the leaders of the people (cf. 12:39; 16:4), and Gentiles (cf. 24:9). These "violent ones" plunder the Kingdom by leading "sons of the Kingdom" astray and causing them to lose their faith (cf. 7:15–23; 13:19–21, 49; 18:6–7; 24:9–11).

49. Cf. n. 48.

Be that as it may, what is noteworthy about 11:12 is the circumstance that it describes the Kingdom as a sphere that is present among men in such measure that it can be said to be vulnerable to attack from the side of its enemies.

If Matthew emphasizes the fact that God is presently at work in his Son to bring his eschatological Kingdom to people, he sketches with even greater vividness the future consummation of the Kingdom. In this regard, the primary figure, as we saw in the last chapter, is no longer Jesus Son of God but Jesus Son of Man.

In our study of the titles of Jesus, we noted that Matthew's use of the terms Son of God and Son of Man is controlled by one principle in particular: whereas the disciples of Jesus confess him to be the Son of God, "men" know him as the Son of Man (cf. 16:13 with 16:16; 14:33). In line with this principle, Matthew pictures Jesus following Easter as, on the one hand, residing in the midst of his disciples as the Son of God (cf. 28:20; also 18:20) but, on the other, as standing before the world as the Son of Man (cf. 13:37–38a). Now in terms of "Kingdom-talk," Matthew quite easily extends this latter thought to the point where he depicts the world in post-Easter times as "the Kingdom of the Son of Man" (13:41), that is to say, as the realm over which the Son of Man rules.[50] Then, too, what the Son of Man does, says Matthew, is to raise up in the world "sons of the Kingdom" (13:38), people who in Matthew's scheme of things are led by the worldwide missionary effort of the church to become disciples of Jesus and so to join the ranks of those who confess him to be the Son of God (16:16–17; 24:14; 26:13; 28:18–20). At the same time, Matthew's notion of the Kingdom of the Son of Man seems to be grander yet: this Kingdom will not be limited to this age but will exist beyond the parousia (cf. 16:28).[51] In other words, the idea which the term Kingdom of the Son of Man appears to express for Matthew is that following Easter God reigns over the world in the person of Jesus Son of Man and, beyond the parousia, will continue to reign through his agency.

But having said this, we dare not fail to observe that the term Kingdom of the Son of Man is not without nuance in the first Gospel. It is a "public" term in the sense that it is oriented toward the world at large and

50. Cf. Kingsbury, *Matthew 13*, 96–98; A. Vögtle, "Das christologische und ekklesiologische Anliegen von Mt. 28, 18–20," *SE II* (TU 87; Berlin: Akademie, 1964), 287–91.
51. Cf. Kingsbury, *Matthew 13*, 98; Grundmann, *Matthäus*, 401.

treats of God's Rule in the person of Jesus as it impinges upon the universe. By contrast, when Matthew speaks of the Rule of God in the person of Jesus as it impinges upon the church this side of the parousia, he never makes reference to the Kingdom of the Son of Man but to the divine authority and the abiding presence with his disciples of Jesus Son of God. Of course at the parousia, when the eyes of the world will behold what until then only the eyes of faith can perceive, then, claims Matthew, the division between the church and the world concerning the mystery of the person of Jesus will cease to exist, and Jesus will openly exercise divine dominion in splendor as the Son of Man.

Keeping these distinctions in mind, we turn to Matthew's description of the future Kingdom. As he sees it, the event that inaugurates it will unfold in the following sequence: the forces of nature will suddenly fall into disarray, Jesus Son of Man will be seen coming on the clouds of heaven in power and great glory, all the nations will be gathered before him, he will separate them into two groups, and he will pronounce judgment on them, thus determining who will "inherit the Kingdom" that has been prepared from the foundation of the world and who will "go away into eternal punishment" (25:31–46; 13:40–43; 16:27; 24:29–31, 37–39, 44, 50).

In painting his portrait of the future Kingdom, Matthew is at pains to show that it is continuous with God's kingly activity in the present. The parables of the Tares, Mustard Seed, Leaven, and Net illustrate this well. Thus, although the major point of the parable of the Tares (13:24–30) is that darnel and wheat are to be allowed to grow side by side until the harvest (13:30a), it is nonetheless from the sowing of the seed by the farmer (the ministry of Jesus Son of God) that the harvest (the consummation of the age and the inauguration of the future Kingdom by Jesus Son of Man) finally results.[52] The twin parables of the Mustard Seed (13:31–32) and of the Leaven (13:33) put it this way: from something most insignificant, like a mustard seed or a little lump of leaven placed in dough (the ministry of Jesus), there issues something most magnificent, like the mustard "tree" or the great mass of fully leavened bread (the future Kingdom).[53] And the parable of the Net (13:47–50) advances this truth as follows: the gathering of the fish (the growth of the church in this age owing to its missionary proclamation of the Kingdom) is neces-

52. Cf. Kingsbury, *Matthew 13,* 63–76.
53. Cf. ibid., 76–88.

sarily followed by the separation of the fish (the church, too, will undergo judgment at the consummation).[54]

As far as Jesus himself and the righteous are concerned, the future Kingdom means, respectively, vindication and the perfect realization of hope. With respect to Jesus, the irony is that the Son of Man who suffers crucifixion at the hands of Jew and Gentile and is utterly rejected is the very one whom God has chosen to return at the consummation as the Judge and Ruler of all (cf., e.g., 17:22–23; 20:17–19; 13:41–43; 16:28; 25:31–46). To Jesus as well the logion applies: "For there is nothing hidden which shall not be revealed . . ." (10:26).

For the righteous, Matthew brings into play a wide variety of word-pictures in order to characterize the future Kingdom as the perfect realization of hope. Matthew depicts the future Kingdom, for example, as a realm the righteous will "enter" (5:20; 7:21; 18:3; 19:23–24; cf. also 23:13), "go into" (21:31), or "inherit" (25:34), and what these idioms signify is evident from parallel passages that tell of "entering life" (18:8–9; 19:17), "entering the joy of your Lord" (25:21, 23), or "inheriting eternal life" (19:29). Of course the contrary is equally true: one can "not enter" (5:20; 18:3; 23:13), be shut out (25:10), or be "thrown out" (8:12; 13:42, 50; 22:13; 25:30) and therefore excluded from the Latter-Day Kingdom. In addition, the bliss that the righteous will experience in the future Kingdom is described in figurative language that refers to Jesus as the eschatological "bridegroom" (25:6, 10), to the consummated Kingdom as a "wedding celebration" (25:10) or as a banquet (8:11; 26:29), and to the righteous as perfected ones who "shine as the sun" (13:43). And the reception of the "reward" that the future Kingdom connotes for the righteous comes to expression in all those sayings that dwell on the reversal of their condition: he who loses his life will find it (10:39); the last will be first (19:30; 20:16); he who humbles himself will be exalted (23:12); and the radical changes enumerated by the Beatitudes (cf. 5:3–10).

The overall purpose of this discussion has been to set forth the salvation-historical dimension of Matthew's concept of the Kingdom of Heaven. This dimension dominates the concept,[55] and one facet of it we have yet to cover more thoroughly is the crisis that the nearness of the Kingdom precipitates for persons, whether Israelite or Gentile. Still, what

54. Cf. ibid., 117–25.
55. Cf. Kretzer, *Herrschaft der Himmel*, 262.

we have learned is that Matthew regards the Kingdom of Heaven as an exclusively eschatological reality: it is openly proclaimed by John, Jesus, and the church in the "time of Jesus" (the "last times"), and such proclamation of the Kingdom is of ultimate significance for Israel and for the nations. In other respects, the Kingdom is a reality that is at once present and future: from the unprecedented activity of God in the person of Jesus in the present there will issue in the future the consummated Kingdom of Heaven. Christologically, the Kingdom draws near in the present in the person of Jesus Messiah, the Son of God, and those who accept the Gospel of the Kingdom join the community of his disciples and experience the Rule of God under his aegis. At the same time, these disciples also know that this same Jesus stands before the world as the Son of Man, that in post-Easter times he works through his ambassadors to lead people in the world to know and confess him as the Son of God, and that at the end of time he, as Judge and Ruler of all, will inaugurate the future, splendid Kingdom to the salvation of the righteous and the damnation of the wicked. Accordingly, the arrival of the future Kingdom means the "public" vindication of Jesus, the one crucified and rejected, and, for the righteous, the perfect realization of their hope.

### The Cosmic Dimension of the Kingdom

The cosmic dimension of Matthew's concept of the Kingdom of Heaven has to do with the oft-maligned notion of the "growth" of the Kingdom. On this score, however, it should go without saying that the old liberal idea that the Kingdom is a social, moral, or spiritual force that will gradually spread throughout the world as it captures the hearts of people is foreign to the mind of Matthew. Moreover, from one standpoint Matthew, too, would reject any suggestion that the Kingdom could be said to grow: he, like his Jewish contemporaries and Israelite predecessors, believes that God is, and always has been, the "Lord of heaven and earth" (11:25; cf. also 6:25–32; 10:29–30).

The thought that the Kingdom grows relates to Matthew's understanding of the course of the Kingdom in the world as a present reality that confronts people in the "time of Jesus." As Matthew sees it, God in heaven reigns indeed over all things, but he has determined in the last times to draw near to humankind in the person of Jesus Messiah, his Son. Still, the nearness of God in the person of his Son and, by extension, in the church's post-Easter proclamation of the Gospel of the Kingdom, is not something unambiguous. On the contrary, it is something that can be perceived only by means of divine revelation (13:11; 16:16–17). Nevertheless, as the church in post-Easter times proclaims the Gospel of the Kingdom to the nations (24:14; 26:13; 28:18–20), persons will in truth be led to acknowledge the Rule of God in Jesus, his Son, and, as they become disciples of Jesus, the Kingdom can in fact be described as growing. Finally, at the consummation of the age, God in the person of Jesus Son of Man will wondrously establish his Rule in glory over all the "tribes of the earth" (24:30). Accordingly, the course of the Kingdom in the world during the "time of Jesus" is that from the "small beginnings" of Jesus Messiah, the Son of God, and his initial disciples (cf. 4:17; 10:7), the Kingdom, through the agency of the post-Easter church (13:47; 28:18–20), "grows" as the gospel is proclaimed to the nations, and, at the last, when Jesus Son of Man shall burst into history, this Kingdom will visibly be established over all.

Several parabolic units in the Gospel document this view of the growth of the Kingdom particularly well. In the parable of the Mustard Seed (13:31–32), for instance, the "mustard seed," which was proverbial among the Jews as the most minute of quantities,[56] is depicted as "growing" until, miraculously, it becomes a "tree" in which the birds from heaven nest, an image which in the OT stands for a mighty empire (cf. Dan 4:10–12, 21; Ezek 31:6). In the parable of the Leaven (13:33), the image is that of the little lump of "yeast" causing the dough to swell until the "whole" mass has become fully leavened. In the parable of the Net (13:47–50), the "drag-net" is described as "gathering in" fish of every kind until that time comes when the good fish must be separated from the bad. In the Interpretation of the Parable of the Tares (13:36–43), the text identifies the "field" with the entire "world" (*kosmos*) over which the Son of Man at the consummation will suddenly be revealed as ruling. And in the so-called parable of the Last Judgment (25:31–46), the Son of Man is portrayed as seated on the throne of his glory with all the nations of the earth standing before him in acknowledgment of his universal Rule. As we stated above, from small, seemingly insignificant, beginnings Matthew pictures the Kingdom as, ultimately and miraculously, cosmic in scope.

## The Ethical Dimension of the Kingdom

By the ethical,[57] or personal, dimension of Matthew's concept of the

56. Cf. Str-B, I, 669.
57. The word "ethical," used in connection with the Kingdom of Heaven, is a tech-

Kingdom of Heaven is meant the new life that results from a person's encounter with the Reign of God. Of course the occasion for such encounter is, again, the presence of the Kingdom in Jesus Messiah, the earthly and exalted Son of God, and therefore in the proclamation by him and his church of "the Gospel of the Kingdom."

In a number of passages, Matthew makes it clear that encounter with Jesus or the Gospel of the Kingdom places a person in a crisis of decision (cf., e.g., 10:14, 18, 20, 27, 40; 11:14–15; 13:9, 43; 23:34; 24:14). In confrontation with the words and deeds of the earthly Jesus, a person faced the choice of "repenting" and "entering" the gracious sphere of the Kingdom (cf. 4:17; 11:20; 21:31) or of rejecting Jesus as the Messiah (cf. chs. 11–12). In confrontation with the church's proclamation of the Gospel of the Kingdom, a person will either "understand" the word (cf. 13:23) or be "baptized" (cf. 28:19) and observe all that Jesus has commanded (cf. 13:23; 28:20), or he will "not understand" the word and hence fall under the power of Satan (cf. 13:19, 38c–39a). Whoever understands the Gospel of the Kingdom may be compared to a "good tree" which produces "good fruit" (7:16–20; 12:33) or to a "good man" who brings forth "good things" out of his "good treasure" (12:35), that is to say, this person, like Jesus Son of God himself (cf. 26:42), "does the will of the heavenly Father" (cf. 6:10; 7:21; 12:50). As such a one, he abounds in righteousness more than the scribes and Pharisees (5:20) and will, at the coming of Jesus Son of Man, be identified by him as one of the "righteous" (13:43, 49; 25:37, 46) who will "inherit eternal life" (25:46) and "shine [in perfection] as the sun in the Kingdom of their Father" (13:43).

On the other hand, those who have fallen under the power of Satan are "evil ones" (cf. 13:19, 38c–39), who may be compared to a "bad tree" which produces "bad fruit" (7:17–18; 12:33) or to an "evil man" who brings forth "evil things" from his "evil treasure" (12:35). At the Latter Day the Son of Man will designate these people as the "accursed" (25:41), and they will be cast into the "fiery furnace" (13:42; 25:41) or into the "outer darkness" (8:12) where they will experience "eternal punishment" (25:46), such as the "weeping and gnashing of teeth" (8:12; 13:42, 50). So again, encounter with the Kingdom means that a

---

nical term. Perrin (*Rediscovering*, 109) correctly observes that it easily lends itself to misunderstanding. What it denotes in the context of the first Gospel is, as we state in the body of the chapter, the response on the part of the individual to the nearness of God's Rule in Jesus Messiah, the earthly and exalted Son of God.

person must decide: will he enter the "narrow gate" and take the "hard way" that leads to "life," or will he enter the "wide gate" and take the "broad way" that leads to "destruction" (7:13–14)?

With this delineation of Matthew's understanding of the ethical, or personal, dimension of the Kingdom, we have treated in general Matthew's concept of the Kingdom of Heaven. Our concern now is to discuss the Kingdom as it relates, respectively, to the kingdom of Satan, to Israel and to the nations, and to the church.

## C. THE KINGDOM OF HEAVEN
## AND THE KINGDOM OF SATAN

Matthew's concept of the Kingdom of Heaven involves a pronounced dualism that pits Satan against Jesus both as Messiah, Son of God, and as Son of Man. The following is an attempt to sketch this.

Matthew's portrait of the arch-adversary of Jesus is that of a transcendent being who stands in unmitigated opposition to the Kingdom of Heaven (cf., e.g., 6:10, 13; 11:12; 12:24–29; 13:39). A striking feature is the plethora of names by which he is known. There is, for example, the term "satan" (*satanas*), which is a proper noun (cf. 4:10; 16:23) and the Greek transliteration of the Aramaic *satana*.[58] In meaning, the equivalent of this term is the common noun "devil" (*diabolos*), which is the Greek translation of the Hebrew *satan*.[59] In addition, Matthew also refers to Jesus' arch-adversary as "the Tempter" (*ho peirazōn*; 4:3), "Beelzebul" (*Beezeboul*; 12:24, 27), "the Evil One" (*ho ponēros*; 13:19), and "the Enemy" (*ho echthros*; 13:39).

Matthew describes Satan, in his opposition to the Kingdom, as one whose power is superseded only by God and Jesus themselves. Thus, Matthew attributes to Satan a kingdom (12:26), which indicates that he, too, is looked upon as one who rules in the universe. Moreover, under his control are such supernatural beings as "angels" (cf. 25:41) and "demons" (cf. 10:8; 12:24), or "unclean spirits" (cf. 10:1). Of course he also enjoys the fealty of humans (cf. 13:38c), and a major way in which he brings his power to bear upon them is through temptation: he endeavors to get them to act or to live "lawlessly" (cf. 7:23; 13:41; 23:28; 24:12), that is to say, in a manner which is contrary to the will of God (cf. 4:1–11; 6:13; 16:23; 27:40). For this reason he is called "the Tempter" (4:3) and "the Evil One" (cf. 6:13; 13:19).

58. Cf. W. Foerster, *TDNT*, VII, 158.
59. Cf. W. Foerster, *TDNT*, II, 79.

Since Matthew shows that the Kingdom of Heaven draws near to people in the person of Jesus Messiah, the Son of God, it is not surprising that in the first Gospel Jesus himself should be the primary target of Satan. Indeed, the first time Satan is directly mentioned is in connection with his desire to tempt Jesus to disobedience and hence to the forfeiture of his divine sonship (4:1–11). In this confrontation, however, Jesus proves himself to be superior to Satan (cf. 4:4, 7, 10–11). But although defeated by Jesus, Satan continues to wield power in the world. As a result, both the Kingdom of Heaven and the kingdom of Satan possess in the first Gospel the quality of "already . . . but not yet," though with opposite tendencies: on the one hand, Satan has already been overcome by the power of the Kingdom of Heaven at work in Jesus, but his capacity for evil has not yet been taken from him; on the other hand, the Kingdom of Heaven has already entered the world in Jesus the Son so as to challenge the rule of Satan, but it has not yet been established in splendor to Satan's destruction and the total elimination of evil.

The clash between Satan and Jesus Son of God in the first Gospel is an ongoing one. Satan is characterized as "the strong man" and Jesus Son of God, in that he casts out demons by the Holy Spirit and brings people into the sphere of God's Reign, as the one who "binds" him and "plunders his goods" (12:28–29; cf. also 8:29). Conversely, Satan and those who do his bidding are depicted as doing violence to the Kingdom of Heaven and as "plundering" it (11:12).[60] A case in point is Satan's enlistment of Peter in an effort to put Jesus at cross-purposes with his Father and to turn him away from the path that leads to the cross (16:21–23). It is precisely to fend off such onslaughts of Satan as this that Jesus teaches his disciples to pray (6:13): "And lead us not into temptation, but deliver us from the Evil One" (or: "from evil"). On another level, Satan also exercises his malevolent will against Jesus through the Israelite crowds (cf. 11:16; 12:39, 45; 16:4) and their leaders (cf. 16:1; 19:3; 22:18, 35; 23:15), who ask Jesus for a sign or who tempt him, not the least while he is hanging on the cross (27:39–43). Indeed, through a parable of Jesus Matthew makes the programmatic observation that Satan is the personal "Enemy" of Jesus Messiah, who has usurped in Israel the allegiance that is due Jesus alone (13:24–30).[61] Nevertheless, as the story of the Temptation at the beginning of the Gospel adumbrates, the repeated attacks of Satan are not sufficient to induce Jesus

60. Cf. n. 48.
61. Cf. Kingsbury, *Matthew 13,* 63–76.

to divest himself of his divine sonship and to bring him from his mission (cf. 16:21).

It follows that, as the arch-adversary of Jesus Messiah, the Son of God, Satan should also be portrayed in the first Gospel as endeavoring in post-Easter times to destroy his church. Externally, he attempts this, for example, through the persecution and affliction of the church by Jews and Gentiles (cf. 13:39a and 5:44 to 5:10–12; 10:23; 24:9). Still, he is active inside the church as well. Thus, Satan subverts the influence of the Word of the Kingdom upon persons who join the church but are without "understanding," or true faith, and so brings them under his sway.[62] But in Matthew's eyes, the mark of those who serve Satan is above all contrariety to the will of God, or "lawlessness" (*anomia*; cf. 13:38c–39a, 41; 7:21–23; 24:12). This, in turn, comes to expression in any number of ways, such as in false speech (cf. 5:37), in a failure to be loving (cf. 20:15)[63] or to be single-mindedly devoted to God (cf. 6:23),[64] in luke-warmness toward the demands of discipleship (cf. 25:26),[65] in an unwillingness to forgive a fellow-disciple (cf. 18:32, 35), and in sins of every kind against the second table of the law (cf. 15:19).

There is one circle within the church, however, to which Matthew calls special attention in warning his community against lawlessness, the so-called false prophets (cf. 7:15–23; 24:11, 24). The false prophets appear to be enthusiasts (cf. 7:23; 24:24), but the thing to note is that Matthew compares them to "rapacious wolves" (7:15) whose deeds are evil, or "lawless" (cf. 7:16–20, 23), and who lead many astray (24:11, 24). At the last, they will be denied entrance to the consummated Kingdom of Heaven (7:21, 23).

So far we have concentrated on Satan as the arch-adversary of Jesus Messiah, the Son of God, and of his church. If, on the other hand, we shift our gaze to the "world," we encounter Satan as the transcendent antagonist of Jesus in his capacity as the Son of Man. Whereas Jesus Son of Man is said to be active in the world to raise up "sons of the Kingdom," Satan is active in the world to raise up "sons of the Evil One" (13:37–39). As before, the mark of Satan's followers is "lawlessness" (13:41), and at the consummation of the age they will be cast into the

---

62. Cf. ibid., 54–57.
63. Cf. G. Baumbach, *Das Verständnis des Bösen in den synoptischen Evangelien* (Theologische Arbeiten XIX; Berlin: Evangelische Verlagsanstalt, 1963), 79–80.
64. Cf. ibid., 77–79.
65. Cf. Kingsbury, *Matthew 13*, 122.

"fiery furnace" (13:40, 42). This thought, in turn, leads us to the final point Matthew makes concerning Satan: his capacity for evil is restricted to the present age, and at the Last Judgment the Son of Man will consign him, his angels, and his "sons" to "eternal punishment" (25:41, 46).

In sum, therefore, Matthew's Gospel evinces a remarkable degree of dualism in its description of the Kingdom of Heaven and of the kingdom of Satan. The antagonists, Jesus and Satan, are locked in mortal combat, and the power of each is cosmic in scope, extending both to supernatural beings and to the world of humankind. At the same time, Jesus in his messianic ministry has in effect already defeated Satan. Even though Satan can wreak havoc on the church, bringing disciples to fall, and raise up in the world those who will do his bidding, he cannot, finally, prevail. In the present time the power of the Kingdom, which the exalted Son of God already wields, serves to strengthen the disciples in their struggle with Satan, and at the last, when the Kingdom of Heaven will be consummated in splendor, the Son of Man will judge Satan and cast him and all who are his into the eternal fire.

One further matter calls for comment. In treating Matthew's satanology, we discover that it coincides perfectly with the pattern of his christology. In the context, for example, of Jesus' earthly ministry and of Israel and of the church, Matthew pictures Satan as the antagonist of Jesus Messiah, the earthly and exalted Son of God. But in the context of the world and of the parousia, he pictures Satan as the antagonist of Jesus Son of Man.

## D.  THE KINGDOM OF HEAVEN
### AND ISRAEL AND THE NATIONS

We have just seen that Matthew views the nearness of the Kingdom of Heaven as a mortal threat to the rule of Satan. Furthermore, since he likewise holds that Satan is at work in both Israel and the world to effect his malevolent purposes, it becomes obvious that Matthew's position is that the Kingdom of Heaven must establish itself on earth in the face of concerted opposition from Jews and Gentiles alike.

We recall that Matthew is eminently concerned to demonstrate that Jesus Messiah, the Son of God, in whom the Kingdom of Heaven draws near to humankind, is sent first of all to Israel (cf., e.g., 2:6, 15; 10:6; 15:24). Through his ministry in Galilee of teaching, preaching, and healing (4:17; 4:23–25; 9:35; 11:1–6), Jesus confronts the crowds with the Kingdom. Their response, however, is one of rejection. They do not percieve who he is (cf. 13:13), and their leaders tempt him (16:1; 19:3; 22:18, 35), demand from him a sign (12:38; 16:1), accuse him of blasphemy (9:3; cf. also 26:65) and of breaking the law (12:10; cf. also 12:2; 15:2), and charge him with carrying out his ministry on the authority of the prince of demons (9:34; 12:24). Hence, the whole of Israel proves itself to be "an evil and adulterous generation" (cf. 12:39–45; 16:4; also 11:16; 17:17; 23:36) which refuses to repent and receive the Kingdom of Heaven (cf. 4:17 and 10:7 to 11:20 and 12:41).

The finality with which Israel rejects its Messiah and therefore the Kingdom of Heaven comes to light in the passion narrative. The animosity of the leaders of the people against Jesus is such that they plot his death and see to it that it takes place (cf. 12:14; 16:21; 21:45–46; chs. 26–27). To this end, they secure the aid of Judas (cf. 26:20–25, 47–50; 27:3–4), of the crowds (cf. 26:47; 27:20–23), and of the Gentile authorities (cf. 27:1–2, 11–38). In the presence of Pilate and at the foot of the cross, however, the crowds join their leaders in total condemnation of Jesus (cf. 27:15–26),[66] and together these two groups function, ironically, as the acknowledged representatives of that people God had once chosen to be his own (cf. *laos*, 27:25, 39–44).[67] Finally, in regard to the Easter-event, although the truth of the matter is that God has raised Jesus from the dead, the Jews perpetuate the slanderous rumor that his disciples came by night and made off with his body (28:11–15).

Accordingly, Matthew depicts Jesus Messiah, the Son of God, as bringing the Kingdom to his people Israel in his person and ministry and as being rejected by them. In addition, in looking back upon the years since Easter, Matthew can boast of no change in Israel's attitude toward Jesus. Indeed, in these years his church has been forced to separate itself from the Jewish community.[68] Two indications of this in the Gospel are the circumstances that Matthew describes the synagogues Jesus visits as "their synagogues" (cf. 4:23; 9:35; 10:17; 12:9; 13:54; also 23:34)[69] and treats the leaders of the people, whether "chief priests and elders" or "scribes and Pharisees" or "Pharisees and Sadducees," as though they had

66. Cf. N. A. Dahl, "Die Passionsgeschichte bei Matthäus," *NTS* 2 (1955/56), 26.
67. Cf. Kingsbury, *Matthew 13*, 26.
68. Cf. also K. Stendahl, *The School of St. Matthew* (reprinted; Philadelphia: Fortress, 1968), xi.
69. Cf. G. D. Kilpatrick, *The Origins of the Gospel according to St. Matthew* (Oxford: Clarendon, 1946), 110–11.

always formed as monolithic a front as do the leaders of the Pharisaic Judaism his church must face.[70]

In charting the course of the recent past, therefore, Matthew shows that if Israel did not receive Jesus' proclamation of the Gospel of the Kingdom (4:23; 9:35), neither has it received the church's proclamation of the Gospel of the Kingdom (cf., e.g., ch. 10; 23:34). As can be seen from the example of its leaders, Israel steadfastly refuses to "enter . . . the Kingdom of Heaven" (cf. 23:13; 21:31). What is more, Israel has even responded to the missionary efforts of the church with persecution (cf. 5:10, 12, 44; 13:21).[71] Thus, disciples of Jesus, particularly "missionaries," are made to submit to such ill-treatment as verbal abuse (cf. 5:11), arraignment for disturbing the peace (cf. 10:17), perjured testimony in court (cf. 5:11),[72] flogging in the local synagogue (cf. 10:17; 23:34), stoning (cf. 21:35), pursuit from city to city (cf. 10:23; 23:34), and even death (cf. 10:28; 21:35; 23:34). In consideration of all this, Matthew employs parables of Jesus to depict Israel as, for example, unreceptive "soil" in which the seed of proclamation is unable to take root and bear fruit and so dies (cf. 13:3b–7),[73] or as "weeds" ("darnel") that are sown by the enemy of the farmer who sows good seed (cf. 13:24–30),[74] or as a "son" who does not repent of his duplicity toward his father and do his will (cf. 21:28–32), or as "farmers" who lease a vineyard but refuse to pay rent and not only beat, kill, and stone the owner's slaves but murder his son as well (cf. 21:33–41), or as "guests" who are invited by a king to a wedding celebration for his son but make light of the invitation and seize, abuse, and kill the slaves of the king (cf. 22:1–8).

As for the leadership of Israel, Matthew is vitriolic in his condemnation of it. The Matthaean Jesus denunciates the "scribes and Pharisees" as

---

70. Cf. Walker, *Heilsgeschichte,* 11–33.

71. On Matthew's treatment of the subject of persecution, cf. D. R. A. Hare, *The Theme of Jewish Persecution of Christians in the Gospel according to St Matthew* (NTSMS 6; Cambridge: Cambridge University, 1967). H. Frankemölle ("Die Makarismen [Mt 5, 1–12; Lk 6, 20–23]. Motiv und Umfang der redaktionellen Komposition," *BZ* 15 [1971]: 57) refers to the perfect tense of *dediōgmenoi* in Matt 5:10 and contends that the persecution of disciples by Jews is, at the time of Matthew, a thing of the past. On the contrary, Matthew's use of the perfect tense in 5:10 suggests the opposite: from his vantage point in history, disciples of Jesus "have been and are still being persecuted" by Jews.

72. Cf. E. Lohmeyer, *Das Evangelium des Matthäus,* ed. W. Schmauch (Meyer; Göttingen: Vandenhoeck & Ruprecht, 1956), 95.

73. Cf. Kingsbury, *Matthew 13,* 32–37.

74. Cf. ibid., 63–76.

"hypocrites"[75] (cf. ch. 23) and charges them with all of the following: not only do they refuse to "enter" the Kingdom themselves, but they also prevent others from "entering" it (cf. 23:13); they search out proselytes only to make of each one a "son of Gehenna" twice as much as themselves (cf. 23:15); they are blind guides who teach people to swear falsely (cf. 23:16–22); they concern themselves with trivia, neglecting the weightier matters of the law (cf. 23:23–24); outwardly they appear "clean" to people, but inwardly they are full of extortion (cf. 23:25–26); to others they seem righteous but in reality they are full of hypocrisy and lawlessness (cf. 23:27–28); while paying tribute to the prophets of old, they put to death and persecute those whom God sends to enlighten them (cf. 23:29–36); they esteem their own tradition of the elders more than the law of God (cf. 15:1–9); and they espouse an evil teaching[76] of which one must beware (cf. 16:6, 11–12).

Finally, Matthew also attempts to address the question as to how it could ever happen that Israel should become so blind and perverse? The one answer he gives we have already noted above: Israel has fallen under the rule of Satan. A second answer he gives is that God has ordained that Israel should not be made privy to the secrets of the Kingdom of Heaven, for which reason the people are "blind, deaf, and without understanding" (cf. 13:10–13; also 11:25). In the case of both of these answers, however, we should observe that there is no intention on the part of Matthew to excuse Israel for its rejection of Jesus and its persecution of the church. Quite the opposite, Matthew goes to great lengths to underline the guilt that devolves upon Israel for its failure to receive its Messiah: all Israel makes itself juridically responsible for the blood of Jesus (27:25);[77] the leaders of the people themselves announce the punishment and loss that the nation must endure for its treatment of the Son of God (21:37–41); and in words of Jesus Matthew declares that Israel is also culpable for its mistreatment of Christian missionaries (23:34–36).

What, then, has resulted from Israel's action? One result has been the destruction of Jerusalem (cf. 22:7). But this is only the physical mani-

---

75. For a proper understanding of this term, cf. S. van Tilborg, *The Jewish Leaders in Matthew* (Leiden: E. J. Brill, 1972), 8–26.
76. In 16:6, 11, the Matthaean Jesus refers to the "teaching" of the Pharisees and Sadducees as "leaven." According to Str-B (cf. I, 728–29) and Schniewind (cf. *Matthäus*, 187), this connotes that their teaching is "evil" (cf. also D. Hill, *The Gospel of Matthew* [New Century Bible; London: Oliphants, 1972], 257).
77. Cf. Dahl, "Passionsgeschichte," 26.

festation of a second result, viz., that God, as Matthew says in a logion of Jesus, has chosen to "take away" his Kingdom from Israel and to "give it" to a "nation which will produce the fruits of it" (21:43). This "nation," of course, is the "church" (cf. 16:18; 18:17), and the "Kingdom" is the Rule of God as a present reality (cf. 1:23; 18:20; 28:20). Consequently, owing to Israel's rejection of the proclamation of the Gospel of the Kingdom by Jesus Messiah, the Son of God, and by his ambassadors, God withdraws his Rule from Israel and Israel ceases to be his chosen people.

Yet a third result of Israel's action is that the proclamation of the Gospel of the Kingdom in the time of Matthew is no longer directed to Israel per se but to the nations (cf. 22:9; 23:37–39; 24:14; 26:13; 28:18–20). Still and all, Matthew is under no illusions as to the reception the nations will give the Gospel of the Kingdom and the church's missionaries. Already in his day he reports in words of Jesus that disciples bear witness to the Gentiles even as they are "dragged before governors and kings" (10:18), that the church is "hated by all the nations" because of its allegiance to Jesus (cf. 24:9; 10:22), that it suffers "tribulation" at the hands of Gentile opponents (cf. 13:21; 24:9, 21, 29), and that members of the church are "killed" (cf. 10:28; 24:9). In view of such happenings as these, it is little wonder that Matthew should see Satan at work in the world raising up "sons of the Evil One" (cf. 13:38–39) or that he should boldly state through the mouth of Jesus that the nations, too, will undergo judgment at the consummation of the age (cf. 13:41–43; 25:41–46), and this precisely in terms of the way in which they have treated those who belong to the church (cf. 25:40, 45).[78]

To recapitulate, Matthew describes the Kingdom of Heaven as confronting Israel in the person of Jesus Messiah, the Son of God, and, following his death and resurrection, in the church's proclamation of the Gospel of the Kingdom. Israel, however, has responded negatively both to Jesus and, since Easter, to his church's missionary efforts. The result is that God has withdrawn his Rule from Israel and now exercises it in Jesus, the exalted Son of God, in the "empirical" sphere of the church. Israel, on the other hand, stands condemned, and the Gospel of the Kingdom is henceforth proclaimed among the nations. At the same time, the nations, too, are hostile to the message of the church, and Matthew warns that at the Latter Day they will likewise have to answer to the Son of Man. But until that day, the task of the church is indeed to proclaim

78. Cf. L. Cope, "Matthew xxv 31–46—'The Sheep and the Goats' Reinterpreted," *NovT* 11 (1969): 37–41.

the Gospel of the Kingdom everywhere, and through this proclamation, in the face of opposition from Jew and Gentile, God in Jesus and in association with the church visits people with his gracious Rule.

### E.  THE KINGDOM OF HEAVEN AND THE CHURCH

Because God has withdrawn his Kingdom from Israel and given it to the church (21:43), "empirically" the church is the place where God in the person of his exalted Son chooses to dwell among people (1:23; 16:18; 18:20; 21:43; 28:20). But as adamant as Matthew is on this point, he is equally adamant in refusing to identify the church with the Kingdom of Heaven. In relating the one to the other, Matthew views them not in terms of identification but in terms of association.

Earlier in this chapter, we spoke in passing of the tension that exists between the present and the future modes of the Kingdom. As Matthew describes it, the church especially is conditioned by the dynamics of this tension. On the one hand, the church in the present does in fact live in the sphere of God's Rule as exercised by Jesus Messiah, the exalted Son of God (1:23; 16:18; 18:20; 28:20). Although God is the Father of Jesus in a way that cannot be predicated to any other human (1:18–25; 2:15; 3:17; 11:25–27; 17:5; 28:18–20), nevertheless, as his disciples the members of the church have become "related" to him (cf. 12:49–50; 28:10) and therefore are themselves "sons of God" (5:9, 45; 13:38) who not only know God as "Father" (cf., e.g., 5:45; passim) but have even been taught by Jesus to address him as such in prayer (6:9). In terms of Matthew's "Kingdom language," the church, as the eschatological people whom Jesus Son of God has saved from their sins (1:21; 26:28; 27:38–54), has in truth been "given the Kingdom" by God (21:43), for it is here that there are "sons of the Kingdom" (13:38b) who hear and understand the "Word of the Kingdom" (13:19, 23),[79] who have been "instructed about the Kingdom" (13:52)[80] and therefore know the "secrets of the Kingdom" (13:11),[81] who seek the "righteousness of the Kingdom" (6:33) and have been entrusted with the "keys of the Kingdom" (16:19), who pray fervently for the "coming of the Kingdom" (6:10) and produce the "fruits of the Kingdom" (13:8, 23; 21:43), and who at the consummation of the age will "enter the Kingdom" (cf. 25:21, 23) and "inherit" it (5:3, 10; 25:34).

79. Cf. Kingsbury, *Matthew 13*, 61–62.
80. Cf. ibid., 125–29.
81. Cf. ibid., 43–46.

On the other hand, despite what we have just said, the church in the first Gospel is by no means to be construed as a pure community of the holy. Instead, it is a *corpus mixtum*. One indication of this is the fact that while Matthew attributes to its members the status of being "the called" (cf. *klētoi*, 22:14), he noticeably reserves the status of being "the elect" (*eklektoi*, 22:14; 24:22, 24, 31) or "the righteous" (*dikaioi*, 13:43, 49; 25:37, 46) for those members only to whom the Son of Man will grant at the Latter Day "eternal life" (25:46). In the present age, the church is caught up in the throes of the so-called Messianic Woes (24:8). Not only does it suffer persecution at the hands of Jews (5:11–12; 10:17, 23; 13:21; 23:34) and tribulation at the hands of Gentiles (13:21; 24:9), but it is also afflicted by internal difficulties, such as the following: there are members who do "not understand" the Word of the Kingdom and consequently are without true faith (13:19),[82] or who are "false prophets" and lead other disciples astray (7:15–23; 24:11), or who surrender their faith because they cannot endure persecution or tribulation (13:21; 24:9–10),[83] or whose lives as disciples remain sterile because their faith succumbs to the cares of the world or to the seduction of wealth (13:22),[84] or who deny Jesus Son of God (10:33), or who despise others in the community (18:10)[85] or betray fellow-disciples to Gentile opponents (24:10) or cause other disciples to lose their faith (18:6).[86] There is hatred among members of the church (24:10), rampant "lawlessness" resulting in lovelessness (24:12; cf. 20:15), lukewarmness toward Christian duty (25:26), an unwillingness to forgive the neighbor (18:35), and other evil that threatens the spiritual welfare of the community (cf. 15:19).

In response to this situation in which he at once affirms the presence of God's Rule in his community but must catalog its many aberrations from the will of God, Matthew directs the attention of his church squarely to the consummation of the age (*synteleia tou aiōnos*) and the inauguration of the future Kingdom by Jesus Son of Man (cf. 10:23; 13:30, 39b–43, 49–50; 16:27–28; 19:28–29; 24:3, 27, 39, 42, 44; 25:31–46). Still, he does this in order that his community might see the present as decisively qualified by the future and recognize that the disciple pursues

82. Cf. ibid., 55–57.
83. Cf. ibid.
84. Cf. ibid., 61.
85. Cf. W. G. Thompson, *Matthew's Advice to a Divided Community* (AnBib 44; Rome: Biblical Institute, 1970), 153.
86. Cf. ibid., 103–107.

life only in the light of the approaching Kingdom. The God who will miraculously establish his Rule "then" is even "now" at work in his Son to motivate the disciple ethically to do his will. In treating sayings of the historical Jesus, James M. Robinson,[87] whose point has been reinforced by Norman Perrin,[88] has shown that the very structure of the logia of Jesus reflect this type of ethical-eschatological tension between present and future; subsequently, R. A. Edwards has termed this kind of phenomenon as observed in the form of selected Son-of-Man sayings "the eschatological correlative" (cf. 12:40; 24:27, 37, 38–39; 13:40–41).[89] Matthew, however, has incorporated most of the logia these authors cite into his Gospel[90] and has even added to their number (cf., e.g., 5:3–10, 19–20; 6:33; 7:21; 16:19). The result is that this ethical-eschatological tension between present and future becomes characteristic also of the relationship Matthew establishes between the church and the Kingdom of Heaven.

In application of this tension to the life of the church, Matthew both warns and exhorts his fellow-members. Negatively, he sternly reminds them that the possession of wealth poses the most serious kind of threat to the disciple who would "enter" the future Kingdom (19:23), that those who cause another disciple to lose his faith or who forfeit their own will be severely punished (18:6, 8–9), that the coming of Jesus Son of Man for judgment will catch unawares those who are not prepared for it (24:36–39, 40–42, 43–44, 50–51; 25:11–13, 24–30), that those who do not do the will of God in the present can be certain that their appeals to the Son of Man at the Latter Day will avail them nothing (7:15–23), and that in this present age they dare never forget that the church, too, will most assuredly undergo judgment at the consummation (13:47–50;[91] 24:45–51; 25:1–13, 14–30).

Positively, Matthew exhorts the members of his community to all of the following: to see their lives in the present as being shaped by God's future promises (5:3–10); to be diligent in offering their (eschatological) petitions to God, especially the prayer that Jesus taught them (6:9–13); to practice a piety that is pleasing to God against that day when he will bestow upon them his eschatological "reward" (cf. 5:12; 6:4, 6, 18;

87. *Kerygma und historischer Jesus* (Zürich: Zwingli, 1960), 161–66.
88. Cf. *Kingdom of God*, 191; idem, *Rediscovering*, 22.
89. R. A. Edwards, *The Sign of Jonah* (SBT, Second Series, 18; London: SCM, 1971), 49–51.
90. Cf., e.g., 5:3, 6; 10:39; 12:28; 18:3; 19:14, 23–24; 20:16; 21:31d; 23:12; 26:29.
91. Cf. Kingsbury, *Matthew 13*, 117–25.

10:41–42); to emulate in the present the Lord Jesus, Son of God, so that each one "takes up his cross and follows" him, thus "finding" his life even while "losing" it (10:24–25, 38–39; 16:24–26); to have no fear of their enemies but to commend themselves to the providential care of the God who can condemn to Gehenna (10:28–31) and to depend upon him as completely as does a child his father (18:3–4); to suffer persecution with joy as ones who will inherit the Kingdom (5:10–12); and to be like faithful slaves (24:45; 25:21, 23) who are totally committed to the doing of the will of God (6:10, 33; 13:44, 45–46),[92] being ever watchful and ready in view of the unexpected coming of Jesus Son of Man (24:27, 32–35, 45–46; 25:10, 20–23).

To conclude, as Matthew understands it, the church of Jesus, the exalted Son of God, is the eschatological people of God whose existence is characterized by a tension between the present and the future. Even now the church lives in the sphere of the gracious Rule of God as exercised by Jesus and has as its commission to proclaim the Gospel of the Kingdom to the nations and hence to invite them, too, to enter this sphere. Although the church lives under God's Rule, it is in no wise immune to the forces of evil. On the contrary, it is exposed in the present to the so-called Messianic Woes. Severely afflicted as it is from within and without, the church is called to see its present situation in the light of the future Kingdom of Heaven. In this way, the members of the community, through eschatological warning and exhortation, are brought face to face in the present with the God of the future Kingdom who would, through his Son, motivate them ethically to do his will and so be heirs of life.

92. Cf. ibid., 110–17.

# Recapitulation

In recognition of the reciprocal relationship that exists between the form and content of biblical documents, we began our investigation of Matthew's Gospel by concentrating on its structure. Matthew divides his Gospel into three main parts with 1:1, 4:17, and 16:21 serving as "superscriptions" for the successive blocks of material. When the subject matter of the Gospel is grouped accordingly, what emerges is a topical outline that highlights the person and mission of Jesus Messiah, as follows: (I) The Person of Jesus Messiah (1:1–4:16); (II) The Proclamation of Jesus Messiah (4:17–16:20); and (III) The Suffering, Death, and Resurrection of Jesus Messiah (16:21–28:20).

Although this topical outline is the principal means by which Matthew organizes his materials, secondarily he also operates with a carefully designed concept of the history of salvation. Fundamental to this concept is the notion of God's abiding presence with his people in the person of his Son to the end of the age (1:23; 18:20; 28:20). In harmony with this notion, Matthew differentiates between two basic epochs: the "time of Israel (OT)" and the "time of Jesus," the latter extending from birth to parousia but first publicly heralded "in those days" by the ministry of John the Baptist (3:1–2). Within this scheme of salvation-history, Matthew's own age, the so-called time of the church, is a subcategory of the overarching "time of Jesus." Theologically, the function of Matthew's concept of salvation-history is to set forth the ultimate significance of the person, ministry, and death and resurrection of Jesus Messiah for all people, whether Israelites or Gentiles.

Taken together, the topical outline that Matthew drafts and his concept

of the history of salvation show that, regardless of the weighty ecclesiological concerns that surface in the Gospel, it is primarily a christological
document and has as its central purpose to inform the members of Matthew's community, against their present situation, of Jesus Messiah and
of his relationship to the Father and of what it means to be his disciple.
With these factors in mind, we posed the question as to Matthew's
understanding of the person of Jesus Messiah.

Because Matthew devotes the first main part of his Gospel to the
theme of the person of Jesus Messiah (1:1–4:16), it was to these chapters
that we looked in order to determine Matthew's fundamental understanding of Jesus. What we learned is that Jesus Messiah is preeminently
the Son of God, that is to say, in his person God draws near to reside with
his own, thus inaugurating the eschatological age of salvation (cf. 1:23).
Furthermore, in analyzing Matthew's use of the title Son of God in the
rest of the Gospel, we discovered that it retains its preeminent position,
for, with the exception of the parousia, it appears in conjunction with
every major facet of the ministry, passion, and exaltation of Jesus. As for
other christological titles, Matthew's tendency is to relate them variously,
but directly, to the title Son of God. "Emmanuel," for example, is Matthew's thumbnail definition of Son of God, "Messiah" receives its further
specification from it, and "Son of Abraham," "Son of David," "King (of
the Jews [Israel])," and "Servant" all function to enhance selected aspects of it, their point of reference being the earthly ministry of Jesus.
On a different level, the term "*kyrios*" (cf. also "the Coming One" and
"Shepherd") does not stand on its own in the first Gospel but is an
auxiliary christological title that always refers to Jesus in some other
capacity: as Messiah, Son of David, Son of God, or Son of Man.

The title Son of Man, however, does approximate in the first Gospel
the importance of the title Son of God. This title is not "confessional"
but "public" in character, and is the name with which Jesus designates
himself during his earthly ministry as he interacts with his opponents and
the crowds, or tells his disciples of what his enemies will do to him.
Following the resurrection, Son of Man marks Jesus as the one who
stands before the world as its ruler and will come at the consummation
to judge the nations. So understood, the title Son of Man is the counterpart of the title Son of God. And if at the point of the parousia "Son of
Man" supersedes "Son of God" (cf. 25:31–46), this side of the parousia
"Son of God" is the ranking title (16:13–20).

In Matthew's hierarchy of christological terms, therefore, the titles

Son of God and Son of Man stand out most prominently, the first as the preeminent predication for Jesus in this age and the second as the sole predication for him beginning with the parousia. Now in the Gospel in general, the most comprehensive concept is without doubt that of the Kingdom of Heaven (God).

The best point of departure for ascertaining how Matthew relates his christology to his concept of the Kingdom of Heaven is the expression "the Gospel of the Kingdom" (4:23; 9:35; 24:14; 26:13; cf. 13:19), for two reasons: first, in this expression these two elements have been conjoined; and second, as the capsule-summary of his document, this expression is of great prominence also in the eyes of Matthew.

As for the constituent terms of this expression, Matthew reveals both by the topical outline of his document and his concept of the history of salvation that "gospel" has reference to Jesus Messiah, the Son of God, and "kingdom" to the dynamic Rule of God that means salvation or damnation for people. When these two terms are combined as in the words "the Gospel of the Kingdom," what they denote from Matthew's perspective is the news, which saves or condemns, that is revealed in and through Jesus Messiah, the Son of God, and is proclaimed to Israel first and then the Gentiles to the effect that in him the dynamic Rule of God has in the "last times" drawn near to humankind. Because the substance of this definition can likewise be found in 1:23, which is Matthew's thumbnail sketch of what it means for him to say that Jesus Messiah is the Son of God, we see from 1:23 and the expression "the Gospel of the Kingdom" how completely Matthew's christology has penetrated his theology, that is, his concept of the Kingdom of Heaven.

At this juncture a seemingly extraneous observation is in order. Concerning the expression "the Gospel of the Kingdom," Matthew, unlike scholars today, does not distinguish between the pre-Easter proclamation of Jesus and the post-Easter proclamation of the church. On the contrary, his great concern is to underline the continuity that he holds exists between the message of the earthly Jesus and the message of his church. It is this concern for continuity that induces him, for instance, to portray the exalted Son of God as enjoining his disciples to teach the nations all that the earthly Son of God has commanded them (28:20), or to employ the identically same expression ("the Gospel of the Kingdom") to summarize the preaching both of the earthly Son of God to Israel (4:23; 9:35) and, following Easter, of the church to the nations (24:14; 26:13; cf. 13:19).

To return to our previous line of reasoning, if we keep in mind Matthew's radical christological modification of his concept of the Kingdom of Heaven, we can review its several features. Matthew attributes to the Kingdom of Heaven salvation-historical, cosmic, and ethical dimensions. Salvation-historically, the Kingdom is an eschatological reality that "presently" confronts people in the "time of Jesus" in the proclamation, respectively, of John the Baptist (3:1–2), of Jesus Messiah (4:17, 23; 9:35) and his disciples (10:7), and of the church (24:14; 26:13; 28:20), and this proclamation is of ultimate significance for the eternal destiny of Israel and the Gentiles alike. Although it is a reality in the present (cf. 11:2–6, 12; 12:28; 13:16–17), the Kingdom has not yet been consummated. At the end of the age, however, Jesus Son of Man will suddenly come in power and great glory, and preside over the judgment of the nations to the salvation or damnation of all (cf. 13:40–43, 49–50; 24:29–31; 25:31–46). At the parousia, then, God will have fully established his Kingdom in the sight of the entire world (cf. 16:27–28).

The cosmic dimension of Matthew's concept of the Kingdom of Heaven has to do with the so-called growth of the Kingdom during the "time of Jesus." As Matthew describes it, from such small and seemingly insignificant beginnings as the kingly activity of God in the person of his Son and, through him, in his church, there will miraculously issue at the end of the age the consummated Kingdom that will embrace the universe (cf. 13:31–32, 33, 36–43, 47–50; 24:29–31; 25:31–46). One point that this thought emphasizes particularly well is the continuity that exists between the Kingdom as a present and as a future reality.

The ethical dimension of Matthew's concept of the Kingdom of Heaven envisages the new life that can result from the individual's encounter with the Rule of God. Such encounter places the individual in the crisis of decision (cf. 11:14a, 15; 13:9, 43): either he will be led to "understand the Word of the Kingdom" (i.e., to "faith") and join the community of the disciples of Jesus Son of God who through him become sons of God and do the will of God (cf. 4:18–22; 5:9; 12:49–50; 13:19, 23), or he will "not understand the Word of the Kingdom" and live under the power of Satan (cf. 13:19, 38c). At the Last Judgment, this decision will prove itself to be of final consequence: the individual will "inherit the Kingdom," or "life" (cf. 25:34, 46), or be consigned by Jesus Son of Man to "eternal punishment" (cf. 25:41, 46).

Correlative to Matthew's description of the kingly activity of God in the person of his Son is his description of the rival activity of Satan. A transcendent, personal being with assorted names whose power is eclipsed only by that of God and of Jesus themselves, Satan is likewise said to have a kingdom (cf. 12:26), ruling in the world over angels (cf. 25:41), demons (cf. 12:24–29), and humans (cf. 13:38c). In his unswerving opposition to the Kingdom of Heaven (cf. 11:12), Satan is the arch-adversary of Jesus Messiah, the Son of God, and of Jesus Son of Man. The principal way in which he exercises his power is through temptation (cf. 4:3), that is, he endeavors to lead people to act or to live in a manner that is contrary to the will of God (cf. 16:23); hence, he is the supernatural fountainhead of all "lawlessness" (*anomia*; cf. 13:38c–39a, 41). Accordingly, Satan tempts Jesus Messiah in an effort to get him to divest himself of his divine sonship through disobedience to his Father (cf. 4:1–11; also 27:40), he is active in Israel to bring the people and their leaders under his rule (cf. 12:39; 16:4), and he attacks the church of Jesus Son of God in order to bring disciples to fall (cf. 6:13; 13:19). In the world at large, Satan is the enemy of the exalted Son of Man, and in this arena, too, he is at work to raise up "sons" who will do his bidding (cf. 13:37–39a). But in the last analysis Satan cannot prevail, for not only has Jesus Son of God defeated him initially by resisting his temptations (4:1–11), but at the consummation he and all who are his will be cast by Jesus Son of Man into the eternal fire (25:41, 46).

Despite Satan's opposition, Jesus Messiah, the Son of God, discharges his public ministry, which in Matthew's Gospel is first of all to confront Israel with the Kingdom of Heaven through teaching, preaching, and healing (cf. 4:17, 23; 9:35; 10:5–7; 11:1; 15:24). Israel, however, is unreceptive to Jesus Messiah, and the cry of the people that he be crucified and their willingness before God to take responsibility for his blood are evidence of their total rejection of him (27:22–23, 25; cf. also 27:38–44). Additionally, in the years since the death of Jesus, the church, through its proclamation, has continued to confront Israel with the Kingdom, but has met with failure and persecution (cf. 5:10–12; 10:17–23; 22:2–8; 23:34–35). In view of this, Matthew believes that Israel has fallen prey to Satan (cf. 13:24–30) and that God has withheld his revelation from this people, so that they have become blind, deaf, and without understanding (cf. 13:10–13). In consequence of Israel's rejection of Jesus and the Kingdom, not only has it suffered the destruction of Jerusalem (cf. 22:7), but God has also taken his Rule from it and given it to the church (cf. 21:43). What is more, the proclamation of the Gospel of the Kingdom is henceforth directed, not to Israel per se, but to the nations (cf. 22:8–9; 24:14; 26:13; 28:19). Still, because the nations, too, display animosity toward the church (cf. 10:18, 22; 24:9), Matthew recognizes that it is only in the face of resistance on the part of both Jew and Gentile that God in his Son visits people in the "time of Jesus" with his Kingdom.

Owing to the circumstance that God has withdrawn his Rule from Israel and given it to the church, Matthew sees the church as the "empirical" sphere in which God exercises his Rule in the person of his exalted Son and this Rule is acknowledged (cf. 16:18–19; 18:18–20). At the same time, the relationship between the church and the Kingdom in the eyes of Matthew is not that of identification but of association. On the one hand, the church is indeed the community of the "sons of the Kingdom" who through Jesus know God as their Father (cf. 5:9, 45; 6:9; 12:50; 13:23, 38). On the other hand, it is also a *corpus mixtum* in which there are false disciples who are without "understanding" (i.e., "faith"; cf. 13:19), or who in manifold ways live contrary to the will of God (cf. 7:21–23; 13:49–50), or who cause other disciples to lose their faith (cf. 18:6; 24:10–12). In addition, the church is also beset by persecution from the side of Israel (cf. 5:10–12; 10:17, 23, 25, 28; 13:21; 23:34) and tribulation from the side of Gentiles (cf. 10:18, 22; 13:21; 24:9). In recognition of such internal and external difficulties, Matthew declares in the words of Jesus that the church is caught up in these "last times" in the throes of the Messianic Woes (24:8).

From Matthew's standpoint, then, the church exists even now in the sphere of the Kingdom, and yet must await its consummation. This eschatological tension between the present and the future is what characterizes Christian discipleship. The call that goes out to the disciple from the exalted Son of God is that he is to construe his present situation as decisively qualified by the promises or, where it applies, the judgment attendant to the future Kingdom, and shape his life accordingly (cf. 5:3–10, 20; 6:9–15; 7:21–23; 10:39, 42; 18:3; 20:16; 23:12). Thus, the disciple goes the way of the cross in obedience to the exalted Son of God against that day when Jesus Son of Man shall bestow on him his eschatological "reward" (cf. 16:21–28).

In conclusion, from this review of the concept Kingdom of Heaven (God), we can see that it does indeed touch on virtually every aspect of the first Gospel. But if in contemporary Judaism, the Kingdom of Heaven was a theological concept in the strictest sense, as Matthew develops it it undergoes radical christological modification. The analyses we have made of the christology of Matthew and of his concept of the Kingdom of Heaven both go to demonstrate that Son of God and Son of Man are the chief christological categories with which Matthew works. In Matthew's scheme of things, if the Kingdom of Heaven will be consummated in the future when Jesus Son of Man will visibly come in power and great glory for judgment, in the present "time of Jesus" it draws near to humankind in the person of Jesus Messiah, the (earthly and) exalted Son of God. Hence, throughout this age it is under the aegis of the Son of God that the church experiences the Kingdom, and its proclamation of the Gospel of the Kingdom aims at making all nations sons of God. In sum, therefore, Matthew establishes a reciprocal relationship between the future and the present: supremely the Son of Man "then," Jesus is supremely the Son of God "now."

# Indexes

## NAMES

## REFERENCES TO MATTHEW